ABOUT THE AUTHORS

After editing over 35 feature films, from *Long Days Journey Into Night* and *The Pawnbroker* to *Goodbye Columbus* and six of Woody Allen's first seven films, RALPH ROSENBLUM is now a director. His recent work includes *Summer Solstice* with Henry Fonda and Myrna Loy, as well as two productions of the American Short Story for PBS and one American Playhouse production. He is visiting professor of film production at the State University of New York at Purchase.

ROBERT KAREN has written extensively on politics, film, and psychology. His articles have appeared in *New York Magazine*, *Gentlemen's Quarterly*, the *Nation*, *Vogue*, *Savvy*, the *Washington Post*, *Newsday*, and elsewhere. He is a contributing editor of *Cosmopolitan*, and he teaches at the New School for Social Research in New York City. His next book is about experiences of power and insecurity in everyday life.

The authors are now collaborating on a documentary film about a student uprising of the sixties.

D1042584

WHEN THE SHOOTING STOPS
...the Cutting Begins

A Film Editor's Story

Ralph Rosenblum and
Robert Karen

DA CAPO PRESS

Library of Congress Cataloging in Publication Data

Rosenblum, Ralph.
  When the shooting stops, the cutting begins.

  (A Da Capo paperback)
  Includes index.
  1. Moving-pictures—Editing. I. Karen, Robert.
II. Title.
TR899.R67   1986   778.5'35   86-11495
ISBN 0-306-80272-4 (pbk.)

Acknowledgments
  Film Quarterly: From "Robert J. Flaherty, 1884–1951," by Helen van Dongen, Vol. 18, No. 4 (Summer 1965). Reprinted by permission of the Regents of the University of California.
  Alfred A. Knopf, Inc.: From *The Parade's Gone By . . .* , by Kevin Brownlow. Copyright © Kevin Brownlow, 1968. Reprinted by permission of Alfred A. Knopf, Inc.
  The photograph on page x: The Paramount cutting room, circa 1927 (the editor is Jane Loring). Courtesy Richard Koszarski Collection.
  The excerpts from *The Producers* by Mel Brooks are reprinted by permission of Mel Brooks.

This Da Capo Press paperback edition of *When the Shooting Stops . . . the Cutting Begins* is an unabridged republication of the edition published in New York in 1979. It is reprinted by arrangement with the authors.

Copyright © Ralph Rosenblum and Robert Karen, 1979

Published by Da Capo Press, Inc.
A Member of the Perseus Books Group.

Dedications

Table of Contents

Introduction
The Hands behind the Seams   1

1. **THE NIGHT THEY RAIDED MINSKY'S**
   Part I: A Month for Nine Minutes   11

2. **THE NIGHT THEY RAIDED MINSKY'S**
   Part II: Life Sentence   21

3. **From a Recording Medium to an Art Form**
   The Invention of Editing   33

4. **Bolshevik Editors**
   The Fanatics of the Cutting Room   45

5. **The Birth of a Profession**
   Technicians with Dreams   59

6. **From the Shadows of Bensonhurst**
    Portrait of the Editor as a Young Man   73

7. **The Office of War Information**
    Apprenticeship with the Documentary Guys   89

8. **Robert Flaherty and Helen van Dongen**
    The Collaboration That Sustained a Legend   109

9. **Making It**
    The TV Pressure Cooker   125

10. THE PAWNBROKER
    Part I: The Re-creation of the Flashback   139

11. THE PAWNBROKER
    Part II: X-Rays of the Mind   151

12. A THOUSAND CLOWNS
    Part I: Flouting Convention   169

13. A THOUSAND CLOWNS
    Part II: A Style Arrived At by Repair   181

14. THE PRODUCERS
    Not Just Another Funny Picture   193

15. GOODBYE COLUMBUS
    The Face on the Cutting-Room Floor   211

16. **My Problem with Directors**   229

17. TAKE THE MONEY AND RUN
    The Film They Wouldn't Release   241

18. **Scenes from a Marriage**
    Working with Woody on BANANAS, SLEEPER, and
    LOVE AND DEATH   255

19. ANNIE HALL
    It Wasn't the Film He Set Out to Make   273

20. **Swan Song**   293

    Thank you   300

    Index   301

WHEN THE SHOOTING STOPS

Introduction
The Hands behind the Seams

"Don't worry, we'll fix it in the cutting room," is a prayer that's been uttered in every language, on every location, in every country where films have been made. Shooting a film is the most expensive entertainment production ever devised. When mistakes are made, or scenes fall short of the director's vision, the immense cost of doggedly pursuing the cinematic fantasy on the set (as wages of cameramen, performers, set directors, makeup artists, and scores of assistants and associates accumulate at union-scale tempo) dampens even the most ambitious director's desire for perfection. And so the cutting room becomes the last-stand corral for everyone's hopes that the unrealized dreams, the dead moments, the inevitable blah sequences from weeks of shooting will finally be brought to life.

But cutting is only marginally a matter of "fixing." When it came into being in 1902, film editing transformed motion pictures from a recording medium into an art form. In its simplest aspect, cutting is about juxtapositions. A man awakens suddenly in the middle of the night, bolts up in bed, stares ahead intensely, and twitches his nose. If you cut now to an image of clouds drifting before the full moon, the audience is primed for a wolf-man adventure. If you cut to a room where two people are desperately fighting a billowing blaze, the viewers realize that through clairvoyance, a warning dream, or the smell of smoke, the man in bed has become aware of danger. If you cut to a distraught wife defending her decision to commit her husband to a mental institution, they will understand that the man in bed is her husband and that the dramatic tension will surround the couple. If you're editing an Alfred Hitchcock movie, the juxtaposition of the man and his wife will immediately raise questions in the viewers' minds about foul play on the part of the woman. If you then cut back to a hospital aide ordering the man out of bed for breakfast, the audience will already be searching for hints about the man's mental state and expecting a significant clue to arise from this interaction.

The cutting room is the domain of the film editor, a man or woman barely known outside the film industry. He is often an introverted and cautious individual who may think of himself as a talented technocrat, a guardian of the tough, mechanical facts of cinematic technique; or as a behind-the-scenes power, like a president's brain truster, unsung but indispensable; or as a creative genius in his own right, a star whose light is blocked by the medieval movie protocol that gives directors and actors almost exclusive credit for a film's success. Whatever his self-image, a key part of his job in the months he will spend absorbed in the seemingly endless footage will be to make his own contribution as imperceptible as possible. No viewer should walk out of that film saying, "I really dug the editing." The final product should have a natural seamless effect, as if it were originally shot just the way it looks on the screen. And if an advertisement ever announces that the film has won an Academy Award for editing, the name of the editor will probably not be mentioned. He inhabits an anonymous world, and various aspects of the trade conspire to keep him anonymous.

Of course, within the movie business a certain amount of lore has built up about the implacable technicians, the strung-out geniuses, the "doctors," the "firemen," the men with "magic hands," and the marvelous feats of filmic endurance and transformation that have gone on in those bleak, windowless cells where most pictures have been cut. Hollywood buffs may have learned that editor Elmo Williams was a major factor in the success of *High Noon*, that he was responsible for the picture's strict correspondence between screen time and real time, and that his device of cutting repeatedly to the old courthouse clock created much of the fantastic tension in that famous film. They may have heard of Merrill White, who was called in one day in 1953 by executives at RKO and asked if he could salvage a disaster called *The Brave One*. "I'll need a year," White is supposed to have said after viewing the original version. Already known as an irascible technician who would curse and threaten a film that gave him trouble, White probably set a record for editorial rage when, several months into *The Brave One*, he came roaring out of his second-floor stall, emerged on the balcony with his Moviola in tow, and in a superhuman frenzy dumped the unbudgeable three-hundred-pound machine to its destruction. (His re-edited version won the author, Dalton Trumbo, an Oscar in 1954.) A very different sort of editor, the ever dapper Paul Falkenberg, is still remembered with delight by film workers in New York. An intimidating, no-nonsense old-timer who once landed me a job cutting the Guy Lombardo TV show, Falkenberg is best recalled for an incident that occurred when MCA invited him to rescue a horrid underseas adventure. The short, balding, penguin-shaped wizard stepped briskly into the screening room, dispensed with the niceties, and proceeded to endure the film. Then, with the lights back on and his features still set in the formal mode of a high-priced surgeon about to deliver a considered opinion, the master announced, "From shit you get shit!" and marched out.

Every so often, in the film magazines, texts, and professional journals, a story arises about a timely feat of editing. And thus those who care about such things may know that during the filming of the climactic chase scene in *Bullitt*, an out-of-control car filled with dummies tripped a wire which prematurely sent a costly set up in flames, and that editor Frank Keller salvaged the near-catastrophe with a clever and unusual juxtaposition of images that made the explosion appear to go off on time. They may have heard that in 1963, when I was cutting *Fail Safe*, the U.S. Defense Department refused to provide me with crucial footage of bombers taking off, and to compensate for the gap I had to take a single piece of stock film with one Air Force plane in it—something I found in a film library—blow it up to various sizes, flop it over, crop the image in several ways, and cut together all these perspectives until it appeared that whole squadrons of bombers were taking off all around the country. They may know of certain movie episodes that owe their emotional power to virtuoso editing: the famous eating scene in *Tom Jones*, assembled one Sunday morning by editor Antony Gibbs; the scene from *Whatever Happened to Baby Jane?*, cut by Michael Luciano, in which Bette Davis dances on the beach with an ice-cream cone; or the sequence in *Cabaret* in which editor David Bretherton took a poorly staged and poorly acted production of a young Nazi boy singing "Tomorrow Belongs to Me" and turned it into one of the most stirring moments in the film.

If you hang around directors, you'll eventually hear other tales—about editors who were grinding bores, who had peculiar habits, who made the long months of professional intimacy a marital ordeal. About editors who were unimaginative mechanics, who were too comfortable with their old habits and rules of thumb to take risks, who stymied young directors with fresh ideas by telling them, "It can't be done." Director Larry Peerce complains of being duped, double-crossed, and bullied during the early years of his career by editors who knew more than he did and took advantage of his ignorance. (He also admits to having threatened the life of one editor because she ate salmon croquettes with cream sauce every day for lunch.)

But there are some questions about film editors that no one knows and no one may ever know. How great was Antony Gibbs's contribution to the entire body of Tony Richardson's work? (In addition to *Tom Jones*, he cut Richardson's *A Taste of Honey*, *The Loneliness of the Long Distance Runner*, *The Loved One*, *Mademoiselle*, and *The Sailor from Gibraltar*.) How instrumental was editor Henri Colpi in the revolutionary film techniques initiated in Alain Resnais's *Night and Fog*, *Hiroshima Mon Amour*, and *Last Year at Marienbad*? What do filmakers Jean-Luc Godard, François Truffaut, and Eric Rohmer owe to their collaboration with editor Cécile Decugis? How great was the imprint of chief editors Margaret Booth, Daniel Mandell, and Barbara McLean on the golden-era films of MGM, Goldwyn Studios, and 20th Century–Fox? The producers, the directors, and the editors themselves have maintained almost total silence on these questions.

This book is a story of film editing. It is based mainly on the experiences of one editor, Ralph Rosenblum—the "I" of the account—and is written by Robert Karen. It is aimed at a three-quarter-of-a-century gap

in our knowledge of how we are entertained, manipulated, and pro-
voked to every conceivable emotion. It is a story of excitement and
distress, of manic anxiety and absurd pomposity, and, most important,
of the work itself. We hope that after reading it, you will no longer think
about movies in quite the same way.

I have been a free-lance film editor—in documentaries, advertising,
television, and movies—for over thirty-five years. Since 1975 I've
lived and worked in a brownstone on West Eighty-fourth Street in
Manhattan. On the second floor of the apartment, down the hall from
the bedroom, is the cutting room where *Annie Hall, Interiors,* and
several other pictures were edited. It is a large room, lined· with two
Moviolas, a teak desk, and five tables, all topped with synchronizers,
film winders, and other little pieces of equipment. On one table
there's a stereo with a small collection of records that have formed the
working scores for numerous films. Metal racks capable of holding
several hundred thousand feet of film fill a small alcove behind the
desk. The walls are covered with memorabilia, photographs, and
Steinberg prints. During periods of dormancy—painful stretches
during which my self-esteem plunges and I become nasty and
difficult to live with—the tables sprout neat piles of magazines, newly
acquired books from the remainder bins at Marboro and Barnes &
Noble, and screenplays that friends and associates have sent me to
read, comment on, and consider producing.

Since I first joined the business in the 1940s, the cozy little New
York City local of the film editors' union has swelled from a mere 150
members to a mammoth 1500. But despite this burgeoning growth in
the field, few outsiders—including actors whose work is so affected by
it—have any idea what really goes on during the editing of a film.
Friends have repeatedly told me, "I know what you do—you take out
the bad parts." Another, more generous view portrays the editor as
the one who "saves" the film, using his bag of cinematic tricks to
overcome the blunders of others. Neither impression is accurate. A
feature-length film generates anywhere from twenty to forty hours of
raw footage. When the shooting stops, that unrefined film becomes
the movie's raw material, just as the script had been the raw material
before. It must now be selected, tightened, paced, embellished,
arranged, and in some scenes given artificial respiration, until the
author's and the director's vision becomes completely translated from
the language of the script to the idiom of the movies. Under the

over-all heading of "editing" are almost all the techniques that distinguish filmmaking from producing a play. The process is as complex and difficult to define as the adjustments, cuts, and shuffling that makes a writer's final product so different from his first draft. And the effort usually takes two or even three times longer than the shooting itself.

Let me set the scene for you as I have come to know it. I am editing *Interiors*. Anguished moans and angry cries burst out of the cutting room and fill the entire apartment as pieces of the uncut film are run through the editing machines over and over again. Four people are working in the darkened space. My two assistants, Sandy Morse and Sonya Polonsky, are winding my selections and rejections from the great mass of film onto small, carefully coded spools. These spools of film, each about the diameter of a salad plate and the thickness of a ten-dollar novel, are sitting in piles of twos and threes on surfaces all around the room.

I sit in a corner at one of the Moviolas piecing together a sequence that was shot from five different perspectives. I work quickly, long lengths of film flying through my white-gloved right hand. I stop, mark the film with a grease pencil, fly on, make another mark, cut, splice together the desired portions, and hang up the trims, pieces of deleted film.

Off to my right, at the large rented Steenbeck editing machine—whose TV-sized screen offers a better view of the raw film than does the traditional Moviola—Woody Allen is viewing and reviewing a tiny piece of action from an early scene. "Scene Seventeen, take two," cries an anonymous voice for the nth time. A prop man races across the twelve-inch screen just before Diane Keaton and Marybeth Hurt appear and begin arguing again. After their short altercation, Woody stops the film. "The second take," he says at last, and, without looking up, Sandy stops winding film and marks his choice in her fat script book.

Several times in the course of the day, Woody and I confer on the editing of a troublesome scene. Once we go down the hall to the bedroom for a more serious discussion. Woody is worried about the episode in which Sam Waterston breaks down. I assure him the whole sequence can be cut out without leaving too glaring a gap.

Five film barrels crowd the cutting room, with long trims hanging into them from an overhead rod. There's a lot of film on the floor—not rejected film, as the cliché has it, but film that's in the process of being viewed or edited or wound. The blast of voices running backward over tape heads repeatedly shatters the air. From my machine a man screams, "So far I have nothing but compassion for you!" Then a Swedish-sounding "!Bhaw-ooo-ai-ya," as I rewind looking for the right place to make the cut. "Compassion for you!" No one pays attention to the sounds emanating from my corner or to the voice of Sam Waterston on Woody's machine as he cries that he is able to care for people only en masse, not as individuals (a sentence that will never make it to the theaters). "Clip! Clop!" as I make the cut and apply the tape in two quick gestures. After four months of this, the film is edited and ready to go to the sound studio and the lab for the finishing touches.

Why so long? Why such painstaking devotion? Because as an editor you are constantly faced with choices that subtly influence the character of the film. Reconsider the man who has just bolted upright in bed from the midst of a deep sleep. You are provided with coverage of the next moments from two perspectives. You have a choice. You can cut from the just-awakened protagonist clutching the blankets to his chest to a stranger standing in the shadows at the foot of the bed, pointing a gun and talking in a menacing fashion. Or you can cut from the startled sleeper sitting up in bed to a tight close-up of his face, which reveals the terror in his eyes as the menacing voice of a gunman, unseen by the audience, is heard on the sound track. Your decision will be based on many factors: the degree of tension you want to generate, whether you want the terror to be muted or to reach climax proportions, your concern about repetitive images and moods, your desire to avoid clichés. Once you decide which way to go, you will have to make other choices—first regarding the selection of the strongest performance (or "take"), then the best camera angle, and finally the exact frame (and there are twenty-four frames in a second) where you will cut each shot and make the transition. The cumulative impact of these little decisions may make the difference between a classic and just plain good entertainment—or between good entertainment and a flop. For although audiences are unaware of editing, they are as affected by it as they are by a writer's style.

No matter how you cut it, really dead material can never be brought to life, but if the raw footage has quality, it faces almost infinite possibilities during the months it passes through an editor's hands. But because an editor's prerogatives depend so much on his relationship with the director, it is impossible to say what his contribution is to any given film. A director may demand absolute control of his picture and give the editor little room to offer creative solutions; or he may walk away, leaving no more than a handful of instructions and an occasional word of encouragement. Under the old Hollywood system editors were often considered strictly mechanics and not expected to offer ideas. But during certain periods, like the heyday of the silent film, the era of the great producer-tycoons, and throughout much of TV's history, certain editors have achieved immense authority and power. In recent years, as the studio system has crumbled and as filmmakers have become more and more inclined to break out of the confines of the script, the editing profession as a whole has begun to come into its own. But even today the situation varies dramatically—from a picture like *Apocalypse Now* that spends years in the cutting and goes through several generations of editors to a less complicated picture like *Slow Dancing in the Big City*, which director John Avildsen virtually edited himself.

Because so much goes on in the cutting room, because it is a major center of film creation, an inevitable tension infects the director-editor relationship. Directors never give special mention to their editors when they lope up to receive their Oscar—lest an overeager critic surmise that the film had been in trouble and was saved by heavy editorial doctoring. And editors, understanding the explosive ego issues involved, wisely stay true to the bent for anonymity that led them to their chosen profession.

When it comes to awards for editing, editors are the first to snigger. "We editors know," says Tom Priestly *(This Sporting Life, Marat/Sade, Deliverance)*, "that we cannot really judge each others' work without knowing the original material. Many a lousy film has been brilliantly edited, and many a brilliant film has been just competently put together."

Nonetheless there are certain films that people in the industry know were "made in the cutting room." This inner-circle recognition offers an editor one of his rare opportunities for ego flight. Among the pictures I've worked on, *The Night They Raided Minsky's* is certainly the foremost example.

**Norman Lear (left) and William Friedkin on the set
of THE NIGHT THEY RAIDED MINSKY'S.**
(Courtesy United Artists Corporation)

1 ■ *The Night They Raided Minsky's*

Part I: A Month for Nine Minutes

When Norman Lear, Billy Friedkin, and I gathered to screen the first cut of *The Night They Raided Minsky's* on a Friday afternoon in the fall of 1967, we were as far apart as three collaborators could be. I was invigorated and optimistic, having just finished a hard-paced three weeks in the cutting room, paring down some forty-odd hours of raw footage into a manageable two and a half. Friedkin, the director, who would later make *The French Connection* and *The Exorcist,* was edgy and preoccupied. He was leaving for England to direct another picture, and although he was already half gone in spirit, he could hardly forget that this film—or whatever became of it—represented the first major opportunity of his career. Lear, the producer and co-author, reverberated with high-pitched anxiety. He had already spent over three million dollars of investor money to finance *Minsky's,* making it the most expensive movie ever produced in New York; his director was about to take off for good; and he was beginning to dread that he had gambled too heavily—that this dangerously old-fashioned story would never be perceived as the exciting "New Look" in filmmaking he had promised.

From the very beginning, the idea behind *The Night They Raided Minsky's* had been to create an "old-fashioned musical with a New Look." The producer, the director, and the people at United Artists were excited by the prospect of the New Look, although what it was and how it was going to be accomplished no one knew. If a New Look could really be said to exist at that time, it was flickering about in four recently released movies that were having a big impact on the industry: *The Knack*, the two Beatles movies, *Hard Day's Night* and *Help!*, and *A Funny Thing Happened on the Way to the Forum*—all directed by Richard Lester. The techniques Lester used with astonishing success had never been seen in commercial films. Actors walked forward and then suddenly backward. People and things popped out of nowhere and jumped around like animated figures. Had anyone dared to acknowledge that the New Look we hoped to achieve in *Minsky's* was essentially a Lester Look, we all might have been saved some anguish; but such an acknowledgment would have been considered inappropriate, if not blasphemous, and so it barely crossed our minds.

To anyone with film sense, the *Minsky's* script quickly revealed exactly how important the New Look was to Lear. It is an insipid story about an impossibly innocent Amish girl, played by Britt Ekland, who bounds into New York City in 1925 looking like a ripe fruit. Seeking to escape her stern and joyless father in order to dance Bible stories on stage, she goes straight to the Lower East Side and the cynical but childlike world of Minsky's Burlesque Theatre, where a pair of vaudeville actors, Jason Robards and Norman Wisdom, vie for her affections. The knavish Robards is also involved in a plot to put Ekland on the stage as "Madame Fifi," who, according to Minsky's crash advertising campaign, will do the "dance that drove a thousand Frenchmen wild." The idea is to goad the overzealous head of the city's vice squad into calling a police raid, only to embarrass him with an innocent Bible Dance. But Ekland, hurt by being played for a fool and incensed over being called a "whore" by her father, goes out on the midnight stage and, incited each step of the way by a riotously libidinous audience, begins bumping and grinding and tossing off pieces of her clothes. When she looks offstage and sees Robards sneering in disapproval, she throws out her arms to him, thereby dropping the front of her dress. And thus, presumably, the striptease is born. Various connivances and conniptions go on in the background, not the least of which involves Minsky's orthodox Jewish father, played by Joseph Wiseman, and Ekland's orthodox Amish father, played by Harry Andrews in wrathful pursuit. It is all very trivial and predictable, and clearly in need of something—the New Look perhaps—to snap it into shape as a piece of compelling cinema.

But as Minsky's father would say, *compelling the first cut wasn't*. What we witnessed for those two and a half hours was some of the least compelling footage any of us had ever seen. There was no pace, no suspense, and not a moment of believable dialogue. Britt Ekland managed to do approximately what was expected of her, gliding through the entire film like a star-stunned ingenue, while Jason Robards, who had been capable of credible performances in other films, waltzed through his part in this one. The vaudeville numbers had genuine quality, but they didn't fit anywhere in the script, and the only interesting dramatic sequences were provided by the marginal character actors. The footage of the re-creations of entire blocks of the old Jewish ghetto in the Lower East Side of Manhattan, including pushcarts, store façades, elevated subway, and six hundred extras, offered a devastatingly expensive backdrop for a silly, inconsequential musical film that could barely be watched for two minutes without a total suspension of one's critical faculties.

The screening over, we sat silently for a while as the extent of Lear's desolation gradually surfaced. "Could you, Billy," he asked Friedkin, "could you do something? Could you and Ralph go back into the cutting room and work tonight and Saturday and Sunday and maybe do some kind of big save by the time you leave on Monday?"

His words had a more chilling effect on me than the screening had had. We couldn't pull it off in two days—that was desperation talk. Besides, I didn't want to give up the weekend. And neither, it turned out, did Friedkin. So we talked for an hour or two more and then parted—Friedkin for London, where he would direct the film of Pinter's *A Birthday Party*, I for home, where I would forget the whole thing, and Lear for a torturous two days of suspended animation.

The next week was gloomy, Lear and I spending several days discussing the film in a general way, hardly knowing what we were going to do to put a New Look or Any Look into two and a half hours of slightly horny kiddie theater. Later in the week we arranged another screening and invited David Picker, an executive vice president of United Artists. "In all my years in film," Picker said afterward, "this is the worst first cut I've ever seen." As we trudged out of the screening room, Picker tried to reassure Lear: "Look, there's no real deadline on this picture—whatever you need, whatever you want to do . . ." his voice tailed off, ". . . whatever you want to do, go ahead and . . . take your time, and do it." And he walked away.

There are three or four big film libraries in New York, each holding millions of feet of film, all of it cross-indexed in scores of ways. The libraries specialize in old black and white film, much of it shot from the period before World War I through the years of the Depression. If you need footage of the opening of a dam in California, a flagpole sitter in Chicago, striking workers in New York's garment center, the collapse of the "Galloping Gertie" bridge in Washington, bizarre feats performed on the wings of airplanes, or old newsreel footage of any of the world's former political, scientific, or cultural elite, it is bound to be wound around any of their thousands of reels.

Grasping for an inspiration, I visited one of the libraries and asked to see a few reels of the Pennsylvania Amish. The men with beards and primitive dress, the horse-drawn carriages, the straight-backed women outside spotless farmhouses hardly suggested the New Look that Lear was pressuring me for, but I ordered a couple of scenes and started work on *Minsky's* first ten-minute reel. It was December 1967, the beginning of one of my longest stints in the cutting room.

The process of turning a first cut into a finished film always proceeds one reel at a time. Each scene is carefully tuned before the next one is tackled. It's the way I imagine a cobra ingests a crocodile, the dead beast going through the snake's digestive system inch by inch, the head being completely transformed by the digestive juices before the neck arrives.

The head of *Minsky's* is the opening sequence of the Amish girl arriving in New York. I worked and reworked this scene, trying to incorporate some of the stock footage. The process is tedious, rarely offering much return on a day's labor, but it yielded my first inkling of how I might transform the film. As I intercut the scenes, I realized that the orthodox Amish farmers looked similar to some of the extras in the original shooting, men with beards and big hats who were supposed to be Orthodox Jews. It seemed a perfect binding element to bolster the important opening minutes. As Britt Ekland arrives in New York, the flash cuts of the Amish would highlight the emotional impact of her entering this alien but strangely similar world.

I ordered more Amish scenes and began cutting again, like a baker adding more yeast to his recipe. After several days, I looked at the remade opening and saw a somewhat enlivened but still disappointing version. I had taken a wrong turn, and, as is frequently the case with editing experiments, many hours of effort were lost.

But I learned something from this mistake. I now knew that the basic approach I had chosen of intercutting stock footage was sound. After several more weeks of editing—with the Amish farmers this time completely eliminated in favor of scenes of old New York—I hit upon my opening formula: the introductory sequence became a vast array of intercutting that establishes the Lower East Side of 1925, introduces the Amish girl, brings Minsky's theater into focus, and works in the title and credits.

The movie begins with words on a title card that are spoken simultaneously by a vaudeville-style announcer (Rudy Vallee). He speaks for just a few seconds, declaring that the film is based on true incidents, that "in 1925 there was this real religious girl and by accident she invented the striptease." Suddenly we are thrown into the midst of a parade from black and white stock footage, the first element of a 1925 montage composed of twenty-nine shots in eighty-six seconds: a female band playing in bathing suits, a couple in a marathon dance contest, a boy and girl hugging in a tenement-lined street, a woman dancing beside a dancing horse, a man scaling the side of a building, a flagpole sitter, pushcarts and peddlers in an overcrowded street which suddenly turns to full color, and so on. I repeated the color trick three times toward the end of the montage to prepare the audience for the color cut of Britt Ekland riding happily on an old elevated city train.

I now bring Ekland into the Lower East Side, and the montage effect continues. At regular intervals I show her progress. She's getting educated by the new sights, and the audience is having an equivalent experience through the use of the stock footage and snippets of footage shot by Friedkin on the re-created set. The Friedkin cuts each go for a few frames in black and white before turning to color, sometimes with the aid of a cue, like the flash of a smile or the sudden flight of pigeons. Gradually the black and white footage yields more and more to the color.

Bert Lahr, an aging vaudevillian (Lahr died during the filming of *Minsky's*), is the second character I introduce. We first see his feet walking along the crowded street. He's wearing shiny "spats," which is also the name of the character he plays. He takes a grape from a fruit vendor's basket. A wagon and driver, more pushcarts. Ekland among the crowd, a shaved-ice seller, 1925 traffic, Ekland catching her first glimpse of Minsky's, the sign announcing the show with Wisdom's and Robards' pictures on it, a quick shot of Robards in his hotel lobby (my editorial signal that this is a character to watch for), Ekland calling out to Lahr—and the first dramatic action begins.

In a few lines of dialogue it becomes clear why Ekland has come to New York and what she is running from: I make a quick cut to her bearded, raging father, then back to Ekland's face wincing with guilt. A sympathetic Lahr invites her inside the theater. I cut to the action on stage, the audience. The music begins, applause, and Pablo Ferro's specially designed flashing titles come on, superimposed over a slightly blurred view of the audience: A BUD YORKIN–NORMAN LEAR PRODUCTION. As the focus shifts back and forth from the audience to the burlesque routine on stage, and as the energy level and excitement rise, I pop the names of the stars on and off the screen, the background taking on a matte finish each time. Eventually I run through all the credits in this way. For several seconds of vaudeville action there are no titles at all. Suddenly I switch to a nighttime sequence of old-time policemen running from the station house to their cars in flickering black and white and color. The vaudeville music continues, mixed with the sound of sirens and engines, but for an instant the picture disappears, replaced by a single flashing black word on a white background: "THE"   The flickering montage resumes, reuniting with its sound track: the prowl cars streaming out of their compound in a single file. As the sound track races on another flashing black word on an all-white background: "NIGHT"
A policeman on a motorcycle.   "THEY"   The cop cars and cycles zooming through town.   "RAIDED"   The police vehicles flickering through the darkness.   "MINSKY'S."

The cops leave their cars and move toward the burlesque palace.

I bring us inside again, in the middle of a Robards and Wisdom routine. Robards: "Hey, Chick, did you take a bath today?" Wisdom: "Why, is there one missing?" Laughter. A judge and a female witness in a courtroom. Judge: "When you were sitting there in the car, and you felt that man's hand on your knee, and then again on the top of your stocking, why, why didn't you scream for help?" Witness: "How did I know he was after my money?" Laughter.

The two-line bits fire off in rapid succession, the effect created by the splicing together of a number of scenes filmed at different times for different parts of the film. Wisdom walks into the aisle of the theater. Audience on both sides, one man asleep. Wisdom: "That was one of me father's jokes." Robards: "What are you, one of your mother's?"

Judge: "Say, weren't you up before me two weeks ago?" A woman witness: "I don't know, Your Honor. What time do you get up?" Laughter. Her response and the laughter are heard as the penultimate titles are superimposed: PRODUCED BY NORMAN LEAR. The audience, another bit, more laughter: DIRECTED BY WILLIAM FRIEDKIN. The vaudeville music starts as Robards and Wisdom make a wildly cheered exit. The camera pans along the laughing audience to end the first reel.

I created the pastiche inch by inch, recut it twenty or thirty times, and worked on it for over a month. In nine minutes there were close to three hundred splices. A single piece of vaudevillian music that I had laid down over the montage sequences became the film's major musical theme. The treacly opening had been infused with enough bustling expectation and playful nostalgia to pass for modern entertainment. Lear found it thrilling.

Norman Lear is a medium-sized man whose single distinguishing feature is a bald head with a thick fringe of gray hair. He's a master at getting what he wants from people, knowing all the subtleties of feeling that make subordinates inclined to give extra and remain loyal. He's positive, encouraging, and friendly, and lacks the gruff characteristics typical of producers. His only transparent manipulative device—one that would eventually cause a blow-up between us—is to offer profuse praise and then ask if the thing praised can't be made "even better." On the whole, he is difficult if not impossible to dislike.

Lear had no intention of returning to Hollywood until *Minsky's* was cut. He set up office in New York and began developing pilot TV scripts, one of which would later become "All in the Family." Days went by without any discussion between us, but he was always accessible if I needed him, ready to drop whatever he was doing in order to see if his New Look was emerging. His office, actually an extension of my cutting room on West Fifty-fourth Street, consisted of some rented furniture and a secretary. He probably never guessed he would be there for almost a year.

Throughout most of that year Lear had to use all his managerial magic to keep my spirits from slipping beneath the minimum working level. Even with the first reel completed, the plot had barely been tackled, and I had only a thin vision of how the dramatic portions could be made to work. I had taken *Minsky's* on not because I believed it would be a great editorial challenge but because I saw it as a lark. I had just come off six months on *The Producers*, a trying experience that pickled my nerve endings, and I badly needed a soothing job. Lear, who had been impressed with my work on *A Thousand Clowns* and had tried to get me to relocate to California (where he had recently produced *Divorce American Style*), had been responsible for bringing me in on this project, and I expected a pleasurable collaboration. The script revealed a frothy, unimportant film full of musical numbers, the kind of thing that might be snapped into shape in six to eight weeks of editing. I loved cutting musicals; I expected a short stretch of mindless fun.

Now I alone was responsible for rescuing what everyone but the irrepressible Lear believed was a hopeless failure. I resented the burden all the more because, while I was being asked to perform the greatest filmmaking feat of my career, someone else's name would be signed to it if I succeeded. This was a difficult barrier for a man who had never liked the adoration that is customarily bestowed on directors. And it was especially difficult after having spent several weeks working with Billy Friedkin, who at that time was in his late twenties and the stereotype of the arrogant kid prodigy. Still relatively unknown in the business—his only previous feature had been a budget movie called *Good Times* starring Sonny and Cher—he leaned heavily on aggressiveness and rank-pulling, which I attributed to the young director's typical fears about inexperience and failure. Now that he was gone, I resented and envied him. Time and again I thought, "I wish I could be in Friedkin's spot; I wish I could be out." Meanwhile, as the weeks wore on, Lear's persistent pressure to make edited scenes "even better" wore my good feelings toward him thinner and thinner. But as the producer, co-author, and sole responsible agent for three million dollars of other people's money, his reputation was on the line. He would not relent until he got his New Look.

About two months into the cutting, Lear called me into his office, closed the door, and, handing me a folder, said, "I thought you'd like to see this." It was a transcript of a late-night television show that Friedkin had appeared on in London. During the interview, Friedkin was asked what his last project had been before leaving the States. "The biggest piece of crap I ever worked on," were his approximate words, "something called *The Night They Raided Minsky's.*"

Friedkin directing Bert Lahr in rehearsal.
(Courtesy United Artists Corporation)

2 ■ *The Night They Raided Minsky's*
Part II: Life Sentence

The chief drawback of *Minsky's'* dramatic episodes was their predictability. The script had aimed for an old-fashioned charm, but, with a few important exceptions, no new twist of sophistication was added to please a modern audience. Jason Robards does succeed in seducing Britt Ekland, and Ekland does ultimately bare her breasts on stage, but the result is neither a fresh New Look nor reliable Old Drama. The first cut revealed a slightly more explicit version of something that had been seen so often before we were sure that audiences would be able to guess the lines before the actors spoke them.

Early in the film Norman Wisdom, who plays a sweet fall guy to Robards' fast smoothy, occupies the vacant afternoon stage to teach Ekland the meaning of burlesque. She looks on with smiling awe (of course) and occasional laughter as he steps into a bucket, falls down a flight of stairs, and throws open an exit door only to run into a brick wall. Her typical expressions are "Oh! Uh! Oh!" They frolic, they embrace, they go out into the streets, where Wisdom buys her a knish, something she's never eaten before. Nothing lifts their adventures above the harmless.

Sometime around the dawn of film a ridiculous short was made of a stiff little boy dating a prim little girl. He drives up to her on a city sidewalk in his kiddie car, steps out, offers his arm, takes her for a ride, buys her an ice cream, and without saying a word, very formally embraces and kisses her—then looks away shyly. I had seen this short on my first trip to the film library, and, unable to resist it, had ordered a print with no particular use in mind. As I intercut snatches of it now with the Wisdom-Ekland sidewalk courtship, it seemed to release the pent-up humor of the scene. This was confirmed when we tested the film before audiences. Viewers would watch silently as Wisdom mugs and Ekland coos; they would chuckle weakly and seem to fear that the scene was slipping irretrievably into embarrassing naïveté. But each time the kiddie short popped in, they laughed with pleasure. Apparently the short not only takes the Wisdom-Ekland absurdity a needed step into the comic beyond, it also signals, much to the audience's relief, that no one is expected to take this mind-bending naïveté seriously. This was a problem that had to be conquered in a dozen different ways throughout the editing of the film.

Take, for example, the moment when Robards provokes a fight between Selwyn, the owner of the delicatessen where the Minsky crowd hangs out, and Trim Houlihan, the pin-striped gangster (played by Forrest Tucker) who serves as the movie's Captain Hook. A disagreement over the price of a bagel escalates, Laurel-and-Hardy fashion, into an all-out war.

> TRIM: Hey, wait a minute. What's that?
>
> SELWYN: You said an order of bagel.
>
> TRIM: That's an order of bagel? One bagel is an order of bagel?
>
> SELWYN: New policy.
>
> TRIM: Two bagels is an order of bagel anywhere in town!
>
> SELWYN: I don't care about anywhere in town. Here you order another bagel, you pay another nickel.

An ensuing exchange of epithets grows into a slapstick fury of bagel-tossing and vest-throwing, each man trying to prove by disposing of his valuable possessions how little money means compared to the "principles" involved. Thinly amusing, the episode is only a minor improvement on the many scenes of grown men fighting that used to force chuckles out of children during long afternoons of silent funnies.

To give it added dimension, I laid down some vaudeville music over the fight and cut it to achieve a choreographed look. The music, an old number called "Gentlemen," has already been used to back up a Robards-Wisdom onstage bit; it lifts the bagel fight out of the context of plot and into the nonsense world of the burlesque stage.

The by now inevitable inclusion of stock footage lifts it some more. The first cut in the stock montage is a piece from an ancient newsreel depicting an Italian immigrant holding an infant child. As the man waves a little American flag, he points across the water to something significant, presumably the Statue of Liberty. To my pleasure and surprise, audiences consistently burst forth with laughter at the appearance of this cut—the land of individual opportunity, where grown men fight maniacally over the price of a bagel! The other stock cuts follow in rapid succession: kids on a pier diving into the East River along with their dog, a fighter attacking a punching bag, postal clerks sorting mail at an incredible speed, Isadora Duncan-style dancers leap-frogging over one another on a roof, the immigrant and child again—an odd assortment meant to suggest the zaniness of the times. Within this context, the bagel business slips safely into a new role as a launching pad for a nostalgic representation of the era.

The cuts range from six to sixty-eight frames apiece—the last ones being the shortest for a speeded up effect. Since there are twenty-four frames to a second, many cuts last only a fraction of a second, and the whole sequence is over in less than half a minute. The vaudeville music that began with the bagel fight continues throughout the stock snippets. Toward the end of the half-minute montage, snatches of Robards, Wisdom, and Ekland running along the street are interspersed with the other cuts. The third time the trio appears, they stay. The music stops abruptly with the first words of dialogue, and we are into the next scene.

Another episode that leans heavily on stock material comes toward the end of the film when Houlihan, who has absconded with Ekland, beats up the pursuing Wisdom and Robards in a penny arcade. It's a brutal scene for all its nonsensicalness, Houlihan batting the two heroes across the arcade over and over again like a couple of fat softballs. By this time the pattern I had established earlier in the film dictated that I again spice the action with a vaudevillian flavor and frenetic editing.

The penny arcade itself is suggestive of nuttiness, being filled with old-fashioned movie scopes that enable viewers to hand-crank animated scenes of cops and robbers, train crashes, and other sensational bits of inanity. I set up the montage in such a way as to suggest a connection between the movie-scope episodes and the fight scene itself. As Houlihan gleefully creams his pathetic opponents, Wisdom flies feet first into a nickelodeon, which—by editorial fiat—suddenly lights up and starts playing. With the music engaged, the montage begins, this time including a man cranking the animated pictures, pedals dancing off player-piano strings, and figurines fighting, along with the now obligatory items: a huge smokestack tumbling down, a falling telephone pole hitting a man on the head and driving him into the ground, a log roller tumbling into the water. A few seconds into the frantic montage, which keeps flashing back to the three combatants, the camera speeds up to create an old-time, jerky-jointed animated effect. Once again, the flood of amusing, ingenious, and unexpected elements mercifully sublimates the original material.

As I became more and more engrossed in this film, my misgivings gave way to some extent. I was beginning to have a glimpse of how the final product might look, and as a result my commitment to the project and my proprietary feelings toward it were growing. But, unlike my experience with any film I've worked on before or since, my anger and suffocation never faded. Nothing could shake my feeling of having been left to revive a corpse—nor suspend my conviction that I would be sticking tubes, and intravenous drips, and cardiac shocks, and artificial respirators onto and into and out of this patient for the rest of my life.

Mornings were most painful. Driving out of New Rochelle each day, I would get unspeakable urges to cross the George Washington Bridge and spend the next eight hours exploring Bayonne, and Hoboken, and Union City, New Jersey. I no longer wanted to see Lear. His one-track mind ("Make it better") had to me become a real-life horror show on the level of *Tarantula* or *The Thing*. Perhaps no amount of gratitude or praise would have been adequate, but Lear's predictable jolly demands made me seethe. At one climactic moment ("It's great, Ralph, but could you make it better?"), I told Lear to stuff it, crashed out of the cutting room, slammed the door behind me, and an hour later found myself pacing Fifth Avenue, dripping with guilt.

Each night I carried this monster show home with me in the form of self-pity or an addictive preoccupation with a difficult cut. My wife would dread hearing my key turn in the door. My kids would stiffen: "Here comes Dad." I yelled. I was surly. I was impatient. But every evening as I left the studio and walked to the parking lot, the same thought would overwhelm me: "Another day has just passed working on two minutes of reel four of *Minsky's*. Two minutes. One hundred eighty feet. All day long. There's got to be something better in life."

Lear, on the other hand, never stopped smiling. Unlike me, he was never surly, or rude, or depressed—all of which just heightened my feelings of guilt. He was so positive, I didn't know whether to cry or grow fangs. And his occasional bursts of inspiration were beginning to strike me as grievous intrusions.

One day he tore into the editing room with a Big Idea. He wanted to go out to a strip joint on Long Island, shoot a live striptease on a bar, and use the footage to open the film. "Don't you see," he cried, "the whole acceptance of nudity today will make a great contrast to the innocent period when the striptease was born!" "Norman, I really don't see it," I moaned, "you're dragging this thing in by its ass." But nothing could stop him. We went out to Hempstead, spent two and a half days shooting lewd smiles, wiggling thighs, and vigorously bouncing breasts, spliced some of the footage into the movie and finally threw it out.

Lear had a number of flash inspirations like that, and some were useful. But in addition to feeling trapped and abused, I was thinking more and more like the director and resisting ideas I didn't agree with. The directorial feeling was most intense during the cutting of certain particularly challenging scenes.

Indeed, for all the puffing up, rearranging, altering, and reviving that went on throughout this film, one scene more than any other needed resuscitation of mouth-to-mouth intensity. It was a crucial scene, a climax of sorts, because it brings the Robards-Ekland relationship to a long-awaited sexual conclusion. Having at that time never directed a movie, it was difficult for me to imagine what I would have done differently in the original staging to make this sequence work. But as an editor, I had created whole new scenes out of discarded plastic, and that was the first thing I set about doing here.

We are about two-thirds into the movie, in the middle of the seventh ten-minute reel. It is the second trip to Robards' hotel room, in which he seeks to give Ekland the single piece of Biblical knowledge she lacks. With Ekland looking and acting like a poof of peach soufflé eager to be consumed, the scene is pregnant with titillating potential. Unfortunately, very little that happens in Robards' room suggests the buildup of enough heat to make this soufflé cook.

To add some lustful expectation, I manufactured a tense preamble. Borrowing some of the edited-out film from their first trip to the hotel, I intercut it with the production number that is being performed at Minsky's the moment they are slipping away. The fleeting montage is accompanied by the music from the performance, an old vaudeville theme called "Around the World" (the tune to which schoolchildren have put the words "All the girls in France do the hula-hula dance"). The music continues throughout the Robards-Ekland cuts—we see them talking but cannot hear their words. In addition to establishing the simultaneity of the two pieces of action, the musical overlay lends a dreamlike quality to the lovers' flight. It's all done in split-second cuts, and the impact is strong:

A close-up of a male performer on stage doing a faggy bump and grind to "Around the World"; Robards and Ekland slipping through the crowded hotel lobby; the male dancer joined by eight females in rope skirts; the Knave and the Soufflé in the brass elevator cage, chatting and smiling and staring into each other's eyes; the burlesque queens bumping and grinding; the two lovers dashing down the dark hotel corridor; close-ups of the motley dancers swaying and leering. The light flashes on in Robards' room, and at that instant the music stops. Action.

The dialogue begins with Robards' kiss. Clearly the lovers still need a dose of editorial foreplay:

> EKLAND: Oh!
>
> ROBARDS: That couldn't have been your first kiss.
>
> EKLAND: The first with a clean-shaven man.
>
> ROBARDS: How was it?

EKLAND: I thought of a melon with a slice out. . . . You want to make love to me?

ROBARDS: How do you feel about it?

EKLAND: I feel to love is to wish to give pleasure.

ROBARDS: And you wish to give me pleasure?

EKLAND: Yes.

ROBARDS: Yeah, well, we've got about thirty-six minutes.

EKLAND: Oh. One thing I wish only, but then it is asking too much. . . .

ROBARDS: What?

EKLAND: I dreamed that the first time there would be a sign to tell me it is right.

ROBARDS: A sign?

EKLAND: Uh-huh. From Him. A sign. The Lord moves in wondrous ways.

Robards becomes irritated by this talk and several sentences later gets angry enough to punch his chest of drawers. Without either of them realizing it, the blow has disengaged his Murphy bed, which slowly descends from the wall. Ekland turns to see the bed magically filling the room, and her face takes on the familiar Dawn-of-Creation expression we've grown to tolerate. It's an amusing joke, the Lord being twisted into the Master Procurer, but it cannot hold up the scene alone, especially alongside the fast pace that's been established for the film.

Two pieces of music were needed to rescue this episode. The first, bursting forth when Ekland spots the miraculous bed, is Handel's Hallelujah Chorus (the use of which is always a sure sign that a film is in danger). As she looks on in wonder, we hear nine peals of "Hallelujah" and yet four more when she walks, arms outstretched, to the delighted Robards.

A loud knock at the door. "Rachel Elizabeth Schpitendavel, this is your father!" We've seen the bearded terror arrive in town earlier accompanied by a selection of stock cuts similar to those that escorted Ekland in. With Mr. Schpitendavel snorting and pacing in the hallway, Robards dashes to fold up the bed and hide in a closet. Here a second piece of emergency music, a vaudeville number, enhances the action, while the cutting aims for choreographed panic. Twice Robards runs to put the bed up, and twice it begins to slide down again accompanied by peals of "Hallelujah."

After a fierce argument, the father leaves in a fury, threatening to disown his daughter if she is not on the one-oh-five out of Penn Station with him that night. But Ekland has a more pressing matter on her mind. She turns to Robards, opting for her new life. He: "Well, we've got seventeen minutes now." They kiss. Sound track: "HALLELUJAH, HALLELUJAH!" A shameless crutch, it nevertheless succeeds.

By the fall of 1968, as I inched toward the completion of the film, I could see that something legitimate was emerging. Until then I'd tackled each scene individually, doing what I could to add to the drama, heighten the humor, and disguise the triviality. I had employed every known trick of editing, from the stylish use of stock footage, extensive dependence on music, frenetic cutting, and over-lapping episodes to the complete deletion of dialogue scenes, replaced instead by snippets of suggestive action. I had used so many opticals, by which I mean all the special effects that have to be processed in a lab—superimpositions, dissolves, alterations in the film speed, recropping a scene by blowing up a desired segment—that for the first time in my experience a film contained more special effects than original photography. As I reviewed the cumulative impact for perhaps the fortieth time, I saw at last that it was holding together. It had style, some genuinely funny moments, and tremendous pace. Even more important, it had developed the liberated grace to laugh at itself. Somehow the mass of clumsy, dated material had been conquered; a silly, uncohesive musical had become attention-holding for close to ninety-nine minutes.

Above all, this emerging *Minsky's* was highly contemporary. One might even conclude it had a New Look. The obvious fact that had eluded us from the beginning suddenly struck me now: The avant-garde quality Richard Lester had achieved in films like *Help!* could only be accomplished through editing. From the moment the Search for the New Look began, *Minsky's* was destined to be a cutting-room picture.

Despite the pressure that had been constantly pumped into the

Minsky's cutting room during that year, Lear and I managed to survive without a real fight. We did have several disagreements, though, one of which was a serious battle that I still regret having lost.

At the end of the film, after Minsky's theater has been raided and we know that it will be closed down for good, we see Bert Lahr on the empty stage fondling the relics of burlesque. When Friedkin and I produced the first cut, I had already begun putting music on the tracks, and for this concluding segment I chose a Chico Hamilton piece called "Thoughts." On it Hamilton uses a jazz bass alongside a haunting voice like that of a Jewish cantor. It is tingling music, and played over the forlorn Lahr alone in the empty theater, intercut with very short black and white snatches of the audience laughing—but without the sound of laughter—it had a powerful, dirgelike effect. One of the last things Friedkin had said to Lear before leaving was, "Whatever you do, don't cut that piece of music." The serious note at the end seemed to crystallize the whole film around an awareness that the burlesque era was truly dead, and that for all its frothiness, perhaps something of value, some innocence, had been lost. It almost ennobled the movie, like a touching truth at the end of a day of mindless frolicking.

But the chilling sequence frightened Lear. He insisted on inserting the brassy David Rose music that is always played alongside a striptease, and the movie was diminished as a result.

A second disagreement was minor and structural, though it did concern an innovation for which the film would be noted by reviewers.

From the first days of editing one of my concerns had been the creation of a smooth blending of the black and white stock footage with the color film. I hoped that one way to make the transitions would be to use some of Friedkin's original color footage in black and white, and I had a black and white work print of the movie on hand for that purpose. One day early in the film I was engrossed in some intricate cutting from stock footage to a sequence from the color film. After cutting it once, I decided to extend the original Friedkin material by reinstating a few frames that I'd trimmed from its beginning. I asked my assistant for the trim. As he rummaged nervously through the film barrel, I became more and more impatient, and finally exploded, "For Christ's sake, forget the trim and give it to me in black and white!" I intended to use the few black and white frames as a temporary filler, but what I saw changed my mind. We now had black and white stock footage, cutting to these few black and white frames from *Minsky's*—which because of the accuracy of the re-created set looks just like another piece of stock footage—and this same scene suddenly turning to color a few frames later. It seemed as if the stock footage itself had burst into Technicolor. The impact was magical.

Using this method I was able to integrate the stock material in a way that added sparkle to the film and avoided obvious, jolting transitions. I became self-conscious about the number of times we used this trick, but Lear was captivated by it, insisted on employing it more times than I thought was necessary, and it became our visual motif. When the film was finally released in December 1968—to generally positive reviews—some of the critics noted that the combined use of color and black and white film was a particularly interesting innovation. In the year-end issue of *New York* magazine Judith Crist wrote, "Director William Friedkin proves his sense of cinema again by remarkable intersplicing of newsreels and striking use of black and white fade-ins to color."

Crist, of course, had no way of knowing that Friedkin may not have even seen the film she reviewed. Indeed, I'd heard that he would be barred from the screenings because of his talk-show blunder and would ultimately have to pay to get in. But as ever when a new movie is released, any mention of the underlying rancors, ordeals, and moments of desperation was strictly taboo. The industry's unspoken attitude is that the production process has been nothing but cooperation, studded with regular bursts of creative inspiration; that the confident smiles on the vice presidents' faces were up there from the start; and that the picture that appears on the screen is exactly what we set out originally to achieve. No one ever talks about the agony of viewing the first cut—even though it is always felt. And as long as films are made, no outsider, neither friend nor colleague, will ever be invited to see that first cut flicker torturously across the studio's private screen.

Key transitional frames from
THE LIFE OF AN AMERICAN FIREMAN.
(Courtesy Museum of Modern Art)

3 ■ From a Recording Medium to an Art Form
The Invention of Editing

E very advance in filmmaking has been designed to make something more real—an event, an emotion, an idea. When moving pictures were still a novelty, an early inventor like Louis Lumière could show a two-minute film of an oncoming locomotive, choke his viewers with terror and delight, and certainly convince at least those front-row spectators who ran panic-stricken for the exits that they were getting their one franc's worth. But novelties wear off quickly, and the devices that once caused onlookers to grip each other's knees soon left them sitting impassively.

In the beginning it was enough to project any convincing representation of motion on the screen. But more inventive minds dreamed up greater delights. Of the primitive creators, a professional magician named Georges Méliès was the most popular and most ingenious. He saw in film the potential not only to record his magic shows for wider viewing but also to embellish them with special effects that heretofore were beyond his reach. Because he could stop the camera in the middle of a scene and make some opportune alterations, or crank the camera back to produce a double exposure, he could make a character vanish in a flash, turn him into an animal or a monster, or, with some additional effort, burst him into a thousand pieces.

In Méliès' little pictures the plot was often used merely as a frame for the wondrous special effects. A typical example from his hundreds of shorts is *The Devil in a Convent*, in which he transforms a devil and an imp into a priest and a choirboy and has them enter a convent. Once inside, the demons change back into their true forms, causing no little consternation among the fleeing nuns. In the end Saint George appears, wrestles with the devil, and liberates the convent from his grasp. In longer tales, such as *Cinderella*, *A Trip to the Moon*, and *The Impossible Voyage*, Méliès used double-exposure dissolves in order to ease the transition from scene to scene. Charming, erotic, imaginative, and poetic, his films made use of such techniques as stop-motion, fast and slow motion, reverse shootings, and animation to put a dynamic and delightful magic theater on the screen.

But despite Méliès' mastery of stage techniques and of certain camera techniques that put him way ahead of his envious contemporaries, he barely touched the mechanics of moviemaking as we've come to know them.

The first man to toy with the power inherent in film was an Edison Company mechanic and projectionist named Edwin S. Porter. What Porter did is so commonplace today that it takes some imagination to recognize how significant it was in his time. When we think back on the films we've enjoyed, we recall our favorite scenes as if they were all of a single piece. That a scene may have been shot on several different days, that it may be composed of scores of little shots lasting only a few seconds apiece, that a close-up of the hero may have been an afterthought of the director's (and shot long after the heroine—to whom he's supposedly speaking—has returned to her dressing room) hardly concerns us. When I was editing *The Night They Raided Minsky's*, I never considered any sequence of film to be an entity unto itself. Of all the burlesque routines that were acted out and filmed in their entirety, not one made it into the movie uncut. Each routine was shot from several angles, allowing me to intercut from one perspective to another. But, more than that, I used the stage material for dashes of spirit and atmosphere, and, instead of showing any routine from beginning to end, I sprinkled it throughout the picture in bits and pieces. Audiences today are so accustomed to seeing film juggled about like this and so capable of maintaining their perspective despite close-ups and flashbacks and sudden shifts in position that they would find it hard to appreciate what a mass of kaleidoscopic confusion a modern film would seem to a turn-of-the-century viewer.

The pioneer filmmakers, like the pioneers in any medium, were severely limited in the use of their tools, and of their limitations none was greater than the way in which they were imprisoned by the events that went on before their cameras. They had no idea that a scene could be composed of bits and pieces. They shot their scenes as if recording a play, and if anything went wrong, they threw away their exposed film and began shooting from the top again. Actors who were shot dead at the opening of a scene would have to lie motionless until the scene was complete—and if there were many retakes, they could spend an entire afternoon biting the dust.

Until 1902, the year that Porter made *The Life of An American Fireman*, what the filmmaker saw is what the audience saw. It was a continuous, unbroken piece of action, shot from a single camera angle, the perspective the all-encompassing, straight-on, eye-level view inherited from the theater. In fact, not only were the individual scenes unbroken, but few moviemakers dared even to break a picture down into scenes. American motion pictures at this time were at most two- or three-minute uncut recordings of humorous or historic happenings. If, as in Méliès' films, a picture was composed of more than one scene (a rarity), no attempt was made to link the last action of one scene with the first action of the next. Each transition was a total break—and this is what Porter changed.

Porter never considered himself an inventive genius. His only goal was to put stories on film, as Méliès was doing. But Porter had a resourceful mechanic's mind, and he turned at once to a search for ready-made components that would make his task easier. He chose to tell the story of a fire rescue, and to kick his project off, he used already available stock footage of urban fire companies in action. To this he added some staged action of his own and then pieced the various parts together as if they were a single event. What did it matter that the elements were originally unrelated? That the mother and child were screaming in a smoke-filled room long after the

Newark Fire Department had gone on parade before the movie cameras? Once they'd been pieced together, no one would know the difference.

Of course in piecing film together like this the assumption was that the audience would make certain leaps of association—for when Porter dissolved from a hand pulling a fire alarm to hundreds of firemen bursting into action, or from the fire engines rushing through town to the mother and child succumbing to the smoke, it was the first time that a film story had been created through the suggestive techniques of editing. As it turned out, Porter's new technique made his drama more real than anything that had appeared on the screen before—so real that audiences exhibited unprecedented anxiety over the fate of the victims and unbridled rejoicing over their rescue. Porter had unlocked the power of editing.

Once the concept of relating two separate pieces of film had been established, anything was possible. You could shoot a man out of a cannon, cut to the same man crashing amid bits of plaster onto someone's dinner table, and the audience would naturally assume that the second motion was a continuation of the first—that the man had not simply been dropped onto the table together with a bag of plaster from a scaffolding a foot or two above, but had crashed through the ceiling as a result of his cannon ride. You could show a battleship being blown to smithereens and then cut to a uniformed man struggling desperately to stay afloat in turbulent débris-strewn waters—and rest assured that the audience would conclude that this was a surviving sailor from the destroyed ship and not some actor desperately trying to look as if he were drowning in the shallow waters off Hollywood and Vine. Editing would not only enable filmmakers to bring dramatic and comic action to life; it could make ideas more tangible, too. In Porter's later film *The Kleptomaniac,* he would cut from a poor shoplifter getting a tough sentence to a rich one getting off lightly, and his viewers were angered by the contrast; while in *The Ex-Convict* he would cut from the former prisoner's humble hearth to the opulent home of the manufacturer who refuses him work. The choice of the cut invited comparison, outrage, and sympathy for the unlucky ex-con.

With the advent of editing, the range of emotions that the camera could stir became endless. No longer dependent on novelties or tricks or confined to recording events, film was suddenly a rapidly expanding medium; it could go as far as the inventiveness of the director could take it. The process of realizing all this potential in editing would take a mere two decades. In that time filmmakers would learn to blend the art of the theater with that of the novel and even the poem. By the mid-twenties masterpieces of artistry and sophistication would emerge that even today stand at the summit of motion-picture achievement. But in the meantime there was groping.

After *The Life of an American Fireman*, Porter's next important picture was his famous eight-minute adventure, *The Great Train Robbery*. He made two advances here. Instead of using dissolves—in which one scene gradually disappears as the next emerges—Porter cut directly from one action to the next, using no visual crutches to ease the transition. This alone was an important innovation, unburdening the young medium of a tedious and unnecessary convention. The other contribution of this film was the use of "parallel" action. When Porter cut from the scene of the holdup back to the location where the telegraph operator had been tied up by the bandits, audiences understood that they were being moved back in time in order to see the development of the story at another place. These small advances greatly enhanced the drama, and Porter's little film was found so exciting that when nickelodeons were introduced a year later, *The Great Train Robbery* was the major attraction for many months, inspiring imitations for years.

Although film technique was marching forward, neither Porter nor the majority of his contemporaries seemed aware of it. Not only did they fail to capitalize on Porter's editing discoveries, but even Porter slipped back into more primitive uncut productions. He seemed oblivious to his own achievements. For several years important clues were left unexamined. At the end of *The Great Train Robbery*, for example, Porter attached a piece of film unrelated to the rest of the story. It shows a close-up of a bandit firing his pistol point-blank at the audience. It never occurred to Porter to integrate this close-up into the story itself. It did not seem possible at the time. Although he had used editing to link the action of one scene to another and to suggest meanings and associations, in 1903 each scene was still composed of one continuous piece of film. To change the camera angle, to move in for a close-up, to cut to simultaneous action and then back again—all that would have to wait for the first true genius of the cinema, D. W. Griffith.

When Griffith initially proposed using a close-up to heighten dramatic tension, his producers warned him that the public would never buy half an actor. But Griffith was an ambitious, determined talent, with a strong sense of drama and a commitment to having artistic impact. With the door to the cutting room opened by Porter, Griffith would not be timid about barging in.

He first broke a scene in 1908 in *For Love of Gold*, cutting in the middle of the action to a full shot of one of the actors. No scene had ever been divided into more than one shot, and this simple innovation would soon cause a minor revolution. It would relieve the director of having to reshoot an entire scene if any part were imperfect—now he could simply resume action from another angle. It meant that actors whose usefulness had ended early in a scene could leave the set. It meant that the tedium of a long scene could be broken and the tempo heightened by fresh cuts and new angles. But Griffith's initial intention was less encompassing. He merely wanted to sidestep the cumbersome "dream balloon," a filmed insert that filmmakers were using to illustrate a character's fantasy or thoughts. By cutting up close to a single character Griffith could allow him to *act out* his thoughts. As in the past, the audience understood exactly what was happening—that despite the cut they were still watching the same scene, only from a zoomed-in perspective—and the dream balloon was banished from the screen for good.

Within the year Griffith took his advance further. While editing *After Many Years*, he cut right up to the face of his leading lady, a transition that shocked his producers. He then cut to the object of her thoughts, her husband stranded on a desert island, and finally back to the woman's face. In one sweeping gesture he had made the first use of a close-up since Porter's throwaway shot at the end of *The Great Train Robbery*, had cut away from a scene without finishing it, and had found a perfect cinematic way of representing a character's thoughts. One can imagine the reaction of the dismayed executives at Biograph. A woman in a room, suddenly a woman's face filling the whole screen, suddenly a man on a desert island—what the hell's come loose here! A genius gone beserk! But once again audiences were able to follow the director's logic, and the executives were greatly relieved.

Griffith's advances in movie technique were soon taking on the force of a one-man revolution. Each year he came closer to making film a worthy rival to his first love—literature—and proving that his adopted profession was more than a workingman's entertainment.

In 1909 he created a high-tension ending that quickly became known as the "Griffith last-minute rescue." By this time rescues of the sort portrayed in *The Life of an American Fireman* were failing to make the adrenaline flow— audience sophistication demanded a more artful representation of danger and suspense. Griffith achieved it in *The Lonely Villa* by cutting back and forth from the inside of a house where a frightened mother huddled with her children, to the bandits outside banging on her door, to the husband racing home to save his family. The impact was riveting.

Griffith discovered that, unlike a playwright, a filmmaker could expand time to meet his needs—the action that took place on the screen during the rescue bore little relation to the amount of time that the actual rescue might have taken. And in the process of juggling these pieces of film, he learned that as each little shot was joined to the next, a rhythm could be created that made the whole flow smoothly. It was the sort of thing viewers would not notice but which would deeply affect their enjoyment of the film.

Though Griffith's discoveries were not all in the realm of editing, even his photographic innovations depended on skillful editing techniques for their successful execution. In 1910 in a film called *Ramona*, for instance, he first used the extreme long shot, a distant panoramic view; and it achieved the greatest visual impact when cut in contrast with the closer shots. The next year, in *The Lonedale Operator*, another last-minute-rescue adventure, he mounted a camera on a truck in order to photograph a speeding train. With this added camera angle, he had a new and thrilling element to splice into the final flurry of last-minute-rescue cuts.

Surprising as it may seem today, at this time the one-reeler introduced by Porter was still the standard length for all movies. Who would sit for more than ten minutes for any one film? But Griffith was beginning to chafe under this limitation, and he was convinced that his films had enough art and artifice to go much longer. To his studio's dismay, he expanded an earlier film into two reels, which initially played at separate showings. But his instinct proved correct, for audiences were soon insisting that the two reels be shown together.

Griffith was constantly making headaches for his bosses. He overshot budgets, paid money for book rights, employed throngs of extras, and utilized expensive and lavish settings. But all this was mere preparation for the two enterprises upon which he was about to embark—*The Birth of a Nation* and *Intolerance*—mammoth projects that were designed to overshadow the spectacle films being made abroad and to reassert his industry leadership. Costing an unheard-of hundred thousand dollars and lasting almost three hours, *The Birth of a Nation* contained all the devices that Griffith had pioneered, and more. The scenes of hand-to-hand fighting, the contrast shots of frozen soldiers and charging soldiers, the symbolic cuts, the startling close-ups, all made the film glitter and move like nothing before. A Southern woman's refusal to marry a Northern suitor is impassioned by a memory cut to a Union soldier killing her brother. Even the final, heroic ride of the Klansmen, intensified by cuts to the galloping horses' hooves, is no ordinary last-minute rescue but a final confrontation of conflicting forces—the evil black man and his terrified white woman captive, the gathering Klansmen, the chilling ride. Some shots were less than a second long, while the scene itself built to a crescendo for many minutes. "It's like writing history in lightning," President Woodrow Wilson said after seeing it. Others, inflamed by the blatant white-supremacist attitude of the film, were moved to less civilized expressions. As if to suggest how far motion pictures had come in just a few years, Griffith's picture did far more than provoke audience fear of an oncoming train, or hat-tossing joy over the rescue of a fire victim. The emotional impact generated by his shrewd cutting technique was such that in city after city, enraged white viewers engaged in mob action and race riots.

As Griffith's mastery of the medium progressed, he cut his scenes shorter and shorter. Instead of following the old theatrical convention of beginning a scene at the "beginning"—say, when a character first enters a room—he would cut directly to the important action. By the time *Intolerance* was released in 1916 Griffith had honed his shots down even further. Each shot, whether of a mob gathering or a striker baring his chest to the militia or a factory manager picking up his telephone, was trimmed down to a single essential fact. Although the film, which skillfully wove together four stories from four different eras, was a financial disaster, its editing achievements and long-range impact on filmmaking were great. "All that is best in the Soviet film," said Sergei Eisenstein, the next great master of editing, "has its origins in *Intolerance*."

As Griffith reached his pinnacle and began his decline, many of the techniques he pioneered were being absorbed elsewhere in the industry. Smooth, sharp, clever cutting became the standby for the action pictures that were keeping the movie houses humming, and two producers who had been briefly associated with Griffith, Thomas Ince and Mack Sennett, were instrumental in adapting his discoveries to the everyday craft of making pictures. At one time Ince wrote, directed, and acted in his films, editing them in the kitchen of his home. As he became one of the biggest producers in Hollywood, he ceased to exercise his other talents, but he kept on editing to the end. His popular Westerns were always tautly cut, and he ruthlessly discarded anything that didn't contribute to the progress of the action. Unconcerned about the original intentions of a film that didn't work, he would recut it, reorder it, and change its meaning if necessary in order to make it entertain, a skill for which he would become known as "the doctor of the sick film."

While Ince was applying his editing talent to the cowboy picture and other action films, Mack Sennett, who considered himself a Griffith protégé, was applying the cut to comedy. The result was the Keystone Cops pictures, whose nonsense flew by faster than the audience could reason—thanks frequently to the editing-room work of Sennett himself.

Although America led the world in filmmaking during these early years, Europe was producing its own cinematic masters, several of them with editing talents every bit the equal of their American counterparts. By the early twenties, European directors, especially in Germany, became engaged in creating a more artistic and sophisticated motion picture as they put the new techniques of photography and editing to subtler psychological, emotional, and aesthetic use. Here, too, Griffith's influence was evident.

Nevertheless, by 1922, when Rudolph Valentino was being cast as a bullfighter in *Blood and Sand,* the magic that editing could perform was still a secret shared by relatively few in the movie business. The producers of *Blood and Sand* expected to pay a vast sum to have Valentino, playing a toreador, superimposed onto stock footage of a Madrid bull ring. They were surprised when film editor Dorothy Arzner said she could turn the trick in the cutting room. Arzner simply intercut close-ups of Valentino making the appropriate gestures with footage from the real bullfights. No expensive laboratory processing was needed—Valentino was clearly, and safely, in the fight.

Although editing was destined to remain the secret power in filmmaking, its effects were being felt on a wider and wider scale—

and nowhere more forcefully than in films with a political or propagandistic purpose. In 1930 film producer and historian Paul Rotha would remark on the phenomenon: "A notable instance was seen at the first presentation of Pudovkin's *The End of St. Petersburg* at the Film Society, London, on 3rd February, 1929. At one portion of the film, the action was worked to a crescendo by gradual short-cutting, with the title '*All Power to the Soviets!*' at the peak of emotion. The audience was observed to start gradually stirring, then muttering, until eventually many persons rose to their feet, cheering and clapping. I do not believe that the word 'Soviets' was of real importance, for had it been 'Royalists' or 'Monarchists' the effect would have been the same, due entirely to the emotions raised by the cutting."

It thus evolved that in the third decade of movie history, while American moviemakers perfected the entertainment capacity of film and leading European directors explored its subtler artistic potential, the power of the film editor to arouse and manipulate—on a scale as yet unimagined in the West—was being wrought to perfection in the new world under creation beyond the Finland Station.

Sergei Eisenstein.
(Courtesy Museum of Modern Art)

4 ■ Bolshevik Editors
The Fanatics of the Cutting Room

> LENIN: "Of all the arts, the cinema
> is the most important for us."
> EISENSTEIN: "I would never have believed that my
> passion for cinematography would one day exceed
> the limits of Platonic love."

When the Bolsheviks took power in Saint Petersburg in October 1917, eight months after the bourgeois February Revolution that overthrew the czar, they were a very different breed of men from the rigid, closed minds that would come to power later under Stalin. Anatoli Lunacharsky, Lenin's first minister of education, encouraged all forms of experimentation in the arts, assuring theater producers and painters alike that any work that "shocked the bourgeoisie" was sufficiently revolutionist for the new regime.

No segment of the Russian arts signified their isolation from the rest of the world at this time more than film. Most filmmakers had fled the country, taking their equipment with them, and film stock, made from the same material that was used in high explosives, was so rare that the postrevolutionary Russian filmmakers would later be said to have produced their pictures "out of thin air."

With domestic resources so scarce, emphasis was initially placed on the reworking of foreign footage. Editors like Esther Shub would take imported films, recut them to adjust the ideological component, and if that meant chopping apart two capitalist features to create one Soviet feature, so much the better!

The Russians approached the theory of filmmaking with a zeal unmatched in the West. If Marx had succeeded in dissecting the capitalist economy and laying bare its workings, then the young poets, theater directors, and writers who took to the art of moving pictures would do the same for film. And if, as Marx said, *work* was the basis for all value in the economy, these cinematic enthusiasts would find in *editing* the basis for all value in film. They maintained that the essential motion in film was not the motion that went on before the camera, but the motion that was created from cut to cut. As they saw it, the true composition of a film was determined at the cutting bench.

Dziga Vertov, the young poet responsible for assembling newsreels of the Red Army during the civil war, was the first aficionado of editing. He proclaimed an end to film's dependence on drama, insisting that its visual qualities were paramount and that through the proper juxtaposition of images in a "cine-essay" any idea could be convincingly represented. He was soon issuing manifestos on the subject and exhorting his comrades to follow his lead. His influence spread quickly. Both he and Shub would prove masters of the "compilation" film, in which newsreel footage and pieces of other filmmakers' works would be welded together to make a documentary feature. In addition to being editing's first enthusiast, Vertov may also have been its first casualty, for his later work was said to be so dominated by editorial effects and trickery that it became painful to view.

The Russians quickly sensed in D. W. Griffith a comrade in cinematic vision. Although the Western nations had put up a trade barrier around the young Communist state, a contraband print of *Intolerance* reached Moscow through the astute efforts of Communist Party members in Berlin, who included the picture (originally impounded by the German government during the war) among the food and medical supplies they were smuggling into the embattled nation.

The print made its way to the film workshop of Lev Kuleshov, a young filmmaker who, like Vertov, had emphasized the importance of editing. Kuleshov and his students would take films apart to get to the essence of what made them work and even try recutting them to see if they could improve on the originals. *Intolerance* was given the supreme workover and was later credited by workshop member V. I. Pudovkin and by Sergei Eisenstein as having had a major influence on Russian film. When *The Birth of a Nation* reached the Soviet Union in the early twenties, Lenin would invite Griffith to take over all Russian film production. But in the meantime, Griffith was accorded the same treatment as other bourgeois directors, and the capable hands of Esther Shub put *Intolerance* into its final Bolshevik shape.

A determination to unlock and reveal the secrets of editing became the passion of Russian directors, and for a time film theory seemed to be a more important Soviet product than films themselves. It was this passion that led Kuleshov to hit on an ingenious experiment that has become one of filmmaking's enduring parables. Using a piece of film depicting the old actor Muzhukhin with a perfectly deadpan expression, Kuleshov intercut identical prints of Muzhukhin's face with three successive images: first from the face to a plate of soup, then from the face to a child playing with a Teddy bear, and finally from the face to an old woman in a coffin. People who saw the finished product naturally assumed that each time the film cut from Muzhukhin to one of the three elements, it was revealing what the actor was observing at that moment. But to Kuleshov's delight, not only were viewers unable to perceive that each cut of Muzhukhin was identical, they frequently praised the actor for his subtle and convincing portrayal of three distinct feelings—joy at seeing the child at play, hunger upon viewing the bowl of soup, and remorse over the dead woman! Clearly there was more power in film editing than met the naked eye.

The Russian filmmakers soon made films that substantiated the importance of their theoretical explorations. The deeply affecting films of Pudovkin and Eisenstein and later Dovshenko quickly established the Soviet Union as an important center in world cinema. Said Eisenstein, who was inclined toward philosophical bombast, of the Russian editing techniques, "We have discovered how to force the spectator to think in a certain direction. By mounting our films in a way scientifically calculated to create a given impression on an audience, we have developed a powerful weapon for the propagation of the ideas upon which our new social system is based."

Eisenstein came to film from the theater. He was a driven man, in tireless study and pursuit of art, whose mind swarmed with new ideas, and who, at least in the beginning of his career, was sufficiently at one with the social upheavals around him and the bureaucrats who watched him to exploit his talents successfully.

He began as one of the avant-garde directors who flourished under Lunacharsky's springtime of the arts. But his extreme theatrical experiments at Moscow's Proletkult Theatre—on one occasion he brought the audience into a factory and forced them to follow the players from location to location within the building—were flailing about beyond the theater's loosest limits.

Aside from several months' study with Kuleshov in 1923, his main early experiences with film were in Esther Shub's cutting room, where he watched her remake bourgeois features and play with the outtakes to assemble experimental concoctions. In 1924 she remade Fritz Lang's *Dr. Mabuse* into a people's picture called *Gilded Putrefaction,* and Eisenstein was transfixed by her performance. The next year he grabbed the opportunity to make his first film with the Proletkult players, and, in true Russian fashion, he was soon making theoretical pronouncements about his newfound medium.

Eisenstein coined the word "montage" to refer to the way a film is pieced together, or "mounted." The word is virtually synonomous with editing, but it carries a more potent charge, the connotation being more "the act of creation" than "the act of arrangement." He spoke of rhythmic montage to indicate the sense of beat that is created from cut to cut, and tonal montage to indicate the play of light and dark elements; he explored directional cutting to achieve continuity of motion by having people or elements of one shot move in the same or opposite direction as elements in the adjoining shot, and he used cutting on form, in which another sort of continuity is achieved through a similarity of structure—say, the roundness of a face giving way to the round opening of a cannon barrel.

Of Eisenstein's editing theories, his most famous is the concept of "shock attraction." By this he meant juxtaposing two images in such a way as to evoke an idea or a feeling that went beyond the sum of its parts. He illustrated his point with Oriental hieroglyphic writing, in which two symbols were joined to make an entirely new idea. Such was the case, for instance, when the symbols for eye and water were combined to yield "crying."

All of this constituted montage. Eisenstein might have been amused by the way Hollywood later appropriated the word—to describe the portion of a film where calendar leaves drift by to indicate the passage of time or snippets of action are pieced together to represent a dying man's memory or stock shots are interwoven for atmospheric effect, as in the opening reel of *Minsky's*—for this was not at all what he had in mind.

By all accounts, Eisenstein was convinced of the revolutionary impact of his work and the theories behind it, and he proclaimed his first picture, *Strike*, to be the "October of the Cinema." Dziga Vertov he assigned to secondary importance—as filmmaking's "February."

In 1925 both Eisenstein, then twenty-seven, and Pudovkin, thirty-two, were commissioned to make films about the abortive 1905 uprising against the czar. The result would be two of the monuments of moviemaking. Although Eisenstein's film has more breathtaking power, the path Pudovkin chose, more in keeping with the narrative style of Griffith, is the one that has so far proved more enduring. Less interested in experimentation, Pudovkin told a revolutionary tale in the traditional narrative way, and he perfected the methods by which editing could make a film an exciting narrative medium. In *Mother,* an account of the experiences of one family caught up in the conflicts of the time (based loosely on Maxim Gorki's book), he broke ground that Hollywood and TV are still tilling. Refining many of the editing techniques Griffith pioneered, he adapted the rapid cut used so advantageously in "last-minute rescues" to the smaller dramas and feelings of everyday life.

In the opening scene of *Mother* the drunken, villainous father comes home looking for something to pawn. He steps on a stool to grab the cherished old clock off the wall, only to be intercepted by his wife. Pudovkin now starts a flurry of quick cuts as the woman tries to pull the man away from his quarry. We see her weary but determined face, her hands gripping his thighs, his contorted face as he struggles to free himself from her grip. A quick shot of the son leaning up in bed. The father's angry, snarling features; her hands clutching his trousers; the stool tipping; the clock being ripped from the wall; a piece of its inner mechanism rolling across the room and keeling over to a stop. There's a sense of stillness as the cutting flurry ends and the camera focuses on the father stretched out on the floor. (We never actually saw either him or the clock crash.) Now Pudovkin continues with shots that last much longer, suggesting a resolution of the action. Astute editing technique of this sort set a standard for moviemaking that still prevails. Pudovkin's insight to allow the part to speak for the whole—the military officer's kid-gloved hands, shown in close-up as the officer menacingly rubs them together—and his use of symbolism—the face of the imprisoned young man when he learns he's about to be freed intercut with shots of birds splashing in a village pond, of a child laughing, and of a swollen brook—would eventually become film clichés. But unlike other pioneer films, *Mother* can be enjoyed today with almost as little effort as a contemporary adventure.

Eisenstein's *Potemkin* is a film of another order. Uninterested in telling a simple story or focusing on the ordeals of one or two people, Eisenstein strove for a symphonic effect in which the lives of individuals were mere elements in a grander scheme. That this effect is rarely sought except by underground and experimental filmmakers may account for the fact that nothing of quite this caliber has since been achieved.

The story is about the mutiny of the sailors aboard the battleship *Potemkin*, the massacre of sympathetic citizens in the port city of Odessa where the ship is temporarily anchored, and the confrontation between the *Potemkin* and its sister ships in the Russian navy. Throughout, Eisenstein displays a mastery of editorial technique that is stupendous.

Early in the film, a young sailor, smarting under the blows of his petty officer and infuriated by an infestation of maggots that made the meat rations inedible, is washing dishes in the officers' mess when he comes upon a plate inscribed "Give Us This Day Our Daily Bread." Overcome with rage, he smashes the plate on the edge of a nearby table. To emphasize the importance of the moment, Eisenstein, who could not rely on dramatic sound effects or musical crutches like the Hallelujah Chorus, chose to show the action through nine different shots lasting a total of just over four seconds. The jagged, overlapping, incomplete action—in which the sailor actually sends the plate crashing twice—is all *effect*. It is as far from a true and simple recording of an event as a cubist painting is from a photograph of the same subject. And its power is terrific.

Many of Eisenstein's editorial effects in *Potemkin* are heightened by the freedom he gave himself to stretch time. One occasion in which this was pronounced was the endless split-second that follows an order to execute a group of insubordinate sailors; while another was the final drama of the film, when the mutinous *Potemkin* is being approached by loyal battleships. The halting shots to the clenched fists, indecisive faces, and wavering rifles of the sailors who have been commanded to execute their comrades extend the tension to an almost unbearable degree; while the shots of the sailors taking their battle stations, the great guns moving into position, the colossal battleships steaming through the seas agonizingly delay the climactic conclusion. In between the use of poetic detail heightens almost every event. When Dr. Smirnov is hastened to the boat's side during the mutiny, we are apprised of his fate by the simple image of his pince-nez—the instrument he'd used to inspect the maggoty meat and declare it fit—slowly dangling from the ship's rigging.

Although the movie is filled with stunning moments, the massacre on the Odessa steps outweighs them all; it remains for editors everywhere the single most intimidating piece of film ever assembled.

By the time we arrive at the Odessa steps, the sailors aboard the battleship *Potemkin* have mutinied and are anchored in the Odessa harbor. Crowds of townspeople have gathered on the steps overlooking the harbor to cheer the mutinous crew. Certain characters are introduced during these moments of good cheer and occasional small conflict—a kneeling mother who lovingly encourages her little boy to wave to the sailors; an older, noble-looking woman wearing a pince-nez, a dark hat, and a white shawl; a young male student wearing glasses; a legless cripple in a dark beret—and these characters will soon achieve greater focus in the massacre. Drifting, laughing, momentarily dramatic, momentarily whimsical, these initial moments on the steps, consisting of fifty-seven carefully chosen shots, each lasting several seconds, suggest the calm before the storm. For everything is occurring within the shadow of the czar's armed forces, who have yet to make their move.

A title card—"Suddenly"—followed by several short cuts, each less than a second, of a woman's head jerking, her dark hair swirling, as she reacts to a horrible sight. Her panicked face screaming. Close views of faces in the crowd contracting in fear. The legless cripple scurries down the steps on his hands and trunk followed by other frightened citizens. Suddenly everyone is moving in one direction, toward the camera, and the rounded top of a lady's parasol fills the screen.

After twelve seconds we get our first glimpse of the source of the panic. A long shot from the top of the steps reveals the fleeing citizens; as they move toward the top of the frame, a row of white-jacketed soldiers, rifles thrust forward, bayonets fixed, emerges at the bottom. A close-up of feet running down the steps, the camera moving alongside them. A long shot from the bottom of the steps of the great onrushing throng. Another close-up, two feet on the steps falling forward, followed by buckling knees. Shot after shot of individuals in the crowd as they make their headlong dash down the steps. Each tiny portrait is charged with power: a little boy sits down in confusion near two fallen bodies and places his hands to his ears to shut out the din of rifle fire. Throughout the massacre, these intimate close-ups of terror and pathos are mixed with long shots of the mad flight.

The mob is bounding down the steps in panic; they seem hardly able to grab each step ahead of them fast enough. Sometimes the camera moves alongside, sometimes it lets them pass. We see the flight from various angles; the pace of the cutting generates an awesome sense of fear. A glimpse of the white-jacketed soldiers moving down the steps in a rigid line, rifles braced, their long stark shadows advancing ahead of them. A volley is fired. The small boy who had waved to the ship falls as his mother rushes on, unaware that she's left him behind.

The rhythm of the editing has now been established. There are the soldiers, the panicked populace, close views of individuals, and finally a thread of personal drama. Eisenstein will keep cutting from one aspect to the other, mixing his themes to compose a mountingly charged symphony.

The flight of the mob. Short cuts from various angles. The fallen little boy, blood on his face. He mouths the word "Mommy!" Cut to the mother. She stops. She realizes the boy is missing. She looks back as others stream by her. In the utter madness of flight, one element is about to move against the grain in solemn counterpoint. The mother's eyes wide with horror. The little boy keeling over as the stampede flies over him. Anonymous boots tread upon the little boy's ankles and fingers. The mother's face fills the screen, horrible with agony. She raises her hands to her mouth and screams. Back and forth from her face to parts of her little boy. A boot crushes his hand. Distorted eyes of the mother, her fingers pressing maniacally against her temples.

A long shot of the masses lunging down the steps toward the camera; a man in the crowd grasps his chest and falters. A close-up of the little boy mangled by boots. The stampeding crowd, individuals dropping. The mother moving slowly against the tide, approaching her child in solemn horror. The faltering man drops. Cut upon cut of the fleeing populace, the backs of their heads emerging in the foreground at the bottom of the screen and disappearing at the top in an endless procession; then coming toward us, faces streaming past the eye of the camera; then from side angles like a forest in flight. The mother approaching the boy surrounded by a group of sympathizers; her compatriots suddenly turn and run in fear. The mother, unaware of anything else, raises the boy in her arms. She cries out accusations. Clumps of bodies on the steps, feet scurrying by.

The mother, carrying the boy, approaches a small clot of people who have hidden behind a parapet by the side of the steps. The woman wearing the pince-nez and white shawl turns to those around her. Title card: "Let us appeal to them." Huddled, frightened faces. The rigid white line of soldiers advancing, firing. The faces of those who will stand and make the appeal. We read their mixed reactions of fear, resolution, and doubt. Others frantically escaping. A view of the group facing up the stairs, appealing to the soldiers. The riflemen, clicking forward, enter the screen from top, their boots arriving first, while at the bottom of the frame the mother, her back to the camera, emerges in the foreground facing them: "Listen to me, don't shoot." The soldiers from behind, stepping over dead bodies as they proceed, their functioning unimpeded by the human obstacles.

A full shot of the woman with the child, facing the camera, looking up the steps. Shadows of the advancing soldiers stretch ominously across her. She mouths the words "My child is hurt." The group led by the older woman appealing to the troops. The mother gunned down, dropping her son alongside her.

A first glimpse of the situation at the bottom of the steps. Mounted Cossacks meeting the fleeing citizens with butchering sword blows. Close-ups of the fearsome Cossacks charging. Another close-up somewhere on the steps of people dropping. An old man tries to lift a fallen woman. The followers of the woman with the pince-nez fleeing. The soldiers marching over the fallen mother and her son. A beautiful young mother with a Lillian Gish face. Her hand on a wicker baby carriage with a baby inside. She is full of anguish, trying to protect the carriage, hesitant to go forward, terrified of the oncoming danger. She bites her lip. A mixture of full shots and close-ups to her hands and face showing her torment. A volley of shots from silhouetted rifles. The beautiful mother's mouth falls open. Close-up of her hands grabbing her stomach around a large silver buckle. Her head swaying. Her clutching hands. The Cossacks chopping at people as they arrive at the foot of the steps. The young mother, blood gushing over her white gloves and silver buckle. Her face. A groan. She falls, slipping out of our view, leaving the wicker baby carriage on the screen. The carriage precariously close to the edge of the steps. Close-up of the wheels teetering at the tip. The boots, the bayonets advancing.

Eisenstein has been defying time as no filmmaker before, showing us detail upon detail of simultaneous aspects of the drama in a film sequence that lasts far longer than a real slaughter could possibly take. The steps have become an endless moment of terror. Now he utterly affronts the linear flow, repeating the collapse of the mother. She crumples against the carriage, and in a split-second cut that hardly gives us time to register its information, the wheels of the carriage tip over the step.

We are now immersed in the waves of people reaching the cul-de-sac at the bottom of the steps. A long shot of the mob, the Cossacks moving through unthwarted, dealing butchering blows with their sabers. Somewhere on the steps an old man continues to try to raise his wife.

The baby carriage slips away as the mother falls senseless against it. We see the baby emotionless within it as it goes clippety-clump down the first dozen steps. The woman wearing the pince-nez, her hat and shawl gone, rivulets of blood on her face, looks back at something (the carriage, we assume) and cries in anguish. A long shot of the carriage gaining speed. A side view of the rear portions of the mob, still scampering helter-skelter down the never-ending steps; the white line of troops advancing mechanically behind them. Puffs of smoke from the row of rifles. The steps littered with bodies. The dying mother's last breath. The baby in the runaway carriage, unaware of danger. The bedraggled pince-nezed woman, her breath giving out. A close-up of her face as she watches in impotent terror. The carriage wheels picking up speed.

A brief close-up of the young student in glasses. A small clot of people on the steps. An old man trying to help a friend as others race by behind them. Commotion all around. A flash glimpse of the student's face, his eyes wide as he screams, his double image revealed in a mirror that Eisenstein has placed alongside his head to intensify the moment. Then the object of his terror: the carriage hurtling by at breakneck speed. The boots of the advancing troops. They pause over a heap of civilians: a close view up the steps of three soldiers from the waist down, their rifles pointing at the heap of fallen people whose hands reach up from the bottom of the frame, pitiably supplicating. A burst of rifle fire and smoke drifts across the screen.

Eisenstein is leaving nothing out. Every angle, every element of the drama is exploited. That everyone should be dead or gone by now hardly concerns us, for film no longer pretends to be an uncut record of real time.

A flash shot, less than a second, of the bounding carriage as it teeters, about to overturn. Close-up of a fierce, long-mustached Cossack giving a *hack, hack* with his sword. In four half-second cuts his face fills the screen, and he utters a horrible cry as his off-camera sword finds its target. It is the woman with the pince-nez. Her bloodied face, blood gushing out of her right eye, her pince-nez demolished, her mouth agape in hopeless doom. We can almost feel her knees buckle. It never occurs to us that we did not actually see the saber strike her. (Any more than we are aware, while watching Alfred Hitchcock's terrifying adaptation of this technique in *Psycho,* of the absence of direct knife hits during the shower sequence.)

Cut to the turret of the battleship *Potemkin.* Title card: "The brutal military power answered by the guns of the battleship." Front view of the battleship. A potent symmetrical shot of the two guns moving into position facing directly into the camera. Card: "Target! The Odessa Theater." The intricate stonework of cherubs. Card: "The headquarters of the generals!" The guns firing. The wall crumbling. The guns firing again. Three shots of stone lions guarding the theater. First a sleeping lion. Cut. A slightly aroused lion. Cut. A roaring lion. Explosion. The theater's tower is enveloped in smoke and begins to crumble.

Again we shift scenes, now to a stirring string of cuts symbolizing the advent of night. We hardly have time to realize that we were never given a resolution to the disaster on the steps. Eisenstein chose to leave the steps with the conclusion implied but not shown. Without a finale there's no drop in excitement, nor even the predictable maudlin knotting of disgust. The transition to the sailors' retaliation, coming as it does just past the height of the action on the steps, demonstrates Eisenstein's determination not to let the breathtaking sequence stand out as a miniature tour de force. He moves ahead so quickly that he does not give us time to reflect upon the magnificent thing we've witnessed.

The massacre on the Odessa steps consists of 157 shots, plus titles, lasting six and three-quarter minutes (four and a half minutes at modern projector speeds). Its nuances and complexities, its rhythms and counterrhythms, its themes and counterthemes, its stark bare images add up to a cinematic achievement of true symphonic proportions. From the technical point of view we could discuss Eisenstein's accomplishments in this sequence for chapters.

At the time it was first seen, the film was a marvel beyond what anyone dared anticipate. Upon previewing an early cut of *Potemkin* with several other cultural and military bigshots in 1926, Lunacharsky jumped out of his seat and said, "We've been witness at an historic cultural event. A new art has been born." It was the first of many such pronouncements. Douglas Fairbanks described viewing *Potemkin* as "the most intense and profoundest experience of my life." While Charlie Chaplin proclaimed the picture "the best film in the world." Future conclaves of film historians would reaffirm Chaplin's rating.

The power of the film is so great and the sense of the moment in history it portrayed so real that sailors who had served on the real *Potemkin* "recalled" fictitious incidents that Eisenstein had inserted in the film for emotional effect. During their 1933 court martial, mutineers from the Dutch battleship *De Zeven Provincien* claimed to have been inspired by the movie.

Amazingly, Eisenstein spent just three months on *Potemkin* from the start of shooting to the last hectic moments in the cutting room. Most remarkable, he cut the whole film in less than three weeks of near 'round-the-clock labor. (His cutting assistant would later serve him with a paternity suit, producing as evidence a photograph Eisenstein gave to her inscribed, "In memory of those nights spent together.")

In his writings and lectures Eisenstein went on at length about theories of editing. He despised the "bourgeois" cinema and actually wrote an article entitled "Down with the Story and the Plot." He would pontificate that "the technique of leaps which produces a comic effect in static conditions produces an emotional one in the case of a dynamic process." As much as I doubt that art can be put together from such principles, Eisenstein's fervid immersion in film theory probably accounts for the facility and quickness with which he composed *Potemkin*. Because of his eager study of traditional art forms, the nature of film rhythm, the effect of offbeat elements, the cubist method of representing action in broken, unfitting pieces, the poignancy of filmic metaphor, he cut *Potemkin* with absolute confidence in what he was trying to achieve as well as the methods he would employ to get there.

But Eisenstein's theorizing was never a substitute for artistic passion, and although it propelled him along, it did not entirely dominate his work. Once he got into the cutting room, he allowed the film to lead him into areas he hadn't expected to go. "The filmed material at the moment of editing can sometimes be wiser than the author or editor," he said. And he acknowledged of *Potemkin*, "I realized the emotive scenes, as the Holy Scriptures say, 'without seeing my creation'; that is, I realized them thanks to the feelings which the events inspired within me."

When I first saw *Potemkin*, I had been in the editing room for about a year and I could well understand the terror the film struck in the hearts of editors, bourgeois and revolutionist alike. Although its naval scenes had become the model for zillions of World War II battleship encounters, the film as a whole had never been equaled. Awing as *War and Peace* or *Moby Dick* might be to an aspiring writer or the Himalayas to a first-time mountain climber, *Potemkin* stands on such a peak that it has become the subject of self-effacing jokes among film editors; they have lived in its shadow for so long, they no longer dare to harbor thoughts of topping it.

Editors Harold Masser, Harold May, George Barto, and Bill Hornbeck in the Mack Sennett cutting room, 1922. *(Courtesy Marc Wanamaker, Bison Archives)*

5 ■ The Birth of a Profession
Technicians with Dreams

EDITOR. Technician who assembles final print of
film from various scenes and tracks available; works
closely under director's control except in routine pictures.
—LESLIE HALLIWELL,
The Filmgoer's Companion

"The studio I became connected with," recalls Bill Hornbeck, one of the top editors of all time, "was the Mack Sennett Keystone. They bought property from my father in 1912 and built the studio there, and one little corner we kept as a home. So I grew up right there with the movies next door to us and would climb over the fence and watch them. And they didn't mind; I was a youngster hanging around, and I didn't cause them any trouble. That's how I got interested. Well, I kept asking for a job, any kind of job, and they said, well, when you get long pants, we'll give you a job.

"When I got out of school I wanted to do something to get in, and it didn't matter what I did. My grandfather was the gateman at the studio and he kept watching for a job, and when one came up, first thing he called me. I was fifteen years old then and working in my mother's restaurant. It was noontime, and I was washing dishes, and my mother was busy as the devil. I quit the job right in the middle of lunch—she never forgave me for that!

"Well, I got on my bike and out I went to the studio and got a job winding film in the lab. They called it a 'film wrapper.' I did that for just a short time. Of course the business was expanding very rapidly with these comedies. We did a film a day, six one-reelers a week, and one two-reeler. We had thirty companies shooting, thirty different directors, camera crews and all. Of course the camera crew was only a cameraman—he didn't have an assistant, he didn't have a focus, he was the works. He loaded his film in the morning, he carried his camera, he put the slate out in front, he unloaded the camera at night, got the negative to the lab, and the next morning he broke the film down, separating out the usable takes—he was an entity of his own.

"Anyway this wrapping thing didn't last very long. I became a printer, printing the daily rushes; stayed in there about a year. Then I went into the dry room where we rotated film on drums until it was dry. Now all this took place in one large building. At first I was interested in the miniature department, the tiny trains and all that, but I soon got fascinated with the editorial end of it, and I would hang out there whenever I had any spare time. The editors had to do their own splicing, so they would get me to do the splicing for free—saying I was going to learn to be an editor. It got so that I would work nights on these reels of film, and I thought, well, I'll be an editor, it won't be long now, and so I have to splice all these reels.

"Well, from drying I went into projection. Being a projectionist fascinated me because now I could watch the films and see what was happening as they went through the editorial stages. Then the war broke out. I was too young to go by six months, but most of the editors were drafted, and they started to use kids. That's really how I got into it so rapidly."

In the early boom years of the industry that Hornbeck describes people were pouring into film from every imaginable occupation—Sennett himself had been a boilermaker—and so it was not astounding that a kid of seventeen would be promoted to film editor, war or no. Filmmaking, the first great collaborative art form, started out, in the United States at least, as democratic as a gold rush.

The pace of the industry heightened the director's need for collaborators. It began with cameramen—Billy Bitzer and Edouard Tissé, the ingenious craftsmen who developed long-standing associations with Griffith and Eisenstein, are two important early examples.

But as the industry grew, so did the number of collaborators upon whom directors were forced to depend. By the twenties scriptwriters and scenarists were making significant inroads on the picture. In some studios scenarists would produce a "continuity," or shooting script, which worked out the picture shot for shot in advance, and while this practice lasted, the director slipped to the second slot in the studio totem. Largely overlooked in the hubbub of growth and excitement and the lengthening list of credit lines was the emergence of the film editor from a mere splicer to a significant contributor to the film's final form.

Kevin Brownlow, a British producer-director and the author of *The Parade's Gone By*, a fine and affectionate account of the silent era, is one of the few film historians to take note of the birth of the editing profession. Among the early editors he interviewed is Clarence Brown, who began his career in Fort Lee, New Jersey, as an assistant to the popular director Maurice Tourneur and quickly graduated to directing his own films with such stars as Rudolph Valentino and Greta Garbo (whose career he launched). "I think I was Tourneur's first editor," says Clarence Brown. "In those early days—nineteen-fifteen—the only two people who knew anything about the film were the director and the cameraman, so they had to edit it between them. I used to watch this process with interest. I once saw Tourneur with twenty pieces of film in his mouth. I got it into my head that I could do it. Within a month I was editing his pictures and writing his titles, relieving him of that end of the business entirely."

In a letter to Brownlow, Dorothy Arzner, who came to cutting from typing scripts and would later be famous as one of the first women directors, recounts her equally informal introduction to the craft, which at this time (1919) was settling down to a recognized specialization: "One cutter, Nan Heron, was particularly helpful. She was cutting a Donald Crisp picture, *Too Much Johnson;* I watched her work on one reel and she let me do the second, while she watched and guided every cut. On Sunday I went into the studio and assembled the next reel. On Monday I told her about it and she looked at it and approved. I finished the picture under her guidance. She then recommended me to keep script and cut the next Donald Crisp picture."

From the very beginning cutting was a profession whose characteristics changed markedly from set to set and studio to studio. Margaret Booth, who began a half-century cutting career in the early twenties, has credited Clarence Brown with becoming the sort of director who would let an editor do his job without interference: "I cut a number of his pictures and never saw him in the cutting room." Indeed, throughout much of the industry a common procedure was developing whereby the editor would cut a portion of the film on his own, screen it for the director, and then make modifications according to the director's critique.

Still, a number of directors jealously guarded the editorial prerogative, sometimes with admirable results. Continuing in the Griffith tradition, filmmakers like Chaplin, Abel Gance, Harold Lloyd, and Buster Keaton were frequently the true editors of their films. Judging from Keaton's account of the relationship, his editor performed the role that would today be ascribed to the assistant editor:

"J. Sherman Kell was my cutter," he told Brownlow. "Father Sherman, we called him. He looked like a priest. He broke the film down and put it in the racks. I'd say, 'Give me that long shot of the ballroom.' He'd get that out. 'Give me the close-up now of the butler announcing the arrival of his lordship.' As I cut them, he's there splicing them together. Running them onto a reel as fast as I hand them to him."

In the major studios, however, the responsibilities of the man with the scissors were growing. Together with the title writer, he worked out the final arrangement of most films, and when a film didn't work, the two men might revise its entire concept by rearranging some of the scenes, or change intended meanings by altering the actors' words on the cards. At Keystone, where Bill Hornbeck in 1921 emerged as the supervising editor, the director had virtually no control over his work once it went to edit. As Hornbeck says: "He was too busy getting the next picture ready. In those really early days an editor would be on each picture. He would work with the director if he was able, and get it down to a pretty darn good cut. About Wednesday of every week, I would take over and do the final cut—getting it down to the fine points with Sennett. But we had to ship a picture every Saturday night regardless of what happened. So down toward the wire, the editor ruled the film—and we didn't get paid the next week if that film didn't go out.

"A lot of times we were forced to make big changes, alter the meanings and so forth. I remember one in particular. Eddie Cline made a picture, and it was overdramatic, overdone—it turned out to be just a lot of baloney—so we wouldn't ship it. Now Pathé was releasing our pictures, and at the end, to fulfill our contract with them, we had to get rid of this one. So we decided to make it a farce. We called it *The Gosh-Darned Mortgage,* put the craziest titles in, and just kidded the whole thing from beginning to end. We thought, well, we'll never get another contract with Pathé after this bunch of crap. But, by golly, when it got to New York, they loved it!"

The cutting room in the twenties was still a primitive arena. Editors cut by hand and tested the rhythm of an edited sequence by pulling it through their fingers as they viewed it. Many were so committed to this archaic process that they were reluctant to use the animated viewers, or Moviolas, when they were introduced halfway through the decade. Only the talkies and the requirements of synchronization would finish off this manual art for good.

One of the silent-era stars, Bebe Daniels, who began acting as a child in 1908 and enjoyed a great success both in comedies and musicals, became friends with Dorothy Arzner while at Paramount in the mid-twenties. Her impressions of Arzner cutting helped capture for Brownlow the flavor of the period:

> One day Dorothy Arzner came to me and said, "Bebe, you could have heightened this scene a great deal." She started to explain, but I didn't get it. "Come up to the cutting room some night and I'll show you what I mean." So I went up with her, and I became fascinated. It taught me more about writing for motion pictures than anything in the world could have taught me.
>
> Dorothy used to hold the film up to the light and cut in the hand. I remember my first lesson; she held the film up and said, "Well, now, look—this is dead from here to here—we're going to put this close-up in here—so we'll go to here. We don't need this—wait a minute, we can come in here. . . ."
>
> Gradually I began to understand, and learned to cut film myself. We used to mark the frame with a wax pencil, scrape the emulsion off with a razor blade, apply the glue, then put the other piece of film on top and press it down hard. Then we'd check our sprocket holes, and examine the cut under the magnifying glass. Dorothy used to cut as we went on those comedies, and it was very helpful to see the cut rushes in the morning. We could keep the pace right. We might have

slowed down as we went along, but seeing the cut rushes kept us to the right speed.

Every night I'd trudge up there and work with Dorothy until seven or eight, then I'd go home with my nails full of glue.

Says Arzner of the same period, "I was a very fast cutter. I cut something like thirty-two pictures in one year at Realart, a subsidiary of Paramount. . . . I also supervised the negative cutting and trained the girls who cut negative and spliced film by hand. I set up the film filing system and supervised the art work on the titles. I worked most of the day and night and loved it."

Whether done by the editor himself or a splicer assistant, negative cutting was the most tedious aspect of the work. It simply meant making a duplicate of the final cut out of all the negative film that had been piling up since the first days of shooting. It was a crucial process, for it was from this negative cut that all subsequent prints would be made. But finding the negative to match each little shot from the finished positive was more complicated than one might imagine. There were no guide, or "key," numbers on the film, as there are today, and it was not always easy to tell the difference between various takes of the same scene. "In the old days we cut negative by eye," recalls Margaret Booth, who cut her first picture in 1924, her last in 1976 (*Murder by Death*), and in between served as editor-in-chief at MGM for thirty years. "We had to match the action. Sometimes there'd be a tiny pinpoint on the negative and then you knew you were right. But it was very tedious work. Close-ups of Lillian Gish in *Orphans of the Storm* would go on for miles, and they'd be very similar so we'd all help one another."

Industry expansion meanwhile presented the editor with new and unexpected challenges. Many pictures had to be cut differently, it turned out, depending on where they were released—such was the variation not only in what people were willing to tolerate but also in what they were capable of understanding. The quick development of motion-picture shorthand, which could propel actors from one scene to another with no transition, was still beyond the comprehension of many new moviegoers, particularly in areas where the cinema was still a novelty. Editors had to make versions suited to their perceptual abilities as well as to their tastes.

With the advent of the double feature, the editor was presented with yet another unforeseen task. In order to include a second film that was somewhat shorter than the top-billed feature, last year's releases had to be cut down by fifteen or twenty minutes to make them a suitable second-run length.

The editor's special services to the industry did not end there. By the late twenties studio executives would occasionally find themselves falling back on him when a struggle with a director over the length, point of view, or artistic approach of a particular film had reached an impasse. In a number of celebrated cases, movies were seized from hapless directors and given to the editor for remaking. This sometimes caused a great outcry, as when Erich von Stroheim's *Greed*, initially forty-two reels long, was cut to ten reels by a studio editor. These battles over the final cut were just the beginning of a struggle between directors and producers that goes on in many forms to this day—the yanking of *A New Leaf* out of the hands of director Elaine May and into the cutting room of Frederic Steinkamp being a recent example, complete with courtroom embellishments. These heavily charged and bitter circumstances would represent some of the few occasions when an editor would have to bear almost total responsibility for assembling a picture. Even then, he would remain unknown.

As editing became more refined and complex, and as its mechanics grew more difficult to master, many directors turned shy of the cutting room, some never venturing in at all. By the early twenties the industry already had name editors who commanded higher salaries and were called in to cut top features. These men and women operated on a free-lance basis, as do almost all top editors today. In the studios, meanwhile, senior editors sometimes had better relations with the producer than the director did, and they used that advantage to get what they needed in the way of additional takes or to see that their point of view over a disputed cut prevailed. In a few cases the relationship between the producer and his favorite editor became institutionalized and lasted for decades. As recently as 1968 director Sidney Lumet complained to a group of young filmmakers, "When I complete a film for Metro, I have to get blood on the floor to protect it from a lady by the name of Margaret Booth, who I'm sure none of you have ever heard of. She was Irving Thalberg's cutter, and to this day she checks every movie made for Metro-Goldwyn-Mayer and can stop you at any point, call off your mix, and re-edit herself. She *owns* your negative."

Another studio powerhouse was Daniel Mandell, who was lured into editing in 1920 after suffering a war injury that terminated his career as an acrobat. Mandell, who eventually spent twenty-four years as an editor for Sam Goldwyn and won three Academy Awards—for *The Pride of the Yankees* (Sam Wood, 1942), *The Best Years of Our Lives* (William Wyler, 1946), and *The Apartment* (Billy Wilder, 1960)—as well as two Academy Nominations, was accustomed to having his way on and off the set—particularly after the director had been given his chance in the first, or "director's," cut: "With some directors I'd listen very respectfully to whatever suggestions they had and, if I thought they merited attention, I'd follow them. Otherwise, I'd ignore them and take the initiative."

"Did you ever get stuck in a situation," we asked him, "in which you didn't have enough film to work with?" "No, no," he said, "because if I thought I needed something else, I'd go out on the set and tell the director to shoot it. There was one director, Henry Hathaway—I did a thing with him called *The Real Glory*—and every time I'd go on the set and ask him to shoot something, I'd get a big argument. But the next day I'd see it in the rushes. I didn't hesitate to make these requests because I always had a good reason. If Goldwyn called me to task, I would say, well *the hell*, I need it, and besides, you don't want to take the chance of going back into retakes, do you?" Mandell, of course, knew that there's nothing a producer hates more than the expense of calling back a group of scattered actors for retakes.

One of Mandell's favorite battles flared up in 1942 during the making of *The Pride of the Yankees*, the story of baseball star Lou Gehrig. Director Sam Wood based a portion of the film on the famous good-bye celebration for the critically afflicted Gehrig at Yankee Stadium, a highly emotional event in which Gehrig and teammate Babe Ruth hugged and cried—a scene that had been viewed by millions on newsreel. "The director, he tried to embellish it more than it was," says Mandell. "I mean we had the newsreels. I ran every newsreel I could get hold of and studied them, and I threw out all the junk that he'd put in—which made him very angry, but I didn't care. I thought, how the hell can you make a scene like that more dramatic? So I followed the newsreels, that's all I did. He wanted to change it back, but I went to Goldwyn, and I won."

When Wood left MGM to begin work on his next picture, *For Whom the Bell Tolls,* the editor of his last film was still haunting him. Mandell had found that Wood had left him too little material to create an important opening sequence. "I took the stuff to Goldwyn and I showed him what he did, and I said, how the hell am I going to make a montage of him learning to be a great ball player out of *this*?" When Wood was apprised of Mandell's complaint, he protested that Gary Cooper, who played Gehrig in the film, was right-handed while Gehrig himself had been left-handed—obviously Wood was limited in the shots he could make of Cooper playing ball. But Mandell had an editor's solution. "It's easy. All you have to do is put the letters on his shirt backward, have him hit right-handed, run to third base instead of first, do everything in reverse, and we'll flop the film over. . . . Oh, we ended up with all kinds of cuts in that one," Mandell chuckles. "A ball player running and sliding into a base, cut to Cooper getting up. There's so many things. Too much to talk about."

Mandell's privileged position depended, of course, on his relationship with Sam Goldwyn, one of the kingpins of the industry. That their dependence was mutual is amusingly illustrated by a memorable practical joke. The incident occurred during the making of *The Best Years of Our Lives*, which swept a handful of Academy Awards in 1946.

"Freddie March has just returned from the war," says Mandell, recounting the film, "and he's coming back for his job. The manager of the bank was saying, 'You know, things don't look very good in the business picture.' Now, I thought it would be so funny to make him say, 'Things don't look very good in the *picture business*.' So I switched the words and ran it for Goldwyn to see what his reaction would be and if he would catch it. He caught it all right, and he said, 'What the hell are we in—the banking business or the picture business!' I said, 'Well, that was the only flaw, and otherwise the take was very good. I can fix that very easily.' So he says, 'Are you sure?' And I says, 'Absolutely positive!' "

Mandell's position was of course a rare one. Most editors, whether attached to a studio or free-lance, whether given a great deal of responsibility or very little, were expected to play a meek role. And whether they had limited imagination and talent and simply did what they were told or were true behind-the-scenes geniuses who added spark and fluidity to everything they touched, all editors were seen as technicians. Even such giants as Mandell, Hornbeck, and Booth failed to achieve recognition anywhere near commensurate with their contributions.

In many respects filmmaking was following the ancient dictum of all collaborative enterprises—that the generals are remembered but not the lieutenants. Still, as the industry developed in the twenties and thirties, the eclipse of the film editor went beyond the time-honored celebration of chiefs. Even cinema aficionados, proud of their appreciation for a cameraman's "soft warm photography," a composer's "stirring score," or even a writer's "brilliant" screenplay, fell silent on the subject of editing.

What accounted for the editor's profound obscurity? A major factor was the way his job tended to overlap the director's. While in some studios it might have been the producer or star he had to please, over the years, especially on important films, the extent of his contribution came to rest chiefly on how much the director respected and encouraged it. It thus developed that outside these two men, almost no one had any idea exactly what that contribution was.

Besides, the very nature of the process tended to obscure talent. Not only was it impossible to assign credit for a masterful editing job, most viewers, aficionados included, had no way of spotting it. The purpose of editing was to cover its traces.

It was a peculiar, ill-defined profession. Many an ingenious editor, convinced of his own vision, would find that much of his career consisted of a subtle, unspoken struggle in which he persisted in taking more editorial liberties than he was offered. If he could make his moves gently, without causing offense, perhaps even hinting that his innovations had been the director's unspoken wish all along, his reputation might survive, and he would be hired to cut another film. Other editors learned to play the mechanic's role, sometimes to the extent of a maddening refusal to take any initiative at all.

Under these vastly vacillating circumstances, who could blame a director for thinking—the question probably crossed at least some of their minds—that giving the editor his due might arouse speculations that would unfairly undermine the director's own prestige? It was one thing to acknowledge the contribution of a set director, a costume designer, or even a cameraman—painful as such acknowledgments might be—but to acknowledge the editor cut too close to the heart of the director's own importance.

Inevitably, the shorthand that grew up around the cutting room mirrored the ambiguous nature of the work. "Fill in the holes!" became the great command that editors were left with. An order that had the ring of "Patch up my grammar when you type the letter," it hardly conceded the magnitude of what was being asked. Even today one can overhear one director asking another, "Who are you using?" when inquiring the name of his current editor. The language reveals the preference to see the cutter as a technical adjunct.

So it was an odd coupling, this relationship between the director and the editor, and because of all the ambiguities that went along with it, and the natural reluctance on everyone's part to rock the boat, even if it was set on a course that was somewhat exploitative and damaging to the editor's dignity, a silent consensus emerged to keep the editor's contribution under the heading of mechanical adjustments. All this was of course belied by the great care that directors, when they had the option, were beginning to exercise when they chose their cutters. The editor's past credits as well as his temperament would be carefully weighed. Because, as editor-turned-director Robert Wise would later note, the collaboration with the editor is the director's longest marriage in film.

As film histories began appearing in the thirties, the importance of editing to the making of the motion picture was gradually acknowledged. In *The Rise of the American Film* (1939), Lewis Jacobs wrote that the Russian emphasis on editing "was nearer the essence of film art" than "the German emphasis on camera eye and mobility," which he saw as a "subordinate tool to the cutting process." Nevertheless, not one film editor is mentioned in Jacobs' book, and the same is true for every major work on film to this day. Reference books like Leslie Halliwell's *Filmgoer's Companion* (1974) may include hundreds of write-ups on producers, musicians, screenwriters, cameramen, directors, stars, long-forgotten grade-B thrillers, and minor character actors, but not one editor. In nine hundred pages, Halliwell's only comment on editors and editing is the quoted definition that begins this chapter.

Barred from status jobs, a great number of capable and talented women moved into editing in the twenties from jobs as negative cutters, script keepers, and typists. Trained from childhood to think of themselves as assistants rather than originators, they found in editing a safe outlet for their genius—and directors found in them the ideal combination of aptitude and submission. Even today, though the percentage of female editors is smaller than it once was, they are far more numerous than women directors. Indeed, Verna Fields

(*American Graffiti, The Sugarland Express, Jaws*) and Dede Allen (*Bonnie and Clyde, Dog Day Afternoon, Serpico*) are the only two editors whose names have ever been known to the general public.

The personality of the men who were drawn to editing as a lifetime career (rather than as a stepping stone to directing) was naturally one of modest ambition and little urge for personal credit. Whereas cameramen organized the American Society of Cinematographers in 1918, the American Cinema Editors (ACE) was not organized until 1950. "They were a quiet group," remembers Bill Hornbeck, himself a man of great modesty, "and they didn't worry about recognition. They probably didn't have sense enough yet to know how important they were."

Self-effacement seemed built right into the job description. When Oscars for film editors were first awarded in the thirties, a dozen or so top editors—apparently determined to keep the awards from going to anyone's head—casually decided on the winner at an annual luncheon. "We didn't give it as much thought as they do today," says Hornbeck, who usually sat on the committee. "I remember one fellow was in the hospital, and we thought it would be kind of nice to give him an award. He won the Academy Award that year."

Like most editors, Hornbeck is loath to gripe about the shadowy status of editors during filmmaking's first century. A legend in the business for his stunning work on *Shane, A Place in the Sun* (Academy Award), and *Giant,* Hornbeck remains unperturbed about his anonymity with the general public.

Q. "How do you feel about the fact that, considering the amount of original work the editor actually does on a film, he gets so little credit?"

Hornbeck: "Oh, I don't know. It's true that they get very little credit for the amount of time and effort and value they give a movie. That's always been the way."

Q. "You never felt any resentment about that?"

Hornbeck: "Oh no, I never felt that I was the only cog. The same thing happens with a lot of others in the business."

And so, for a bunch of interlocking reasons, the first generations of film editors have been forgotten. Of course, they bear an accountability for their fate—many of them chose the profession precisely because it allowed them to use their vision and imagination without putting their self-worth on the line. To wield the power of creation without bearing ultimate authority or responsibility was a perfect formula for a cautious personality.

The early editors never protested or organized or promoted themselves. They might get together and bitch about certain directors—so-and-so doesn't know what he wants, so-and-so never shoots enough, so-and-so shoots too much—but something very basic within them reinforced the most pronounced vassalage in movie-making. "*I never thought I was the only cog,*" explains Bill Hornbeck, one of the genuine pioneers of film, whose work in England during the thirties has been credited with a significant increase in the quality of British film production, who edited Frank Capra's famous *Why We Fight* series of World War II, and who then went on to cut some of the best postwar pictures. "*How did you hear about me?*" asks three-time Oscar-winner Daniel Mandell, a man who could make a dead courtroom scene like that in *Witness for the Prosecution* come kinetically alive and who retired in 1966 after performing similar feats for sixty-eight other movie features.

Most assuredly, here was a profession that would demand every ounce of your craftsmanship and inner resources yet spare you the limelight's scrutiny. For certain people this was a satisfactory compromise; for others, as I would discover from personal experience, it was a painful one.

Ralph and Jack Rosenblum, circa 1931.

6 ■ From the Shadows of Bensonhurst
Portrait of the Editor as a Young Man

One of the fondest memories of my youth is seeing two pictures on a Saturday afternoon at the Marboro Theatre in the Bensonhurst section of Brooklyn, coming out about five o'clock, and getting a frankfurter with mustard and sauerkraut. I still get the taste every Saturday between five and six.

I became an avid moviegoer just as the talkies were coming in. The spectacular 1926 version of *Ben-Hur*, with a chariot-race cutting sequence that still rivals the best, was reissued with sound effects in 1931, and for a long time that was my favorite picture. Even at six I could identify with chilling excitement with a story about a slave who was finally set free. Another of my favorites was an obscure science-fiction fantasy with Richard Dix called *TransAtlantic Tunnel*. It was the story of a zealot who, fired by his own single-minded determination, built a tunnel from New York to London. The prospect of someone forging ahead on such an outlandish project in the face of near universal opposition was exalting.

In general, the films with a social statement of some kind—*I Am a Fugitive from a Chain Gang* (1932), *Blockade* (1938), *Grapes of Wrath* (1940)—made the greatest impression on me. Had either the Marboro or Benson theaters given me the option to view some of the great documentaries that were being made at this time, I probably would never have seen another *Snow White* or *Wizard of Oz*. Entertainment films, no matter how good, were just wishful thinking to me, and the people who made them could never stand on a par with those who dealt in hard facts.

An early tendency toward isolation, even more than my love of the movies, has always been linked in my mind with my becoming a film editor. An unhappy, silent boy, prideful, and easily hurt, a fat boy with a weird sense of humor and an unchildlike awareness of the absurdity of things, I usually sat in the back of the class, and had few friends. Most important, I had a speech impediment that made me extraordinarily self-conscious.

Because I stammered, every day had its secret agonies. At school, the roll call was like a fuse that burned in my direction. I got stuck on h's. The struggle to say "Here" left me shaken for the rest of the morning. Other situations I could get around by carefully choosing the opening letter of the first word of my sentence. But I never volunteered in class and said as little as I could in all circumstances.

Every Friday morning the entire population of P.S. 186 would gather in the giant, windowless auditorium with its row upon row of connected metal folding chairs, and after we said the Pledge of Allegiance and the Lord's Prayer and listened to announcements, one of the sixth-grade classes would entertain us. One by one the students came onstage to recite or sing or play an instrument. The performances were hardly stirring, but I observed everyone with fixed attention. I never smiled or grimaced or enjoyed or judged them—all I could think about from the moment they came onstage was the day when I would have to take their place.

When my class's turn arrived, I was assigned to recite John Masefield's poem "I Must Go Down to the Sea Again." To hide the awful ordeal of preparation from my family, I spent the time before dinner practicing the poem in the closet of the bedroom I shared with my brother Jack. It is unnerving to look back and realize how important small, enclosed, secluded spaces have been to me from the time I was a child.

The morning I recited my two stanzas of Masefield's poem still echoes as the most dreadful experience of my life. Waiting in the wings to go on was like packing all the roll calls in the world into a single nightmare. I would rather have gone out there naked than reveal my defect to all those people. I had no idea who went ahead of me or what he said. When it was my turn, I went out drenched, as if to slaughter.

The whole thing must have taken two minutes. I felt very alone and nearly blind with anxiety. I had to speak loudly because we had no microphone. Just the same, my voice seemed to get lost in the cavernous room, where it mingled with the sounds of restless students turning and shifting and coughing. I froze once or twice, and during those moments I became so hot and so red I was sure they noticed and wondered what was wrong with me. "Hey, what's taking him so long?" "Come on, Ralph!" "Cat got your tongue, big boy?" "Spit it out, fella!" But no such humiliation occurred. As I walked back into the wings, the tone of the place remained unchanged—as if they not only hadn't noticed my stammer, but hadn't noticed me at all. The perfunctory clapping gave no hint of rejection or pity. Another kid had come and gone and stumbled through his stupid recitation. For the rest of the day, and for several days afterward, I forgot entirely about my stammer, and felt debased instead for having done such a half-hearted job. These conflicting anxieties, a fear of exposure and a drive to excel, have badgered me all my life.

Most of my childhood coincided with the Depression, and in mine and many other families personal unhappiness was often sealed behind a wall of financial woes. It was an era when Hollywood became the national diversion, a double feature cost twenty-five cents, and if it didn't make you forget one form or another of depression, it at least packed a lot of ephemeral pleasure into three mindless hours.

I realize in retrospect that children are great fans of fast editing. The films that were breaking new ground in editing at this time were gangster pictures like *Little Caesar* (1930), *The Public Enemy* (1931), and *Scarface* (1932), and we kids loved them as much for their malevolent content as the pace with which it poured over us. The advent of sound had initially put a severe cramp in editing style—noisy cameras could not move in for close-ups, and the requirements of synchronization made the old editorial liberties impossible—with the result that for a year or two some very stilted and static films were produced. But once the industry engineers surmounted these obstacles, fast, tight cutting came back with a vengeance, often—as Arthur Knight recounts in his book *The Liveliest Art*—accompanied by equally punchy dialogue:

> In a typical scene from *Little Caesar*, the gang is discussing the fate of one of its members:
> "Eddie's turned yellow. He's goin' to rat on us."
> "He can't get away with that."
> "Get Eddie," says Little Caesar. And the scene cuts abruptly to a church exterior, with Eddie coming down the steps. A long black car swings ominously into view; there is a burst of machine-gun fire and Eddie lies sprawling on the steps. Followed by a flat cut to the next scene, Eddie's funeral.

The only difference between me and the other kids who packed the movie houses in those days was that by the time I was fourteen or so I knew the name of the actor who played Eddie as well as the guy who knocked him off. There seemed to be a pool of about thirty-five or forty of these character actors and actresses—Marc Lawrence, Edward S. Brophy, Ruth Donnelly—who got used over and over again for the minor roles in all the Hollywood films, and knowing their names and spotting them was a hobby I shared with my best friend, Buddy Levine. We realized that nobody else knew them, and so it became our private joke. We weren't film buffs, just early trivia nuts, and we even bought those terrible movie magazines to bolster our useless knowledge.

Perhaps because I was so inhibited myself, when it came to comedy I leaned toward the coarse, the lowdown, the exhibitionistic, and the flamboyant. The Three Stooges, Charlie Chase, the Ritz Brothers, and Laurel and Hardy were utter nonsense (unlike Chaplin and Keaton, who had to be taken more seriously) and thus my favorites. The Ritz Brothers had only to walk into the frame for me to feel tickled and succumb to the stomach contractions that would lead to all-out laughter at the first ridiculous joke. To see one of the Stooges indignantly bang together the heads of his errant comrades—as the dubbed-in sound effect of something like two coconuts clonking echoed through the theater—was pure organic delight.

The editing of these comedies in the twenties and thirties contributed greatly to the general quickening of cuts and transitions in American pictures, and although the action was nonsense, the thought that went into its presentation was not.

The British director David Lean (*The Bridge on the River Kwai, Lawrence of Arabia, Doctor Zhivago*), who was a top editor (*Pygmalion, Major Barbara*) during the years I frequented the Bensonhurst theaters, reveals in an old article the delightful diligence, the scientific resolve, that was being applied to film comedy during this decade. Analyzing two unedited shots from an imaginary Laurel and Hardy movie, Lean demonstrates a cutting-room technique I would later learn to apply to the work of Woody Allen, Herb Gardner, and Mel Brooks—*making an alliance with the audience.*

In Lean's first hypothetical shot the renowned ninnies are running down the street for several seconds until Hardy suddenly slips and falls. Lean's second hypothetical shot begins with a close-up of a banana peel lying on the sidewalk and ends with Hardy's foot entering the frame, stepping on the peel, and skidding. "Now where," asks the director with an earnestness that Eisenstein would have approved, "would you cut the close-up of the banana skin?" The smoothest, straightest, and most obvious way to cut the scene would be to show the two men in flight, cut to the close-up of the banana peel as Hardy's foot enters the frame, follow his foot halfway through the skid, and then cut back to the full shot of the two men as Hardy tumbles to the ground. But as Lean points out, the smoothest is not always the funniest, for it overlooks the opportunity to let the audience in on the joke before the characters in the film have any idea what is about to befall them:

> The answer lies in a very old comedy maxim: *Tell them what you're going to do. Do it. Tell them you've done it.* In other words the scene should be cut like this:
>
> 1. *Medium-shot of Laurel and Hardy running along the street.*
>
> 2. *Close-up of banana skin lying on pavement.* (You have told your audience what you're going to do and they will start to laugh.)
>
> 3. *Medium-shot of Laurel and Hardy still running.* (The audience will laugh still more.) *Hold the shot for several seconds of running before Hardy finally crashes to the pavement.* (The odds are that

the audience will reward you with a belly laugh. Having told them what you are going to do, and having done it, how do you tell them you've done it?)

4. *A close-up of Laurel making an inane gesture of despair.* (The audience will laugh again.)

Laurel and Hardy alone generated some fifty films during the Depression years, many of them shorts that played on Saturday afternoons, and I'm sure that I saw almost all of them. But the fact that I took in a minimum of four pictures a week hardly qualified me as a fanatic. I was never taken to a play, television did not yet exist, and until I discovered books in my teens, I had no other form of entertainment. To a youth whose sole happiness derived from secret fantasies, it was inevitable that the movies would be a major influence. All the same, the thought of a career in film never crossed my mind. It was foreign, it was California, it was irresponsible, it was un-Jewish. It was glamour and fulfillment of a sort that I never dared to believe I could achieve.

I was born in 1925, the year, according to *Minsky's*, that also gave birth to the striptease. But there was nothing comic or sensual or seductive about the Brooklyn Jewish community where I spent the first twenty years of my life. Bensonhurst was tidier, stabler, and more genteel than the commotion-prone Lower East Side where the newcomers thronged, but its lessons and ways were those of impoverished immigrants hanging on desperately to the niche they had made for themselves. Thrift, self-improvement, and a thudding practicality ruled everything, a heavy-spirited regime that was molded into permanence by the weight of the Depression. Ten years later when Woody Allen was growing up in the same milieu, its values and oppressive conformity would still prevail.

The one film I've seen as an adult that evokes the buried sorrows of my childhood is *The Gambler*. James Caan, a teacher and compulsive gambler, squanders his money on a football game, then calls his mother. They have a drink, and once again he puts the touch to her. She knows exactly what the money is for, and you get the feeling she's tried for years to stop him, because he's always in debt up to his ears, but reluctantly she writes out another check. As she hands it to him, she tells him that whatever problems he's created for himself, her love for him is undiminished. She puts her arm around his neck and kisses him—and I, sitting in the audience, close to fifty years old now and immune to most forms of sentimentality, begin to weep. Because this sort of love, this motherly affection, is foreign to me. And the lack haunts me even into my fifties.

The circumstances of my mother's life demanded qualities of courage and fortitude, and these she developed to an extraordinary degree. But expansiveness was alien to her, and her stabs at love always landed in the realm of custodial care. She cleaned us and fed us and took care of our material needs with a devotion that just now, when she is eighty-two and growing incapacitated, I am beginning to admire.

There's an old Jewish folk tale about a powerful woman who claims that her husband makes all the important decisions for their family. When questioned about her own contributions to the household, she states modestly, "Oh, I handle the finances, deal with the tradespeople, pay the landlord, decide where we will live. . . ." Well, then, what are the important matters reserved for the man of the house? "Oh, *well*, he makes all the decisions on politics, philosophy, and international affairs."

And so it was with my family, although whether my father thought that much about international affairs is difficult for me to say, since, unfortunately, he almost never spoke to me. In unselfish moments, I can begin to understand my parents. Being poor, emigrating from Europe, starting over with a new language, surviving in this country through some of the worst years we've known. How can you help becoming overwhelmingly tight, obsessed with preserving what you have? That they created a household atmosphere of near total terror over where the next dollar would come from—a spirit-crushing preoccupation that, on special occasions, holidays and such, might be tempered down to a level of extreme anxiety—is understandable considering the extraordinary hardships of their lives.

My favorite relatives had something of the offbeat about them. Uncle Morris, the kosher butcher, was a bootlegger. They said he loved "Stollard," which was the family code name for Stalin, but more important to me in retrospect were the little errands Uncle Morris had me run for him during the last months of Prohibition, when I was seven years old. I'd go to his house, which was in our neighborhood, and Morris would give me an address and a package to deliver, a brown paper bag with a heavy bottle inside. I'd wander through the streets of our half working-class, half middle-class community, past row after row of tidy one- and two-family dwellings, thinking my thoughts, and never have any idea what was in the paper bags I carried. I loved doing these errands for Uncle Morris because he was a softspoken, gentle man, very unlike the rest of my relatives.

My mother's sister, Aunt Bessie, was known as the eccentric in the family. Her eccentricity consisted of such minor exploits as inviting friends to her house for dinner. This was unheard of. Aunt Bessie, too, was a favorite.

Our own household lacked cultural inclinations, conformity reigned over our habits and furnishings, and we rarely did anything strictly for pleasure. My mother must have sensed the longing Aunt Bessie's dinner parties aroused in me, for I remember her saying, "Oh, *well*, it's nothing to get friends to visit you if you're going to feed them. Of course she has a room full of people—they're all getting a free two-dollar meal."

Mother was generous, though, when it came to ladling out the guilt. My older brother, Jack, choked on his rations and rebelled against her continually; fights and trouble always swirled around them, and they never stopped yelling. I must have determined at a very young age that I did not want to repeat this drama and stepped back into the private, bleak role of an obedient and helpful child.

When I was eight years old, Jack was bar mitzvahed. Of all the events that took place on that day, I remember just one. It burned indelibly into my eight-year-old mind. Jack delivered a speech. It was a long speech to what seemed to me a throng of several hundred admiring relatives who had crowded into the synagogue. I knew my parents expected me to get up there and do the same thing on a Saturday morning four and a half years hence, and I knew just as clearly that this would never happen.

One of my first friendships was forged cutting Hebrew class on weekday afternoons. Henry Morris and I would walk the streets for two hours and do all sorts of ridiculous things—put our faces against the windows of restaurants to bother diners, go into bakeries and fool around—nonsense to keep ourselves occupied. It took the synagogue authorities nearly a year to notify my father that for the five dollars or so a month he was paying I hadn't been attending at all.

Both my parents were stunned. My mother had no way of dealing with this quiet rebellion. My father sat me down to talk about it, and I responded with all the force I could muster: "I'm not going. I will not be bar mitzvahed."

We were surrounded by relatives on all sides. My father's brothers, my mother's sisters, all religious people who observed the holidays. The shame my parents felt over my rebellion must have been great. Until a week before my thirteenth birthday, they both tried to believe that somehow my bar mitzvah would come to pass. But I was inexorable: I would never make that speech. Finally my parents settled on an arrangement that spared them any further pain. The weekday temple on the ground floor of the synagogue, a small room that was used mainly by old religious men, was opened for me when the telling Saturday arrived. Surrounded by my parents and four ancient men, I spoke my three lines of Hebrew and the ceremony was over. We never talked about it again.

By the time I was thirteen I was beginning to have some sense of myself. Like many adolescents, this included a great deal of agony over the parts that didn't quite fit the accepted norms. My refusal to speak in class had given me an undeserved reputation for arrogance. I did not like being thought of as arrogant, but I learned from it my primary lesson in self-defense: by being silent and showing no emotions I could become forbidding—a characteristic that both hampered and protected me during my early years as an editor. Around this time I was also discovering an inclination toward slightly eccentric pursuits. I determined that I would never become a teacher or a dentist, the sorts of professions that at the time were the goals Jewish parents pressed on their sons. I had learned to smoke when I was twelve and had developed the custom of hiding in the bushes of the park across the way from Seth Low Junior High School and indulging in this vice. All told, a troubling lack of wholesomeness pervaded my secret persona.

One of the gifts I received for my bar mitzvah was a small radio that I would play at night. In those days NBC and CBS were broadcasting the big bands, starting at 11:00 P.M. from Chicago and Cincinnati and all the cities where people used to dance in hotels. I would stay up till one every night and play the radio very softly and savor what soon became my first love—jazz. Artie Shaw, Glenn Miller, Jan Savitt, Benny Goodman, they all drove me wild. From the big bands I graduated to the black bands, Count Basie, Earl Hines, Jimmie Lunceford, Andy Kirk, Chick Webb. And for the first time I had both a friendship and a dream. The friend was Buddy Levine. Buddy was everything I wasn't. To me he seemed outgoing and gutsy, and, what's more, he appeared to have a great relationship with his parents. He also loved jazz, and the two of us began collecting records. The little money I made from baby-sitting went directly to the Commodore Record Shop in Manhattan. We started a jazz correspondence, set up fan clubs for the various bands, sent for pictures of the band leaders. We knew every band in the country.

The dream, of course, was to become a black jazz musician. I began studying the saxophone. It was a desperate act that, needless to say, went without parental encouragement. I remember practicing on a hot summer's day when I was fourteen or fifteen. I couldn't bear to be heard, so I squeezed into the closet and played there. The saxophone lasted about six months. Subsequently, I discovered reading, and, entranced by the work of an Italian psychiatrist named Cesare Lombroso, inventor of the "criminal type," I determined to become a criminologist. This, too, was short-lived.

My love for jazz gave me an identity of sorts, and, more sure of myself, my sense of humor and oddball behavior became more pronounced. I sometimes enlisted Jack in my exploits, like infesting a Passover Seder with trick wine glasses and other obnoxious delights. But Jack and I remained basically at odds. I envied his more rugged, durable personality and the success I imagined he had with girls. To him I was a fat little nuisance who was willful and got away with too much. He knew how to get under my skin in a way that aroused my frightful temper, once causing me to hurl my treasured radio across the room at him. It smashed against the wall and burst into eighty pieces, which Jack quickly and guiltily swept up and threw away.

Unlike my dream of a career in jazz, the jazz obsession itself never died. I could name the soloist, the theme song, the record label, and some of the specialty numbers of every major band in the country. In a fit of sweet, compulsive orderliness, I decided to catalogue all this information in a filing-card system and give each band a grade. The catalogue eventually included some two-hundred entries—right down to the Grade D groups that had strings and played only in the Midwest—and it reminds me of nothing so much as the catalogues I would soon be keeping of millions of feet of uncut film.

Buddy and I had meanwhile begun to haunt the jazz spots on Fifty-second Street. We'd sneak up to Harlem on Sunday afternoons, when the Golden Gate Ballroom and the Savoy Ballroom staged a "battle of the bands" in which two or three of our groups of heroes would play in succession. When my father found out that I had spent these Sunday afternoons in Harlem, he lunged for the bicarbonate of soda. Years later I read an autobiographical book by Mezz Mezzrow, a white jazz clarinetist who lived in Harlem and always cáme on as black, and in a strange way it brought back those adolescent days and the inexplicable thrill of my jazz passion.

Jazz. To this day I cannot play a musical instrument, but the importance of jazz to my life and my work has been pervasive. My love for music has been the single greatest influence on the development of my editing "touch," and early in my career I developed a capacity to use music as an auxiliary editing tool. In one way or another all my frustrated musical yearnings have squeezed their way into my work.

The relationship between film editing and music has been noted on many occasions. In his 1974 memoir *Don't Look at the Camera*, Harry Watt, the British documentary director, was drawn to the musical analogy to explain the importance of an editor:

> While admitting he cannot turn dross into gold, [the editor] can so alter a director's clumsy or tentative efforts as to make them almost unrecognizable. What he can do is to give tempo and emphasis. We all know that tunes picked out on one finger by some illiterate in Tin Pan Alley become lovely pieces of music when played by a skilled band. Somewhere along the line that tune, which, of course, had to have musical potential, was dissected, rearranged and orchestrated by the backroom boys. A film editor is an orchestrator.

Sometime in 1966 at a big party held in Central Park's Tavern on the Green to celebrate the release of Sidney Lumet's *The Group*, I had a conversation with the *New Yorker* film critic Pauline Kael during which I confided to her about the love I'd always felt for jazz and my secret childhood ambition of becoming a saxophone player. Kael, whose reviews are enriched with an encyclopedic knowledge of literature, film history, and biographical detail, somehow misfiled this information in her magnificent memory bank. In 1971, when she reviewed Ivan Passer's *Born to Win*, the misfiled data was retrieved, and I became one of the few film editors ever to receive an undeserved credit:

"Passer's sense of America is very sharp," wrote Kael, "and the rhythm of the picture, edited by Ralph Rosenblum, who was once a jazz musician, is active, volatile."

But if jazz and my friendship with Buddy and my trips to midtown, to Harlem, and occasionally to the Polo Grounds in the Bronx were the secret celebrations that kept my teenage years alive, their decline as I turned sixteen left me with little to fall back on. The year still registers as an emotional calamity. Buddy and most of my lesser friends, guys who were two years older than I because I had been skipped twice in school, were drafted or enlisted to fight in the war. And my father became paralyzed.

My father is a dim shadow. Silent. Worried. Unexpressive. Impatient. All his life he did piecework in the garment center and fretted during the months of no work. He was a sewing-machine operator and always aspired to become, oddly enough, a "cutter," the one who scissored the pattern. I knew very little about him except that as a boy he had made his way on foot from Russia to Belgium, where he boarded a boat to New York. Aside from this one heroic act, his life was full of negatives. He lamented that he had never studied dentistry or accounting, professions that had been open to him and more suited to his intellect. Throughout my boyhood I was always told that my father could not take me to a ball game, to a circus, to a vaudeville show because he had tried to do all these things with my brother and had been disappointed or distressed by the results. *Took Jack to the ball game—he ate too many hot dogs and vomited. Never again! Schlepped Jack all the way to Madison Square Garden to see Ringling Brothers and he was bored. Never again!* My father did take me skating once, when I was about six, but I landed on my ass, and he got fed up, and that was probably the last time we did anything together. As it turned out, I was twenty-five when I first saw the circus—with my wife, Davida.

Although the actual cause of my father's paralysis was a cerebral hemorrhage, it seemed to represent an organic decision on his part to bring the grinding routine of his life to a halt. With that stroke I graduated from an oddball kid to the sole breadwinner in my family.

By this time I had had adequate warning that I could never go to a *pay* college, but I had fantasized all the same about attending one of the Midwestern universities, particularly one of the Big Ten because I loved football. True to my nature, one that had caused me to memorize the names of grade-B actors and revel over a file on jazz bands, during my senior year at high school I had sent away to these schools for their catalogues. Despite all this fantasizing, I assumed that I would go to Brooklyn College in the end. Now, suddenly, because of my father's illness, this fallback was snatched away. I found myself at sixteen with a paralyzed father at home, complete responsibility for my family's support (Jack, too, had been drafted), and not an inkling about what I wanted to do with my life. The things that turned me on all seemed as impractical as the saxophone. If I didn't fail for lack of talent I would surely fail for fear of failure. I wasn't yet aware that all the things that meant something to me, like becoming a writer or a composer or a musician, had one quality that was laden with taboo—standing on a hilltop and proclaiming myself.

For the next year I worked in the shipping department of the garment factory where my father was last employed. The shipping department consisted mostly of older black men and a few Italian kids, no one that I felt I could relate to. What's more, having been denied Brooklyn College and brought up to believe that knowledge and self-worth were intimate partners, I was becoming gripped by a new obsession: self-education.

The factory was located at 500 Seventh Avenue right off Thirty-eighth Street. I would spend my lunch hours at Herald Square, sitting on a park bench across the street from Macy's, under the clock whose mechanized figures would bang out the hours. There I read some of the most exciting literature of my life. The sensation of imbibing Dreiser, Tolstoy, Henry James, Ignazio Silone—every molecule in my body told me I was being enriched.

Meanwhile, at home I was listening to Prokofieff, Tchaikovsky, and Beethoven. I spent hours and days learning about classical music, to the point that by the time I was eighteen or nineteen I could listen to a Beethoven symphony and identify both the number of the symphony and the movement being played. I could identify all the piano concertos. This was proof of the success of my noncollege education.

Unfortunately, I knew no one with whom I could share this burgeoning knowledge. I was too shy to hang out on the Brooklyn College campus, and the girls I was introduced to at the time could barely carry a conversation across the street. Afflicted with my stammer and a nagging insecurity, I was nonetheless filled with a secret belief in my own superiority. "The superiority of the afflicted" is what Woody and I would later call it.

In keeping with the rigidity of a family life from which I desperately wanted to be free, at the age of sixteen I still saw intellectual growth as a process of memorization. You can't read this important stuff and file it away—you've got to be able to *quote* it. You should read *Portrait of the Artist as a Young Man* and then, in the best of all possible worlds, be able to *recite* it—because it's so damned important. Years later Malcolm X's autobiography would stir me more than any book I'd ever read, because, similarly consumed with the need to educate himself, he had spent most of his first term in prison reading and memorizing the dictionary.

After I had worked in the garment factory for about a year, someone told me about a civil-service exam, and without much thought except of escaping the pushcart and the rack, I took the test. I passed easily and soon received a notice telling me to report to the Office of War Information on Fifty-seventh Street to take a job as a clerk-messenger. I was so pleased I never returned to the factory to pick up my last check. They'd liked me there and called my home to see what had happened to me, and even left a message assuring me that the job was still mine, but I was so filled with shame and anger over having been subjected to that existence, of having followed so dreadfully close in my father's footsteps, that I never returned their calls.

It must have been my first or second day at the OWI that I caught a glimpse of the cutting rooms. Row after row of dim cubicles in which film that had been shot all over the country was being assembled into propaganda documentaries. In solitude and concentration, each editor worked his creations unencumbered by human relations, audience reactions, or even, for that matter, the judgment of the world. For who knew what an editor did? And who was to say if it was bad?

Above: Sidney Meyers.
Below: Willard Van
Dyke and Larry
Madison (at camera),
filming STEELTOWN, USA.
*(Courtesy Museum
of Modern Art)*

7 ■ The Office of War Information

Apprenticeship with the Documentary Guys

A great many of us learned our craft very well,
because we had almost unlimited money and an
atmosphere in which we could learn freely. No, we
didn't make the films we wanted to make. Rarely
did we. But we worked together carefully and
closely, so it affected all of us, and
perhaps it affected the field.
—WILLARD VAN DYKE

I arrived at the Office of War Information in the spring of 1943, armed with a hardship draft deferment (because of my father's illness), troubled by a secret inner mixture of arrogance and self-rejection, and filled with the hope of discovery. The offices were spread across several floors of the Argonaut Building at 224 West Fifty-seventh Street, right off Broadway. They were bustling with educated people from all over the country. For a boy who had never been outside New York City, who had never known a "free" woman, who had never witnessed an animated conversation that didn't concern the price of chopped meat or the ingratitude of a feuding relative, who had never known anyone who was excited by culture or the arts, who had thought all his life that the world was almost equally divided between Jews and Italians, this was a debut of cosmic proportions. To my great pleasure I was assigned to the Overseas

Motion Picture Bureau down at 35 West Forty-fifth Street in the jewelry district.

The OWI at this time was already the subject of considerable political controversy. The propaganda that was being churned out to stimulate the war spirit at home was often found unnecessary, paternalistic, or otherwise insulting, while the OWI as a whole had to contend with the traditional American suspicion of propaganda and the fear that it would somehow be used to support New Deal policies and to help President Roosevelt win a fourth term. Little of this affected us at the overseas bureau, however, where our products were strictly for foreign consumption. In fact, during my entire three years at the OWI I was ignorant of any controversy, ill will, or competitiveness. It was an enthralling new world, and I was deep beneath the storms.

The idea of the OWI overseas bureau was to counter the vast sums that the Germans and Japanese were spending on propaganda of all kinds—radio broadcasts, pamphlets, magazines, and films. While some of our own "psychological warfare" was geared to frighten and break the resistance of enemy populations, the special job of the Motion Picture Bureau was to make friends for America. Films featuring various aspects of the American way of life—small-town democracy, the European heritage, the functioning of government agencies, the industrial process—all with an emphasis on ordinary people and their labors, were chosen with the idea of correcting a set of prejudices that had sprung up about America—largely as a result of the success of Hollywood pictures abroad. They were each produced in twenty-six languages for distribution to allies, neutrals, and liberated nations. The voice-over commentaries were translated and renarrated at the Foreign Language Section, the department where I began work as a messenger.

One of the administrative people at the Foreign Language Section was a woman named Helen Gwynne, who must have been close to forty at that time. Helen struck me immediately as the most extraordinary woman I had ever encountered. She had been married twice, had worked in California for the *Hollywood Reporter*, had flacked for one of the big New York nightclubs, and had rubbed up against and walked away from a lot of wealth. Now she was writing, publicizing, administrating—a tough, independent woman and the first person I latched onto at my new job.

Rosemarie Hickson, who was only about three or four years older than I but far more experienced, also became a friend, and as a member of this triumvirate I was first delivered from the Bensonhurst *shtetl* and introduced to the world I came to think of as the Twentieth Century.

With Helen and Rosemarie I first ate Chinese food. I was astounded to discover that these women could go into a Chinese restaurant and, without asking, know the difference between moo goo gai pan and egg foo yung. I had never graduated from coffee-shop food, and here I was eating Chinese, Japanese, Mexican—going straight to a Ph.D. What these two women thought of me, I can only wonder. But they must have been surprised at my encyclopedic knowledge of jazz. And in return for all the sophistication they showered on me, I took them to jazz concerts. One day—much to my embarrassment—they even took the subway all the way to Bensonhurst to see my family and the house I'd lived in almost since the day I was born—whereupon my mother became overwrought with the alarming idea that I was about to form an unhealthy attachment to an overaged, non-Jewish woman. The three of us were inseparable until late in the war, when Helen got restless and took an assignment with our bureau in India.

The Overseas Motion Picture Bureau occupied four entire floors, the halls of which were lined with cubicles where films were in various stages of production. In one room the bureau chiefs, Robert Riskin and Philip Dunne, might be viewing the rushes sent back from Youngstown, Ohio, by Willard Van Dyke, who was shooting *Steeltown*. In another room John Houseman might be preparing the script for *A Tuesday in November,* a film about the electoral process. Down the hall Gene Fowler, Jr., might be editing *The Autobiography of a Jeep* (narrated with great anthropomorphic wit by the jeep itself), while just within earshot Fredric March finished recording his voice-over for *The Valley of the Tennessee.* Elsewhere a sound editor might be editing the score for Henwar Rodakievicz's *Capital Story,* a film about the U.S. Public Health Service's efforts to track down a dangerous pollutant, while next door a staff group lingered for a final glimpse of the bureau's first production, *Swedes in America,* starring Ingrid Bergman.

It was like an international documentary headquarters. Helen van Dongen, the Dutch-born editor who had cut the films of Joris Ivens; Boris Kaufman, the brother of Soviet director Dziga Vertov and a renowned documentary cameraman in his own right, who later shot

On the Waterfront, Baby Doll, and three of the four pictures I edited for Sidney Lumet; Alexander Hammid, a Czech filmmaker who had photographed and co-directed *Crisis,* the anti-Nazi picture on the rape of Czechoslavakia; Willard Van Dyke, a former still photographer who was on the way to becoming America's Mr. Documentary; Waldo Salt, who later won Academy Awards for the *Midnight Cowboy* and *Coming Home* screenplays—these were some of the people I found myself mingling with. Because they made movies, they were like gods to me. And because they made fact films about the realities of everyday life, they were even greater gods.

Of them all, an editor named Sidney Meyers who before the war had helped found the left-wing documentary collective called Frontier Films was most important. Having never seem film cut, or even guessed that such a process existed, I was amazed to look over Sidney's shoulder and observe him chopping and joining and, with quick confident strokes, making relationships with raw footage that I never thought possible. I determined that my first promotion had to get me into one of these rooms with Sidney, and by the end of the war he became my mentor.

It has been said that editing is directing the film for the second time. In documentary work, editing is often directing the film for the first and only time. Until he gets into the cutting room, the documentary filmmaker is mainly involved in information gathering. His reliance on cutting as the chief tool for molding his work has made him an important contributor to the development of editing technique.

If I've become known for anything as a feature editor, it is a facility for shifting around the original components of a film, knowing how and when to drop whole sections of dialogue and replace them with musical overlays, and generally feeling comfortable taking liberties with a script—skills that are relatively standard in the documentary field. Working in Hollywood, especially in the old days, gave you little idea of the real potential of film; the emphasis was always on following the script, and only the most daring editors proposed radical diversions. To a documentarist, a script was a plan that helped get you going in the morning—certainly nothing that was ever intended to cramp your creative impulses as you went along. My apprenticeship with documentary filmmakers enabled me to face a picture like *The Night They Raided Minsky's,* know that I had to piece it together from scratch in the cutting room, and not crumble in panic.

It was exactly the sort of problem I was trained for. Although, after I left the OWI, my career took a long and unsatisfying turn through advertising and television terrain and then passed through the promised land of some thirty feature films, I never lost my love for the documentary, and in my struggle to become a director, documentary is the form I've returned to.

The documentary sprang up like a weed wherever people had passionate statements to put on film. One of the earliest forms was the "compilation" film pioneered by Esther Shub and Dziga Vertov. Because these works on the upheavals of the Russian Revolution and its aftermath were forged entirely in the cutting room—of old newsreel and private footage dug out of musty basements, film archives, and personal collections—the editor/directors had to fight at first for their right of authorship.

Another form of documentary was pioneered by the Russian director Victor Turin in *Turksib*, a 1929 film about the construction of the Turkestan-Siberian railway. Turin's subject could easily have been seen as a routine industrial labor, but through the subtle use of editing he brought out the inherent drama of the event. After viewing it at the Scala Theater in 1930, Paul Rotha commented on the film's propagandistic power, "The spectators in London were just as eager for the railway to be opened as were the peasants in Russia!"

Elsewhere in Europe film aficionados and ideologues joined cinema clubs to screen forbidden revolutionary works like *Mother* and *Potemkin*, surreptitiously recut newsreels for left-wing viewing (reassembling them for return the next day), issued manifestos on the true purpose of the film, and saw in documentary an opportunity for political and artistic expression. From this milieu came Joris Ivens, a leftist Dutch director who made celebrated pictures in Holland, Belgium, Spain, China, Russia, and the United States during the turmoil years of the thirties. His editor, Helen van Dongen, would become my second teacher.

The title "Father of the Documentary" is often reserved for the American director Robert Flaherty, on whose final picture I served as assistant editor. Flaherty's 1922 Eskimo film, *Nanook of the North*, was a surprise commercial hit, and it seemed, as a result, that exotic travelogues would fit into the Hollywood system. But after spending three years shooting his second picture, *Moana*, an idyll about the coming of age of a Samoan boy, Flaherty was forced to stand by as his producers at Paramount released it as *The Love-Life of a South Seas*

Siren, a subterfuge that insured a box-office fizzle. Thereafter the documentary remained an outsider's art form in America.

The OWI held regular screenings of the documentary films that had been made abroad. In this high-spirited, home-front, democratic milieu, the lowliest messenger was welcome to attend these viewings and discover worlds that were still unknown to the Benson and the Marboro theaters. My education was sudden and intoxicating. For the first time I was exposed to the two major documentary trends that were doing battle before the war began, and each in its way packed jolts of awakening.

John Grierson, who headed the British government Film Unit and whose name has become almost synonymous with documentary film, believed in the power of film to educate. His celebrated cluster of filmmakers not only perfected the imaginative educational use of film, they made pictures that captured the special qualities in what otherwise passed for humdrum existence. With pictures that ranged from the story of the men who sorted mail on the Postal Special from London to Glasgow, to an exploration of housing ills and cures, to a dramatic statement on the importance of savings accounts, the British Film Unit served in both spirit and tone as the model on which the OWI propaganda was built.

If the British films made me dream of faraway places, egalitarian principles, and the dignity of simple lives, *Triumph of the Will*, my first glimpse of Nazi documentary, sucked me into my seat as if I were being electrocuted. Technically a record of the 1934 Nazi party congress at Nuremberg, Leni Riefenstahl's mythic chiller was hard-core propaganda with a melodramatic, antihumanist bent. Edited to produce a pace of irrestible forward energy, and photographed to create a sense of omnipotence and unbreakable mass unity—with endless ranks of soldiers, torchlight parades, haranguing speakers, and cheering crowds—the film terrified me, much as it had terrified audiences all over Europe.

The Nazis had been the first to recognize the power of film as an instrument of war, and when Hitler's panzers drove into Poland, his camera crews were right alongside them. *Baptism of Fire* was the picture that resulted. A year later *Victory in the West* recorded the capitulation of France. In Russia, England, and the United States a similar mobilization of documentary talent was underway, and filmmakers who had lived through years of sparse employment suddenly had jobs with overtime. Out of the British Film Unit came titles like *London Can Take It* and *Target for Tonight,* while in the Soviet Union top directors like Pudovkin and Alexander Dovshenko busily edited footage from a thousand miles of front. Seen today on television retrospectives, these wartime compilations are still as breathtaking as they were for me in the early forties because of the superlative Soviet editing.

When the United States entered the war in 1941, it started spending upward of fifty million dollars a year on propaganda films. The various military services had their own film units, of which the Army Signal Corps was the most important, accounting for Frank Capra's celebrated *Why We Fight* series. The directors John Huston, John Ford, and William Wyler left their studios to learn the art of documentary, and with the collaboration of studio editors like Bill Hornbeck created films that ranged from training material for soldiers, to edited compilations on various war themes, to on-the-spot reportage of great battles. Naturally this material also came through the OWI. Although various Signal Corps productions have achieved lasting recognition, I was most profoundly affected by the uncut reels of Corps film that were shipped almost daily into our offices toward the end of the war, most of which have never been shown publicly and may even have been destroyed. This was the film that the Signal Corps cameramen shot as they poured into liberated concentration camps all over Europe, film that we screened in silence and agony and disbelief.

The OWI was set up in 1942 to consolidate all the information services of the government's far-flung and burgeoning propaganda machinery. And, as it turned out, it was at the OWI that the bulk of the country's documentary film talent, people who had developed as artists and craftsmen during the last years of the Depression, found their battle stations. It was the first and last time that American documentarists were brought together in a mass collective effort, and it was an historic moment in filmmaking.

When Robert Riskin took command of the OWI Overseas Motion Picture Bureau, he was well established as a playwright and scriptwriter, known especially for his work with Frank Capra. His screenplays included *It Happened One Night,* for which he won an Oscar, *Lost Horizon,* and *You Can't Take It with You.* He was married to the blond screen heroine Fay Wray, who was, of course, better known for her liaison with an enormous ape.

Because the United States was far behind in documentary filmmaking, Riskin had a large job on his hands. Dramatist Robert Sherwood, who headed the OWI's massive overseas propaganda effort, groaned that he had only frivolous Hollywood pictures to show in the liberated zones of North Africa. Wallace Carroll, who headed the OWI London office, reported that in 1943 London's central film registry listed five thousand documentary films of which "only three were American and they were out of date. At that time, the American film companies in London had two hundred gangster films in their vaults, but not one film about the Tennessee Valley Authority. The crowds that stormed a London theater to see the stirring Soviet documentary film *One Day at War* were also treated to a Hollywood film called *Orchestra Wives*, which told the story of a touring jazz band and the petty rivalries among the wives of its members."

If filling the holes in two decades of American filmmaking neglect was a stout challenge, Riskin was faced with an equally arduous job in forging his unlikely unit into a cooperative alliance. Here, after all, was a Hollywood man heading an organization composed mostly of documentarists, people who had always been viewed in Hollywood as poor relations—filmmakers who ran around making pictures no one wanted to see, using hand-held cameras, in crews of two and three. Riskin could lavish on his documentary cousins unlimited industry resources including the best Hollywood scriptwriters (whose scripts the documentary men invariably found absurd and unusable), but could he respect them and win their trust?

The group that hashed out ideas and assignments typically included Riskin, his production chief Philip Dunne (a Hollywood screenwriter whose credits included *The Last of the Mohicans* and *How Green Was My Valley*), and documentary men Irving Lerner, Irving Jacoby, and Willard Van Dyke. "There was a feeling on our part," recalls Van Dyke, "that Riskin didn't know his ass from his elbow because he was a Hollywood guy."

As the meetings became sticky, Riskin's celebrated nervous habits would surface. "He had a wedding ring that was composed of three interlocking rings," says Van Dyke, "and he would take that off and would play with it. Then he would reach into his pocket and get change, and if he had four quarters, two nickels, and a penny, he'd shift them around until the penny was in the middle, and then the two nickels and the four quarters—and he'd sit there and play with them, and the thing was to get symmetry. He was a great gambler, a professional. People would give him a thousand bucks and send him to Las Vegas. He was really a terrific guy, a nice guy, but not our kind of guy."

I'll always remember the impression Van Dyke made on me—a dazzling dresser, the nattiest man I'd ever seen; an aristocrat with an egalitarian self-confidence that seemed to include rather than belittle those around him. His first affinity among the "Hollywood guys" was for Dunne, because, as he puts it, "Dunne wore button-down collars and so did I." When we visited him in his Upper West Side apartment to interview him for this book, Willard was seventy-one years old and retired after a fruitful decade as a top TV documentarist and as the director of the Museum of Modern Art's film department. Though he no longer wielded a camera, his facility for nailing the essential detail was still acute.

"Riskin couldn't help feeling uncomfortable with all of us," says Willard. And when it was decided to do a documentary story of the Tennessee Valley Authority, Riskin reached into the Signal Corps for Shepard Traube, who had directed *Angel Street* on Broadway. "Traube came over to the OWI and he listened tolerantly to what was being said to him. Finally Riskin turned to me and said, 'Willard, you've worked among those mountain people—tell Shep the kind of thing that he might run into.' Well before I could open my mouth, this guy who had new bars on his shoulder as a captain in the Signal Corps said, 'Dò you see these bars? They'll do what I tell them.' "

Alexander (Sasha) Hammid, who was languishing in Hollywood at this time, unable even to get into the cameraman's union, was asked to join the OWI and to go right to work as Traube's cameraman. A quiet, unassuming man who could walk through a room like a whisper, Hammid was immediately put off by Traube's grand style: "One day we happened to come to a location that I liked very much, and so I grabbed a camera and started shooting. That got him terribly mad—that I dared to shoot without consulting him."

Traube incited a minor rebellion among the crew, and after two weeks Riskin reluctantly turned the project over to Hammid. "Sasha went down and made a beautiful film," says Van Dyke with pleasure. "He was a documentary guy."

The chauvinism of the documentary guys was the chauvinism of the foot soldiers. They were proud of their ability to go onto a location and patiently get the feel of a real situation; to work with nonprofessional actors and gently guide them away from their self-consciousness; to operate out in the field with limited personnel and none of the fancy equipment available on a studio set. At times their contempt for their rich relations in The Industry was ill concealed: "Every picture made in Hollywood was confined to a studio set," snorts Willard. "The idea of sending a camera crew to New York if you wanted New York streets just wasn't done. If you wanted a New York street, you built it on a Hollywood set."

The simmering conflict between the two camps began to froth and foam when Josef von Sternberg (*The Blue Angel, Shanghai Express*) volunteered his patriotic services and was assigned by Riskin to do a film called *The Town*. Von Sternberg was known as a master of lighting and camera work, for having created through his careful photographing of Marlene Dietrich the current romantic screen "look," and for his great arrogance. He was anything but a documentary guy. And the OWI documentarists felt both snubbed and secretly elated at the thought of what might happen.

The idea behind *The Town* was to present the life of a small town in the Midwest. What the people looked like, what happened on Saturday afternoons when the farmers came to sell their produce—to capture the feeling of living in a very American place. A little town in Indiana was chosen, and one day in 1943 von Sternberg arrived there with an OWI crew that included unit manager Ben Gradus and cameramen Larry Madison and Benji Doniger.

"When the initial rushes started coming in, we didn't know what he was trying to do," says Willard. "It was embarrassing. He was approaching it as if he were photographing Dietrich. He couldn't stay away from the camera and when they went inside he usually pushed Larry aside and began to do his own lighting. He had the trees painted with silver paint so they would reflect the light just right. He had a contempt for the exposure meter. At one point he was on top of a station wagon and a big crowd was there. Doniger, who was an absolutely wonderful, wild, crazy New York fella, was going around taking readings, and through the bull horn von Sternberg said, 'Mr. Doniger, would you please come to the truck.' So Benji comes over, a wide-eyed, full-of-citrus-fruit nice guy, and von Sternberg said, 'Mr. Doniger, I wish you would put that annoying instrument away. We do not measure the intensity of people's dandruff.' Well the whole town heard it, and Benji was humiliated."

Riskin smoked Dunhill cigarettes with their paper cigarette holders, and, according to Willard, "The point at which Riskin began to tear those things up and bite 'em and chew 'em and spit 'em out, you knew something was up." Night after night Riskin, Dunne, and Van Dyke watched the rushes coming back from Indiana with Riskin breaking and chewing his Dunhill cigarette holders into thousands of pieces. "Finally Riskin turned to me and said, 'Willard, go out there and save this picture.' And I said, 'Not on your life.' Nobody was going to go and either save von Sternberg or step on his toes. It wasn't professional to do that."

In the end von Sternberg surprised everyone by producing a pleasing portrait of the town and the way people lived there, an effort much like many of the other OWI movies. The documentary guys were a little reluctant to admit this, however, and for a long time afterward *The Town* led their list of "East Toilet, Ohio" pictures—compulsory stories of the folks from nowheresville, heavy on the schmaltz and light on the content.

Ultimately the prejudices faded. The documentary guys gradually realized that no one had a better critical eye than Riskin or a sharper ear for dialogue than Dunne. While the Hollywood brass, for their part, were soon impressed with the documentarists' fieldwork and cutting-room dexterity. "In documentary practice," wrote Dunne in a postwar appreciation of the documentary skills he observed at the OWI, "a film editor is also in effect a writer, using a Moviola instead of a typewriter. Give a good documentary editor an idea and he will express it for you in film: pictorial image, mood, and tempo. His function is more often creative than editorial."

Each morning, although I'd already eaten breakfast, I arrived at the eighth-floor office with coffee and a danish, which to me were symbols of entry into the adult world. Helen Gwynne would be compulsively finishing off *The New York Times* crossword in ink, and I got a certain thrill just being alongside her as this virtuoso performance neared completion. My first run of the day might be to pick up some piece of equipment, deliver a script to the home of one of the composers, like Aaron Copland, who were scoring our films, or make a run to the film lab. Much of my time was spent in transit between our office and the main offices up at the Argonaut Building.

I was drawn to editing by almost every aspect of my childhood experience. The darkness, the isolation, the power of the process over the emotions of millions of people who never knew it existed, the alchemical secrecy. When my promotion came through in 1944, my first job as an assistant was in the cutting room of the foreign-language department, where the films were remixed with translated narrations. I bided my time there until I was moved over to assist the chief editor, Sidney Meyers.

Sidney was a balding man with a horseshoe band of orange fringe and miscellaneous stray wisps. He was always a little stooped, even when he wasn't bending over his Moviola, and he was always gentle. He struck me as someone who was more interested in the deeper issues of life, in philosophy, in political ideas, in questions about music—he had been a violist before becoming a filmmaker—and rather less concerned about who was having lunch with whom and where. I always thought of him as a man who would be more inclined to be paternal and protective toward a pretty girl than seductive. Looking back, I believe he would have been happier if he had been a little tougher.

Sidney was my mentor and my surrogate father. I talked to him about things that I'd never discussed with anyone else—poetry, music, philosophy, and filmmaking—and he told me there was a basement auditorium in the Museum of Modern Art where I could see some of the great films I'd missed. My favorite recollections are of Sidney and me sitting out on the stairwell having a smoke—cigarettes were strictly forbidden in the cutting rooms during the days when nitrate stock was still in use—and spending maybe fifteen minutes, maybe a half hour, talking about all these things that had been important in his life and were becoming important in mine. He told me what books to read, and certain pieces of music to listen to, and he filled me with so much inspiration that there was never a thought of turning toward another career after the war. In the months we spent together, months of moments that had titanic importance to me but were probably little more than pleasant for Sidney, he never castigated me or lost his temper or discouraged me in any way. He never tried to warn me, as I hear myself warning so many would-be filmmakers today, that film is a desperately competitive business and difficult to break into. Although he was at least twenty years older than I was, I have no memory of him talking "sense" to me about anything.

How different Sidney was from a certain West Coast film editor who also wound up at the OWI. A contemporary of Sidney's, he saw cutting as a mechanic's job with no creative potential. He had to drink his lunch to endure the afternoon, so painful and monotonous was the business to him. Once, when I wanted to discuss a current movie, he looked at me as if I were crazy—"I don't go to the movies," he said.

During this time, I was still living with my parents in Bensonhurst, although my daily excursions into the Twentieth Century had given me a spiritual divorce from my old environment. My mother could hardly be approached on the subject of filmmaking, and my paralyzed father was beyond communication. I remember trying to tell my uncle Morris, the butcher and bootlegger and lover of Stalin, one of the few relatives I really enjoyed, about my new profession. Morris was over seventy then. I had to explain patiently that films are photographs, that they are arranged in a cutting room—and Morris looked at me, and he listened, and he seemed quite interested. When I finished talking, Uncle Morris rearranged his face and said, "So when are you going into business for yourself?"

Only my OWI family stood solidly behind my filmmaking future. Helen Gwynne convinced Irving Jacoby, who had just founded the Institute of Film Techniques at City College, to let me attend his first course by acting as his helper. Two nights a week I carried, threaded, and ran Irving's 16 mm projecter and saw films I never knew existed.

In Irving's class I first saw Pudovkin's *Mother* and the British Film Unit productions *Song of Ceylon* and *Night Mail*. Watching now for the editor's contribution, I spotted the technique that had made them classics.

The drama of Harry Watt's and Basil Wright's *Night Mail* was clearly the product of editing. The film's ability to generate excitement over the task of dropping off mail sacks from a speeding train—two men preparing the sack, the rails whirring by, the scenery, the wires overhead, the local dogs transfixed as the train flies by, the approaching sack catcher, the men releasing the sack, outside the train the sack caught in a web—could only have been imparted at the cutting bench. Some pair of hands at a Moviola somewhere (R.Q. MacNaughton's, as I later learned) had made that excitement communicable.

In Basil Wright's *Song of Ceylon* I could see how cutting was used to a more lyrical effect. A mingling of human and elephant feet, cut to the elephant's trunk lifting the rider, cut to the elephant's impervious face. We are awed by the elephant's immense servile presence because instead of standing back and observing the whole action at a distance, we are invited to share certain intimate and suggestive details. The young shirtless man scaling the coconut tree, the sound of a ship's whistle, cut to the ship itself. See! See how the sound had prepared the way for the cut, made it seamless and unquestionable? Again, the work of editing.

Another film I remember was Leo Hurwitz and Paul Strand's *Native Land*, a 1942 attack on antiunion oppression in the United States. One scene in particular left an impression on me, the burial of a man who had been killed in a strike. The enormous grief of the widow is communicated with almost unbearable intensity by showing her bending over her husband's newly dug grave again and again and again from different angles and distances. The impact of this simple repetition is heartrending. Of course the viewer knows he is being manipulated, that he is being made to see the same action over and over, but the effect is no less powerful.

Because I was an apprentice editor, my mind preyed on transitional effects. Irving might discuss the eloquent, timeless images in Dovshenko's *Earth*, but my eye was on the cut: the terrified face of the child, the mother's arm coming through the air to strike it, sudden cut to the peasant's whip following the arc of action begun by the arm and landing with a smack on the ox's back. Today most of these editing techniques have become commonplace, and some have become cliché. But they were fresh then. And what made them truly exciting was going to work the next day and watching Sidney perform these tricks as if he had been raised on them. How could anyone make that mass of prosaic detail Willard was shipping back from Seattle into a cohesive film? And yet in a series of quick cuts from cattle to fishing to grain to timber to mining to farmland—with the action of each cut moving in the same direction across the screen—Sidney could weld together a theme in a way that was so natural the viewer never consciously appreciated the technique behind it.

Willard's *Northwest, U.S.A.* was an attempt at a portrait of the people and industry of Washington and Oregon. It had no more compelling element to link its themes than the fact that a Soviet plane had recently flown over the North Pole from Moscow to Seattle—an achievement that promised to make the Northwest an important international crossroads. Like so many other OWI films, the combination of Willard's powerful images, Ben Maddow's commentary, Walter Huston's narration, Norman Lloyd's score, Sidney Meyers' cutting, and Riskin's and Dunne's shrewd critiques somehow managed to fill the vacuum, an incredible triumph of form, style, and technique over lack of content.

To say that Sidney played a major role in this is an understatement, for the challenges he faced were mammoth. "The material was as good as we could make it," says Van Dyke, "but it was thin, and I thought that Sidney did a hell of a job with it. In my case, I was constantly feeling, *Jesus*, I wish I could have gotten *this*, we only had *this* amount of time, we got stymied on *this*—and I was grateful that the editor brought as much as he did to it and pulled the thing together."

"Sidney would get a film," remembers Irving Jacoby, "and he would look at it and say, 'Oh my God, this terrible shit, I have to make a film out of it!' And then he would work on it for some months and, by God, it got better and better and better all the time. Not another inch of film was added, mind you. But as it became his, it became better, and toward the end it was very fine. Then the director had to fight for his credit!" (Actually Jacoby himself had to fight for his director's credit once—over his OWI compilation film, *The Pale Horseman*, a powerful account of the epidemics that might follow the war. The editor who challenged Jacoby for the director's credit—and almost got it—was an unusually confident young cutter named Peter Elgar.)

Not everyone was satisfied with Sidney's work, however, as Willard reveals in comparing him to producer and editor Irving Lerner: "Irving and I worked together hand in glove. Irving was always looking for the clear narrative line, so that you wouldn't lose the message. Then within that he would look for the connectives—and he was always coming up with brilliant connectives. Sidney more often tried for a kind of ambiguity that would show off his contribution. Rather than what the film needed to say, it was what *Sidney* needed to say."

Willard cites *San Francisco, 1945,* his film about the founding of the United Nations, as an example of Sidney's occasional gracelessness as a collaborator. "What happened in San Francisco happened behind closed doors. They were not going to let us in. We didn't have the material; there was no way to get the material. So what we all had to do was to kind of fake it. There were minor disagreements on emphases and where the fakery ought to be and so forth, and my feeling was that Sidney was often less interested in the straight statement than in showing how clever he was."

The problem with Sidney was that he was an editor who really should have been a director. He had a lively, inventive mind and he could not bear to have it constantly subordinated to the needs of another man's picture. He proved his capacity as a director after the war when he made his celebrated movie *The Quiet One*, a feature-length film about the private world of a young Harlem boy and his experiences at the Wiltwyck School. But partly because funds for documentary film took a dive after the war and partly because of the limits of his own personality, Sidney spent most of the remaining years of his career in the cutting room.

Sidney's office was on the eighth floor, which had been set aside entirely for editing cubicles. The standard cubicle, never more than twelve feet square, contained two four-foot tables, a wall lined with metal racks to hold reels of film, a couple of high stools, a Moviola, and a big, free-rolling film barrel with numerous pieces of film hanging into it.

The Moviola was invented in 1919 and came into use around 1925. At the time, editors were still jerking film through their fingers before an overhead light to get a sense of the motion and to estimate the best place to break. Although many editors resisted the alteration of their physical routine that the Moviola required, its peep-show viewer offered a much better sense of how the edited film would look on the screen.

The basic Moviola has hardly changed in forty years. It is a chunky machine full of switches and swivels and interlocking parts almost all of burnished steel and aluminum, first black, now green. Its legs support a waist-high base upon which rests the four-inch viewer that points up toward the hunched-over editor at something like a 45-degree angle. Stretching up above the viewer from the back end of the base are two metal arms that are fitted with sprockets for reels. One sprocket holds the silent footage, which runs past the viewing head. The other sprocket holds the sound track, which runs over a standard magnetic tape head. Two foot pedals control the motors that keep everything moving. The editor can run sound and visual reels separately or in synch, and make separate splicing marks on each. Sidney sometimes ran through whole ten-minute sound and picture reels this way, marking them with a grease pencil, before handling them over to his first assistant for cutting.

As Sidney's second assistant, my job was also strictly mechanical. I kept in contact with the laboratory, helped the negative cutter match the negatives for the final negative print, helped prepare the negative title role, attended the recording sessions where the translated narrations were being made—just a few of the scores of tedious tasks that go into making a movie. One of the great features of the OWI films was their sound tracks, many of which were original scores by Aaron Copland, Morton Gould, Norman Lloyd, or Virgil Thomson. I would prepare for these composers a cut-by-cut "shot list" of the film with a description of each shot and the number of seconds it lasted. After viewing the unscored film and getting an emotional sense of it, the composers would use these shot lists to write their precisely timed scores.

Morton Gould recorded his score for *San Francisco, 1945* in a completely empty Carnegie Hall. An extreme perfectionist, he wanted the acoustics and timing to be immaculate. As he conducted, he seemed to be everywhere at once, with one eye on the orchestra, one eye on the score, and one eye on the stopwatch that was held just beneath his nose by Sidney's second assistant. I was then twenty years old and so pleased with myself that had Gould indeed had three eyes, I would not have noticed.

Not all the OWI films had original scores, and when stock music was needed, Max Goberman was the maestro of the sound track. Max was a New York conductor and musicologist who worked for the OWI as an independent contractor. He was a slight, spunky, outspoken man who achieved a somewhat Mephistophelian appearance by dint of a very pointy Van Dyke beard. Once when I brought him a script, I asked Max how he managed to find just the right piece of music for all the propaganda films he was scoring. Max pointed to five records and said, "This is my whole music library." The library consisted of Tchaikovsky's *Sixth (Pathétique) Symphony*, Stravinsky's *Firebird Suite*, Moussorgsky's *Pictures at an Exhibition*, Tchaikovsky's *Fourth Symphony*, and Rachmaninoff's *Second Piano Concerto*. Somewhere in the wings were two or three other Russian recordings, but these were the five he depended on over and over again, and in the thirty-five years since then, I have come to depend on them too. If you think of film action in battle terms, Tchaikovsky's *Fourth Symphony* and Stravinsky's *Firebird Suite* are great for the battle scenes—tanks, infantry, bombing—all the conflict and frenzy. They are followed magnificently by cuts to Tchaikovsky's *Sixth* or Rachmaninoff's *Second Piano Concerto*, portions of which are always perfect to lay down behind refugees, wounded soldiers, or devastation or pain of any kind. The

Moussorgsky is an all-purpose record, flexible enough to use for both a climax and a dénouement.

Max's little room at the OWI had a Moviola, records, and a turntable. As he watched the edited picture, he would record portions of his five records onto optical sound track, which he would then cut into perfect synchronization with the film. Because he always record-ed much more than he needed, he had a whole library of leftovers—a can of Moussorgsky segments here, a can of Rachmaninoff segments there—that he could dip into for each new picture. One of my thrills as an assistant editor was to be sent into Max's empty room one day with instructions to use his outtakes to score a five-minute sequence from one of Sidney's films. I no longer remember the film, although the afternoon is still vivid—it was the day that President Roosevelt died.

In the end some forty films were made during the three years of the OWI's operation. Technically brilliant but terribly restricted in content, most seem bland and uninteresting today. The films that got the best reception abroad were those that had some real (if re-created) drama, like the struggle of the French immigrants to a New England town in Helen Grayson's and Larry Madison's *Cummington Story;* a single person to focus on, like *The Window Cleaner,* who takes us on his odyssey across the face of the Empire State Building, talking the voice-over narration as he goes; or some offbeat humor like Joseph Krumgold's commentary in *The Autobiography of a Jeep.* Film writer and educator Richard Dyer MacCann (who got the story from OWI overseas chief Robert Sherwood) recounts the reception the jeep film received in Normandy shortly after the Allied invasion: "At Cher-bourg, when the ruins were still smoking and the peninsula was still not secure, the OWI showed a feature, a newsreel, and *The Autobiogra-phy of a Jeep.* The jubilant, liberated Frenchmen, touched by the warm humanity of this little film about a quarter ton of metal and motor, burst into shouts of '*Vive le jip! Vive le jip!*' "

Reportedly the most popular of all the OWI films shown overseas was Hammid's 1945 portrait of the renowned conductor Arturo Toscanini. Prepared for release to coincide with the liberation of Italy, *Toscanini: The Hymn of Nations* shows the seventy-eight-year-old expatriate celebrity conducting the NBC Symphony performing the Verdi composition from which the picture takes its title. Produced and edited by Irving Lerner, with Burgess Meredith narrating, the film portrays the dignity, nobility, and, by implication, the antifascist resolve of Toscanini in heroic proportions. One of the longest of the OWI pictures (thirty-one minutes), it was also its finest piece of propaganda.

If it did nothing else, the OWI documentary unit filled the enormous gap in historical and educational material on the America of its time. Few of those who went to public school in the fifties realize that their basic film diet as students was the OWI movies that had been made available by the U.S. Office of Education at print cost to teach American youngsters about their country. Wrote film historian and critic Arthur Knight in 1958 of the OWI work, "It was a priceless collection."

Both the Cold War, which made the examination of domestic problems taboo, and the arrival of television killed off most possibilities for government and private sponsorship of documentary filmmaking after the war. By the early seventies, when the documentary began to flower again, the work and the reputations of men like Willard Van Dyke, Sasha Hammid, and Sidney Meyers had sunk anonymously into the general pool of film knowledge. In 1977, when Irving Jacoby, who founded film studies at City College, returned to apply for a job, no one there knew who he was.

The OWI collection has similarly been lost to memory. Not even a simple list of the three or four dozen films produced by the Overseas Motion Picture Bureau has been preserved. "The Battle of Stalingrad was the important thing," says Willard, "not the fact that we made a film about the Pacific Northwest and had a hell of a time doing it. The idea that future generations would be interested really never crossed our minds."

Hollywood was, of course, irrevocably changed by the war experience. Location shooting for documentary flavor became the standard new form—if you wanted New York streets, you went to New York and shot them. But the full-length nonfiction feature became a rarity. It would remain for the old master Robert Flaherty, who had nearly invented the genre with *Nanook*, to make its postwar swan song with the final film of his life—and my first feature job—*Louisiana Story*.

Robert Flaherty and Helen van Dongen in their makeshift Louisiana cutting room.
(Courtesy Museum of Modern Art)

8 ▪ Robert Flaherty and Helen van Dongen
The Collaboration That Sustained a Legend

> Do this again and you will be immortal, and
> excommunicated from Hollywood,
> which is a good fate.
> —CHARLIE CHAPLIN, JEAN RENOIR, and
> DUDLEY NICHOLS in a telegram to Robert
> Flaherty after the West Coast premiere of
> *Louisiana Story.*

In the summer of 1948, when I was twenty-two years old and star-struck by the people who glistened at the heights of the motion-picture industry, I was riding in a cab with Robert Flaherty, on whose film, *Louisiana Story,* I had just finished working as the assistant editor. Flaherty was a great rumpled man with a wide fringe of white hair and the sort of broad, fleshy face that made his Irish nose look like a beak. He was sixty-four then but appeared to be over seventy, as perhaps befits someone who had achieved almost Biblical stature to people all over the world. His voice was deep and slightly graveled, with that rich, confident cadence that, when applied slowly and purposefully to the narrations of his films, lent them a tone of mystery and timelessness, as if the fables he told were not about specific people but about the struggles of the whole human race.

For several months after *Louisiana Story* was completed, I assisted Flaherty in the tedious business of seeking a distributor for his independently produced film. It was not a happy time for Flaherty, for once again he was returning to do business with the commercial studios that had made him an outcast and that he detested. But he was a warm and irrepressible raconteur, and whether we were break-fasting on his awful, over-brewed and blackened tea in his room at the Chelsea Hotel or performing our desultory rounds, he charmed me with stories of the Cajuns of the swamp country, of Irish writers, of famous people and faraway places.

Our errand on this particular day was to screen his picture for one of the big Hollywood companies—MGM, Columbia, or Paramount. As I held the door of the cab for the man who had climbed in and out of igloos, who had been carried on a litter by Samoan chiefs when he was ill, who had been borne by elephants in India and cabin cruisers in the bayou, I could not help but notice how awkward Flaherty looked in this midtown business setting. He didn't seem to belong in the cab, and he didn't seem to belong in New York. He could fit in almost anywhere, except in the one arena where the power lay to bolster his forever frustrated career, and it was easy to see that Flaherty understood this all too well. As we rolled through the stunning cavern of upper Park Avenue, Flaherty stuck a chubby thumb toward the towering symbols of modern civilization and with a wonderful disdain that momentarily righted all balances, he said, "This has all the warmth of a well-marbled lavatory."

Flaherty's reputation was based largely on three films: *Nanook of the North* (1922), his famous picture about the Eskimos with whom he had lived for two years; *Man of Aran* (1934), a film created during a two-year sojourn with the Aran Islanders off the coast of Ireland; and *Elephant Boy* (1936), a big studio-sponsored production in which Flaherty's stirring scenes of India were adulterated by studio additions and editing. Scattered between were numerous failures including three Hollywood-backed pictures in the South Seas.

He was known in the profession as an uncompromising innocent, a difficult collaborator, a man with no sense whatever of the commercial realities of filmmaking. Yet he had the knack of capturing moments that stirred people very deeply, and this capacity, this love and gentleness and extraordinary tenacity, made him a legend of a kind we no longer have today—as well as a constant, if resistible, tempta-tion to producers. In 1931, after Flaherty's negotiations with Soviet motion-picture authorities to film the dying cultures of Central Russia fell through, John Grierson invited him to join the British Film Unit, hoping to point Flaherty's loving lens at Britain's industrial craftsmen. But Flaherty's love was a love that needed to linger, and the prohibitive costs of his production routines forced Grierson to take the picture—*Industrial Britain*—from him and edit it without him.

Flaherty was essentially a lonely and misunderstood man, much abused in his own profession. Even documentarists who hailed him as their founder and flocked to his side during the filming of *Man of Aran* had, by the time that film was finished, largely dismissed him as irrelevant and even blind. He had no interest in exposing the economic, political, and technological travails of modern man—these things embarrassed him. And few of his politically conscious colleagues could appreciate the importance of the enchanting fables—however naïve—that had won him his audience.

Only in *The Land*, a film he made for the U.S. Department of Agriculture in 1939–41 on land abuse and rural unemployment, did he turn his camera to human suffering, injustice, and folly. Unfortunately the Japanese attack killed all government interest in its themes and the film was never commercially released.

Unsuited to propaganda work, and therefore inactive through most of the war years, Flaherty was sixty-two years old in 1946, when he was offered his final opportunity to make the kind of film he loved best. Standard Oil of New Jersey, aware that Revillon Frères, the French furriers, had sponsored *Nanook*, asked Flaherty if he thought he could make a film about the oil fields. They would finance the picture, he would own it, and, most important, he would be left alone to film it as he saw fit.

Flaherty drove thousands of miles through the Southwest with his wife and frequent collaborator, Frances, seeking an appropriate setting for the film. When they came to Louisiana they were immediately enchanted by the French descendents and their picturesque way of life. After steeping themselves in Cajun history and legends, they happened one day to see an oil derrick gliding up the bayou, towed by a launch; they knew they had found the theme for their film. "Almost immediately," said Flaherty, "a story began to take shape in our minds. It was a story built around that derrick which moved so silently, so majestically into the wilderness, probed for oil beneath the watery ooze, and then moved on again, leaving the land as untouched as before it came."

I was barely a year out of the OWI when Helen van Dongen, whom I had met there a few times, called to ask me to be her assistant editor on the film. During part of the preceding year I had worked for Max Rothstein's hole-in-the-wall editing service, and although Max paid me assistant's wages, he let me cut without supervision. Becoming a real assistant again seemed like a step backward, so I turned Helen down. Three days later I called her back in a cold sweat, much relieved to discover that the job was still available.

I had almost made the first serious error of my young career. Not only was this my chance to get back into the big leagues and work on a feature-length film, but it was an opportunity to work with the tiny, serious-minded woman who had traveled the world with director Joris Ivens, her first husband, and was known to those who cared about such things as one of the giants of the cutting room. As Paul Rotha and Richard Griffith wrote in *The Film Till Now* of Helen's long association with Ivens: "They worked on equal terms as joint creators, a collaboration which has been one of the most fruitful in film history but which has tended to obscure Helen van Dongen's own quite distinct talent. . . . No one at work today observes more subtly the implications and possibilities of isolated shots, nor has a surer instinct for the links between them."

In the summer of 1947 Helen rented a room at the old Deluxe labs on Tenth Avenue and Fifty-fifth Street, and that's where we worked until the summer of 1948. Within a few days I saw that this would be a very different relationship from the one I had had with Sidney Meyers. Helen did not treat me like a son, and she was not interested in my education. She never paused at the Moviola to show me why she chose one cut over another. She never paused to chat or ruminate or philosophize. In fact, pausing was not in her nature. She was indefatigable, and she devoted her energy to the single purpose of conquering the two hundred thousand feet of film—thirty-seven hours' worth—that she'd brought back from Louisiana.

My apprenticeship with Helen formed the bedrock of my cutting-room technique. Her rigid professionalism struck a responsive chord in me, and her orderliness reinforced my own working style. At this time in my life, I fretted a great deal over whether my free-lance career would hold together. I still had to support my family, and because I had no college education, the only alternative to film editing seemed to be another job in the garment factories. So I thought much less about how I would become a full-fledged editor one day and much more about doing a good job, working hard, being a little inventive sometimes, and becoming accepted by the people I worked for. I thus fell quickly into Helen's pace, and I eventually understood that within the crisp efficiency of our work habits there was an intangible warmth.

Because I rarely spoke, whether in the cutting room or at screenings, I was practically invisible. But I observed things very closely. And of the things that interested me, nothing was more remarkable than the relationship that had developed between the expansive director and the cool cutting-room virtuoso twenty years his junior.

Never was there a greater disparity between two people. If Flaherty was ebullient and disorganized, Helen was contained and disciplined. If he was politically removed, she was immersed in some of the most political pictures of the era. If Flaherty overspent his time and his budgets, driving his producers and collaborators to despair, Helen operated with a machinelike constancy. If he was informal and garrulous, she was more than slightly forbidding, with a taut mouth that rarely yielded a smile during working hours, and a firm, single-motion, masculine handshake. If Flaherty was raised in the Canadian wilderness among Indians and backwoodsmen and knew little of urban civilization until he was an adult, Helen was brought up by a French mother and had the civility of the Old World embedded in every word and motion.

Flaherty liked to stretch things out, and never seemed concerned about finishing—perhaps because he wanted to make each precious job last as long as possible. His lackadaisicalness and ingenuousness could be startling. During one of his rare visits to the cutting room, Flaherty came up to the table where I worked, examined the synchronizer, and started fiddling with its wheel. Then he looked at me and said, "What is this for?" I politely explained that the synchronizer is a cutting tool that enables you to keep the sound track and the picture on two separate pieces of film and yet still in synch. But I was momentarily stunned. This was a man who had been making films before I was born, and I was explaining a piece of film equipment to him. It seemed so odd; he was such a giant; I was baffled.

My guess is that Flaherty was intimidated by Helen and everything she represented—from her businesslike manner to the complexity of her skills. Sometimes he would clam up when she made specific suggestions about how to arrange a sequence, suggestions that went beyond his own thinking at that point, or walk away without a word when she screened a scene that was so finely edited he felt jarred by its unfamiliarity.

But somehow Helen managed to work within Flaherty's emotional confines without either threatening him or sacrificing her own self-esteem; and not an unpleasant word passed between them. Never having worked with an egocentric director, I had no idea of the inner acrobatics Helen performed to bring this off—or the extent to which my own career would be devoted to repeating them.

It is a revelation to have Helen's own account, certainly one of the most poignant in film-editing history, of how she held this most improbable collaboration together. Her story, which appeared in *Film Quarterly* twenty-five years later, begins in 1940, when Flaherty invited her to Washington to cut *The Land*. Awed by his reputation, eager to make a good impression, and frightened by the thought of working with a new director whose habits might be strange to her, she made her way down long, bleak corridors to his office at the Department of Agriculture, where she found him seated behind his desk reading a newspaper:

> "Hello," he said cheerfully, getting up and extending his hand, "your name is too difficult so I'll call you Helen, O.K.?" and then, without pause or interruption, held forth on the bad state of the world. This took several hours of the first morning (and was to take as many hours of every following day so long as the film lasted). Then he said abruptly: "Come on, let us screen some film."
>
> It took us several days to screen through most of the rushes. In the office I found a long "script" written by someone in the Department of Agriculture. It did not look much used and appeared to have little connection with the rushes I was seeing. During these screenings I waited for a word of explanation from Flaherty as to what some of the scenes represented, expected him to disclose his plans, hoped for some word of enlightenment as to what he had in mind. But he just sat there, rubbing the left hand through that fringe of white hair, smoking, and groaning. Back in the office, after some more desperate sighs, he would start his monologue again, repeating almost verbatim a news report he had read about the war in Europe. He would also speak in

general terms about the fantastic abundance he had seen during the shooting. Other topics he continued mentioning were: the waste of human lives, the destructive influence of civilization, and the killing of human skills and crafts through the introduction of machines; but on these subjects we had as yet no film. He would repeat this day in and day out, by telephone if I had not yet come in, over and over again, until it became an incantation.

After about three weeks we had done no more than screen the same material over and over and still he never came to the point where he would make suggestions, outline a possible narrative, or divulge his intentions. Each time when the lights would go on again in the screening room, he would groan: "My God, what are we going to do with all that stuff." How would I know, if he did not?

In this fashion, Helen gradually became familiar with everything Flaherty had shot. She longed to begin editing but dared not make the smallest suggestion for fear it would be contrary to his plans—whatever they were.

In desperation I wrote to Joris Ivens, explaining that all Flaherty did was talk about the war and attack machines in the morning, screen the same stuff all over again in the afternoon, and tell stories about *Elephant Boy* in the evening, but never, never a word about what kind of film he was trying to make. I could see, I wrote, that he might not need a script but he ought to have a plan or at least an idea! What did Flaherty want from me? Companionship to relieve the boredom of looking at uncut scenes all afternoon? Ivens, who does not like to write letters and shifts the ones he receives from pocket to pocket until they are beyond answering, wired back, "Observe, look, listen. Love, Joris."

To Helen's great relief, Flaherty soon left his office at the Department of Agriculture to go off on a second shooting trip.

Before he left, I asked the inevitable question: "What shall I do with all the film we have and all the stuff you are going to send me?" "Oh? Well, you just go ahead," he said. During his absence I screened *Nanook* and *Moana* repeatedly, trying to see if I could discover any particular method in his assembly that could be applied to *The Land*. But there was too much disparity between the themes, and it was no help to notice that, whenever he got stuck with the visual story line in these two silent films, he would flash a title on the screen and proceed until he got stuck again. I occupied myself with an initial selection and grouping of our rushes.

Then a breakthrough. Helen noticed that there was a relationship between Flaherty's endless monologues and what happened on the screen; that his daily litany was his way of slowly perfecting the voice-over narration that he would one day record. She began to listen to him very carefully no matter how often he seemed to repeat himself, and soon she found that she was beginning to see the film through his eyes. Slowly, she discovered the signs that gave her the direction she needed for editing, and to the end she depended on these signs, for Flaherty disliked direct questions about film theories and could become almost inarticulate in response.

> When I had assembled some part of the film and did not want to proceed beyond a certain point, I would ask him to come to the projection room. With one eye I would watch the screen, with the other one, Flaherty. What he did not say was written all over his face during these screenings: the way he put his hand through his hair or squashed out that eternal cigarette; the way he shifted position on the chair, sometimes rubbing his back against its rungs as if it were itching; these gestures would speak more than a torrent of words.

Helen's ability to decode Flaherty's unspoken intentions must have won her passing grades from Flaherty on a whole battery of professional and personal tests, for when the offer came through from Standard Oil, he immediately asked her to join the crew on *Louisiana Story* as editor and associate producer. Because she was with him from the beginning this time, everything was less chaotic. But Flaherty continued to resist all forms of organization, which he treated like intrusions. If he saw something he liked, no matter how extraneous, he shot it, sometimes thousands of feet worth, and then brought it back to Helen to fit it in. When there were gaps, Helen felt confident enough to *request* certain shots, and Flaherty might eventually comply—but only months afterward when he had seen the need for them himself. When Helen returned to New York after a year on location, the rushes were barely assembled.

Our rushes were air-shipped daily to New York [Helen continues] and the laboratory returned them daily. Flaherty would continue to look at the rushes night after night. He seemed happiest when they were screened the way they were shot. Untouched, unorganized, unshortened, they contained all the possibilities, all the potentialities of all the ideas he had in mind, and with his unlimited fantasy and vision he saw behind the screen, behind this incompleted material the story he had envisioned. "It's going to be great," he would say in general. But when the scenes were separated into categories, or put in a somewhat chronological order, though still in full length, he began to worry. An "arrangement" had occurred, and gaps began to show. The slight order disturbed the wild flight of fancy. His expectations began to fade. The circle always repeated itself: elation when seeing untouched rushes with all their promises, black moods and despair during the formation and growth of the sequence, until that moment when the composition was fairly completed and he began to see that the old magic he had wanted to instill had taken hold.

As a realistic matter of time was involved, I could not forever let him indulge his enjoyment of unarranged rushes. Sometimes I suspected that he would be perfectly content to do nothing but shoot, screen whatever he shot, and bewitch everyone with his enthusiasm about "what a wonderful film this will make."

Half of the large porch surrounding the house had been screened in and closed off. It was my cutting room and off limits to everyone. It was the only place where I could work undisturbed. Flaherty came into it only once: to have the picture taken which is now the frontispiece of that large volume *The Film Till Now* by Paul Rotha and Richard Griffith. He avoided coming in, because it would involve him in details he apparently did not want to know about.

I would search for scenes which might complete a sequence or give it just that atmosphere which was still lacking. Then I would go to Flaherty with suggestions with which I hoped to get his reaction. I often met with a cold shoulder; perhaps he thought that I wanted to take the initiative away from him or wanted to push my ideas to the foreground. "Give me the rushes for screening tomorrow, I want to look at them," he would counter and then, as if to protect them from contamination, would not return them for a while.

As time passed I would try out my ideas by myself. If I

thought they worked, I would put the sequence back the way Flaherty had last seen it, always leaving in just *one* change, making it as perfect and as smooth as it ought to be in the final version, meanwhile also always tightening my composition just a little more every time. If I had achieved what I had in mind, I would hand the sequence to Flaherty for screening, and if he did not get restless right away, I knew I had been successful. I was wise enough not to point out what I had done. Then would come that encouraging moment when he would exclaim: "She's going to come, she's going to come," referring to the sequence he had just seen. Then, somewhat with mistrust: "Did you change anything?" and I would say: "No, I don't think so. Just tightened it up a little." Because of his apprehensions, his doubts, and hesitations the process of editing dragged considerably.

The opening scene of *Louisiana Story* is one of the most effective of the whole movie. We are in the bayou country, lingering on the tiniest of nature's treasures, a dew drop, a lily pad, and then moving on slowly to alligators and other wildlife, and finally a boy paddling quietly in his pirogue. Then Flaherty's soft, inviting voice opens the narration: "His name is Alexander, Napoleon, Ulysses, Latour . . ." Each name, carefully chosen to evoke the spirit and culture of the place, is separately enunciated in Flaherty's slow, cherishing cadence. There's a feeling of hushed mystery, the opening of a fairy tale.

As described in Flaherty's script, we are supposed to "move through the forest of bearded trees" and be "spellbound by all the wildlife and the mystery of the wilderness that lies ahead." And to make sure Helen had enough to work with, Flaherty shot just about everything in the bayou. "We had scenes," she lamented, "of alligators sitting on their nests, slithering through the water, basking in the sun, or rearing their ugly heads from a mud-patch in the swamp-forest; strange and magnificent birds perched on tree-tops or sitting on branches sticking out of the lily-pond; snakes gliding up trees, lotus-leaves reflected in the clear water, dewdrops on the leaves, flies skimming the water, a spider spinning its web, Spanish moss dangling from huge oak-trees, fishes, rabbits, fawns, or skunks, and others too numerous to mention."

Hours upon hours of such shots, many of them as spellbindingly beautiful as Flaherty had prescribed, shot by Flaherty's young cameraman Richard Leacock, were stored in cans labeled "scenes for introduction." If Helen wanted to select a dewy leaf or a muddy alligator, we might spend an entire day just screening the appropriate material. Her patience was extraordinary. She could sit and look for hours, hoping to find the single detail—the raised eyebrow, the bird ever so slowly rising out of the water—that would implant just the right meaning, just the sense of muted anxiety or primeval timelessness she needed to perfect a scene.

The film presented more editorial problems than anything I'd ever imagined. Walking through miles and miles of takes and retakes were untrained local "actors"—people of the region—who performed Flaherty's story about a half-wild Cajun boy whose father leases a piece of land to the oil company. Flaherty was a master at working with nonprofessional actors and astutely allowed them to ad lib their lines. But when retakes were shot, they ad-libbed different lines, making the job of selecting the best moments from each take and piecing together the ideal performance a nerve-wrecking enterprise. If Helen cut from a medium shot to a close shot of the actor who was speaking, the juxtaposition might work visually and fail verbally. If she tried to cover the rough edges by cutting momentarily to the reacting face of the actor who was listening, she often found the face so expressionless that the moment was dead. If she cut the sound track and rearranged whole sentences to make newer, livelier sentences, they would only in the end prove too long or too short to match the action. The more she experimented the more frustrated she became, until finally, very much against her will, she determined to put the sequence aside and hope for better luck in the future. Her solutions were ingenious. In several instances she found that by overlapping the voices as if they were interrupting each other, all the juggling would fall miraculously into place.

But, of course, her problems didn't end there. The pace of the nonprofessional performances was so sluggish that she had to trim them down in order to speed them up and maintain the rhythm of the picture, an intricate cutting process equivalent to the surgical paring of notes from an operetta. In traditional Hollywood method, an actor brought his face back to "rest" before changing expressions from one emotion to the next. But Flaherty just kept the camera running while calling instructions to the boy to alter his expression or change the direction of his head. The results left Helen little room for error in choosing the cut that would be both the right emotional length as well as the right emotion, for she had no padding on either end. In those days, every time you rejected a splice and recut something, you lost a single frame of film—such was the nature of the irreversible glue-splicing process we used—and the more you changed your mind, the closer you came to all-out panic. True, we could have ordered a reprint from the lab if she had cut herself into a hole. But when you wanted them to dig a single foot out of two hundred thousand feet and still wanted to stay on good terms with the lab and not get your negative scratched, you had to think twice before making that call.

Day in and day out, month in and month out, Helen struggled to turn an untrained raccoon into a Hollywood actor, to build a climactic confrontation between the boy and an alligator with only a few shots that actually showed the two in battle (most of the alligator splashing wasn't even shot at the same location), piecing together the introduction to create the hush of eternity promised in Flaherty's and Leacock's photography, and composing and choreographing the shots and the intricate sound effects for the finest piece of editing in the film, the sequence that became known as the "ballet of the roughnecks."

Although the oil rig had a dramatic presence when Flaherty first saw it gliding silently into the bayou, he discovered after shooting its operation for weeks in daylight that it was about as interesting to watch as an office building. Only after dusk, illuminated by the huge floodlights and with the sounds of drilling shattering the still bayou night, did the derrick come to life and infuse Flaherty with the exhilaration he had felt when it first appeared. Hours of film were shot of the huge drill hammering downward, of the men threading the chains that rapidly unraveled as the pipe descended, of the charged moments when another giant pipe flew up the length of the derrick to become part of the great downward plunging shaft, of the tense intervals when the men performed carefully timed and dangerous motions—securing each section of fast-moving tubing to the next, controlling the engine pressure—of the boy quietly climbing onto the rig, his bare feet shining against the black, oil-slicked platform, of the confident smiling faces of the workmen in the midst of all the commotion. There were shots from the base of the rig looking up its towering height, shots from above as the powerful drill descended, and hours upon hours of clanging and rattling and whirring recorded on a dozen sound tracks.

Helen first edited the visual sequence. Because it was strictly a cutting-room job, Flaherty had to leave its composition entirely to her, a situation that initially made him morose. He was further disappointed when he first saw the silent cut footage; but he was elated several months later after Helen added the sound. It was the climax of the film and it is still as stirring to watch today as the fiercely edited battle scenes from World War II.

My job was to be able always to put my hands on whatever Helen wanted. To do this, I had to develop a photographic mental recording of everything we screened, to catalogue it, and to refile every snippet of it with an iron will that can only come from the fear of having to search through a two-hundred-thousand-foot haystack. We worked like a hospital operating team, Helen riveted to the Moviola, marking her cuts, me feeding her the shots she needed, putting away the trims, cleaning out the film barrels of the "maybes" that had become "no's," and, of course, scraping, gluing, and splicing her cuts.

Each day we started fresh at nine, broke for an hour lunch, broke again at four for coffee or tea, and wrapped up at six—all 350 cans of film neatly awaiting our next stubborn incursion. The smoothness with which Helen and I worked was a revelation to me, and I was secretly thrilled to note at the end of each day that no matter how much film we handled, no matter how many splices we made, no matter how much frustration we endured, our cutting room never looked as if a stitch of work had gone on there.

After seven or eight months of this, we had a two-hour rough cut of the entire film, but in the two years since he began *Louisiana Story,* Flaherty had used up his budget. Not only couldn't we get all the finishing touches—lab work, the optical effects, the titles—but Virgil Thomson had yet to write the score and Eugene Ormandy had yet to record it, all of which meant a gap of something like fifty-eight thousand dollars. So Helen and I stopped working and took a vacation, while Flaherty went back to Standard Oil to promote more money. This took weeks of persistence on his part, since the people at Standard Oil were not jumping to lay out more money for a film they had commissioned almost three years earlier, and none of the executives would acknowledge having the authority to okay the funds. (A year later, when the picture was finished and it got a spectacular press, and *Life* magazine gave it a giant spread, and Standard Oil was mentioned everywhere, everybody in the company seemed to claim responsibility.)

When the funds finally came through in the spring of 1948, I set about preparing a shot list for Virgil Thomson. It was a thrilling time because Thomson, who was one of my heroes, was coming into the cutting room regularly to look at the picture. The shot list was a laborious procedure. In seventy-five minutes of film there are hundreds and hundreds of shots, each of which had to be described one at a time in words, feet, and seconds. When at last I finished, I took the manuscript to the Chelsea Hotel, where Thomson was living, and the five-minute visit I expected turned into a three-hour conversation. He spoke at length about the scores he wrote for *The River* and *The Plow that Broke the Plains*, two thirties films by Pare Lorentz that are still considered classics of American documentary, and I left feeling significantly closer to the world I longed to join.

When the score was finished, I was sent by train to Philadelphia to deliver it to Eugene Ormandy at the Philadelphia Academy of Music. Ormandy asked me if I would like to hear the concert that night, and he put me in a box above the stage. Moments like this, and the fact that I was getting my first screen credit, were the things that meant everything to me in these early days of my career. I was too young and naïve to be aware of the emotional trials of being an editor, of the aggravations Helen had endured, of the difficulty of maintaining one's identity. These issues were far, far away. The only career anxiety I understood was economic survival.

Once completed, the picture was lauded everywhere. The nation's great fabler had again made our mundane world sublime. When the second edition of *The Film Till Now* appeared in 1949, this is what it said about *Louisiana Story*:

"There must have been thousands of 'educational' films produced during the last fifty years which tried to show 'the wonders of industry' through the eyes of a child. The wonders of industry as they presented them remained more incomprehensible than wonderful, and the children were those familiar textbook ones known as John and Mary Smith. Here the boy is as palpably real as the swamps he lives in, and the process of oil-drilling is observed and described with a clarity and drama unmatched in my experience of seeing films. This is a *real* educational film; it is also a poem, and the two things work together."

All the same, *Louisiana Story* did not give documentary filmmakers the momentum they expected, and despite Flaherty's and Standard Oil's happy collaboration, no similar private funding offers were made.

Within a few years Flaherty died, Helen remarried and retired to Vermont (where she lives today), and, after kicking around in the nooks and crannies of New York's nascent film industry, I went to work as a full-fledged editor for the medium that helped to kill the documentary film, TV.

Setting up for "The Guy Lombardo Show."

9 ■ Making It
The TV Pressure Cooker

On Tuesday nights all through the fall of 1948 clots of people gathered outside the big hardware stores in Bensonhurst. For sixty minutes they stood immobilized by the magic rays emanating from the new mahogany-encased video sets on window display. They were watching the Milton Berle show, an incredible cultural phenomenon and the first national obsession since the war. Businesses all over the city closed early so that proprietors could rush home in time to join their families for this great communal event. Often they squeezed into their living rooms in the company of a dozen or more friends and relatives, for televisions were still rare in 1948 and those without muscled their way in wherever they could. In my family Aunt Bessie was the first to have a TV, and not since my brother's bar mitzvah had I seen so many relatives in one place.

By the early fifties almost every middle-class household had a television set, and shows like Milton Berle's were creating the biggest and most lucrative advertising market ever known. The TV boom transformed New York's film business from a sleepy little collection of documentarists, film services, and Hollywood representatives into a raging madhouse full of ambitious technicians, fast-talking ad men, desperate actors reaching for Eldorado, producers and directors replacing each other in an endless swirl of hirings and firings, and, above all else, pots and pots of money.

Like thousands of other people who are drawn into the safe areas of publishing, music, or filmmaking, I began cutting TV commercials because I was overcome by insecurity. My father, who finally died in 1947, had been spiritually crushed by free-lance work, and I was haunted by his experience. Getting married when I was twenty-two and having two children by the time I was thirty only increased my anxiety.

My fears were not entirely unrealistic, for I learned in the postwar years how difficult it was to make any headway in the film business. Aside from my year on *Louisiana Story*, my pre-TV experience consisted of a series of short-lived jobs alternating with periods of unemployment and one dreadful return to loading trucks in the garment center. There was Max Rothstein's editorial service, where I cut Panagra Airlines travelogues of Latin America, excerpted "moral message" scenes from feature films for an outfit called Teaching Film Custodians, and synchronized the dailies for a Hollywood picture that was being shot in New York called *Carnegie Hall;* some on-and-off free-lance assignments making promos for Standard Oil out of Flaherty's leftover film; a year at the United Nations film section, where I developed a reputation as a troubleshooter for my ability to take aimlessly shot footage of some "interesting phenomenon" and mold it into a usable short of some kind; and finally an editing job at a peculiar company called Obelisk Films, which consisted of five Jewish executives who produced Bible stories for the Catholic Archdiocese of New York. When in 1950 I got word of a job opening with a new production company called Tempo, where the pay was $125 a week and the work was steady, I was primed to go.

The company was set up by one of the top animation artists from Walt Disney. He had come East to make animated TV commercials, and because even animated commercials usually included some live action, Tempo needed a film editor. It was one of the first and it quickly became one of the biggest commercial houses in the business.

Most of the commercials we produced were thirty- and sixty-second spots for products like Maxwell House Coffee, Vicks Vaporub, Ajax (bum-bum, the foaming cleanser), Colgate Dental Cream, and other household products. Technically speaking, these early ads were the simplest work imaginable. There's a dancing coffee pot or some such thing with a jingle about Maxwell House exploding flavor buds; cut to a man tasting a steaming cup of coffee while his lovely, crisp wife looks on expectantly; cut to the best take of his reaction ("Hmm, that's *delicious!*"); cut to the sign-off; and you're through. But nothing is ever that simple in the advertising business.

At noon the ad guys would march into the cutting room to view the work. A single executive could have looked at the spot a couple of times (two minutes), requested a change or two (ten minutes), and been out by twelve-fifteen. Instead, six high-priced executives butted heads over the tiny Moviola screen and discussed every possible "nuance" of the ad. "Is the wife's smile convincing enough? Let's see take seven on that again." "Look at the way he holds his pinky—it bothers me." "Would it be better if we had him say, '*Hmm*, that's delicious!' with the accent on *Hmm?*" And so forth.

Just the same, you'd imagine they'd figure out what "nuances" they wanted, tell me what takes to use, and be out by twelve-forty-five. But no. For I soon realized that while all this was painfully boring to me, the ad men liked to prolong their visits to the cutting room as long as possible, cherishing every volt of artistic energy that surged through their systems. Whether they were requesting a closer close-up on a tube of toothpaste or asking me to shorten the pause before the jingle ("Brush your teeth with Colgate!") burst forth on the sound track, they always managed to sound as if they were constructing the Taj Mahal. In a single afternoon with a group of advertising executives, I heard the words "creative," "innovative," and "concept" more times than in the previous five years with professional filmmakers.

Every few days another set of dailies came in for another product with another narrator reading a sixty-second message in an endless number of variations. I was amazed that they could go on for so long—seventeen, eighteen, twenty-six, thirty-two readings of the same paragraph and still they kept going. On one occasion I was confronted with twenty minutes of dailies in which a freckle-faced kid had to stuff himself with Instant Royal Pudding until he vomited. Twice a minute he'd stop shoveling, look at the camera, lick his lips, force a grin, and say, "Royal Pudding is so *delicious!*" or "Royal

Pudding is *so* delicious!" or "Royal *Pudding* is so delicious!"—until he finally covered his mouth and puked off camera.

With practically all these commercials, the most convincing reading came by the second or third try—a five-year-old could spot it—and by the fourteenth I had no idea what I was listening to any more. But down at the studio it took three hours just to light the set and get everything ready. With executives from B. B. D. & O., or Benton & Bowles observing and correcting every move, the producer was not going to let the narrator or the actors do five takes in five minutes and then go home. It just wouldn't seem right. It would be too simple. Somebody wouldn't be getting his money's worth. The deeper nuances wouldn't emerge. Besides, the agency guys didn't want to go back to the office. They wanted to stay right there on the set where they could be creative. So they spent hours telling each actor to be a little more exuberant, to be a little less exuberant, to try this word, to try that word—until at the end of the day they could finally return to the office and grumble, "We pulled it out of them."

But when all this material came into the cutting room the following day, in thirty-seven readings there was never one that was good enough to assure the ad men that they'd still have their jobs the next week if they chose it. So they had me splice together bits of takes fourteen, twenty-five, and thirty-two to make the Single Perfect Reading (which to me looked identical to take three) and finally departed in a state of hypercreative exultation. Any thought I had of redeeming the situation by cracking a joke or making light of the whole enterprise was out of the question. The agency guys were grimly serious about their calling.

This kind of work was all right for a week or two. It had its curiosities. But after a few months at Tempo, I was morose and close to broken, for I knew I was using almost none of the skills that had landed me the job in the first place. At night bad dreams about exploding flavor buds and foaming cleansers with catchy jingles and forced smiles began to bother me. In the one nightmare I still recall, I was stuffed into a Maxwell House jar and exploded into ten thousand pieces when they poured the boiling water on me. At work, meanwhile, for the first time since I began cutting film I started to have daydreams about becoming a feature-film editor. During the next eight years those reveries grew into the most profound hunger I've ever experienced.

In 1951 I moved to Transfilm, the largest production company in New York, located, oddly enough, in the same offices where I had once worked for the OWI. I was brought in to cut commercials, having developed a reputation for being fast and reliable. But I soon proved that my training and talents went beyond commercial work, and when Western Union contracted with Transfilm for a fifty-thousand-dollar industrial documentary, I landed the assignment. The other three editors in the company, all of whom had seniority over me, resented this, and I was at a loss for how to react. Trying to be falsely humble and one of the guys struck me as the lowest form of appeasement. I turned aloof in response to their hostility and told myself I didn't give a damn what they thought. I became feared, disliked, and isolated, and sometimes felt as if I were walking right over them for my own success. But I shoved all that aside. The Western Union film was a serious assignment, and I considered myself an editor for the first time. Despite the office politics, I couldn't wait to begin work in the morning.

Alistair Cooke was hosting a quality CBS program at this time called "Omnibus," one of the showpieces of television's Sunday-afternoon "cultural ghetto." In 1952 the producers began coming to Transfilm for special projects—a short on tugboats, a documentary on William Faulkner, who had just won the Nobel Prize—and again I was selected to edit. The "Omnibus" directors were invariably astonished by my knowledge of music and film structure, and in a short time they were treating me as a collaborator rather than a technician. Three years later, when I set up my own editorial service, "Omnibus" hired me as supervising editor.

Late in 1952 Gene Milford, an established motion-picture editor of twenty years standing both in Hollywood and New York (in 1932 he was nominated for the first editing Oscar), a man I had met a few times and always thought of as the person to call if you were an editor looking for work, recommended me and another young editor, Sid Katz, to cut a new Sunday-afternoon CBS series called "The Search." The show would take viewers to a different university each week and report, documentary style, on all sorts of current research.

Sid and I cut "The Search" for the better part of 1953 and 1954. Seat-belt research at Cornell, brain research at Tulane, a passionately cut show on speech-defects research at the University of Iowa. The directors and cameramen—many of them old acquaintances from the OWI—shot as much as twenty hours of film for each half-hour program, giving Sid and me substantial editorial challenges. "The Search" years still stand out as the most sane and rewarding of this entire period; but the show was a loser and was killed after a single season.

When the end came, I couldn't face another company job with office politics. If I had to cut crap again, I wanted at least to be working for myself. At the time Sid and I were using cutting rooms that CBS had rented for us in the studio district on Twelfth Avenue and Fifty-fourth Street, and I said, "Sid, let's just stay right here and set up our own editorial service." That's what we did, and, as it turned out, we timed the TV wave right at its crest.

When Gene Milford came back to New York from the West Coast in 1956 and paid his young protégés a visit, he found us really swinging, with three employees and more business than we knew what to do with. All sorts of commercial work—Jergens, Buick, Texaco, Philip Morris, Robitussin; independently produced pilots by old-time stage personalities and by newcomers, like Dick Van Dyke; industrials; promos; everything. Milford, who figured he was about ready for another stint in New York, said, "Hey, you guys've got a terrific thing here—I'd like to become the third member of this company." And thus MKR Films was formed.

Gene's presence meant more expansion and more work—mostly for me and Sid, since Gene was already in his mid-fifties then and inclined to long lunches and other perquisites of established success. Nonetheless, as part of our company he cut three Elia Kazan pictures, *Baby Doll, A Face in the Crowd,* and *Splendor in the Grass.* (In 1954 he'd won the editing Oscar for Kazan's *On the Waterfront.*) His reputation brought in more TV pilots, and soon we were cutting regular weekly shows as well, such long-forgotten programs as "Wanted" and an early "I Spy" with Raymond Massey.

The next five years were a blur of ceaseless pressure and nonstop work. We cut everything. Somewhere in the midst of cigarette ads and TV comedies I cut a series of documentaries for a medical advertising firm that included all sorts of bloody tumors and explicit operations I would have averted my eyes from in a theater. It was just part of the numbing quantity and diversity of material that passed through our cutting rooms during those boom years. I would have been giddy—or in this case nauseated—if our frantic schedule hadn't pushed me completely beyond feeling.

I once suggested to Gene and Sid that we stop accepting so many jobs, but they said, "Ralph, if you're not expanding, you're going backwards," an American business maxim I've never fully understood. But I was just thirty-two and still basically insecure; and despite our frenetic pace, windfall incomes, and a month's backlog of work, as far as I knew the entire television industry could sink into the Atlantic the next day and I'd be back loading trucks in the garment center. To escape that clawing financial insecurity, I was ready to subvert my personal life, and to some extent I did. In any case, my protests were few and muted, and we never turned away a job. Although we stuck to our own accounts, in an emergency we'd split a job three ways and each edit a separate portion. I never got home before eight, and worked around the clock when necessary. And MKR Films quickly became the biggest editorial service in the city.

I was becoming known in the business now as someone for whom no deadline was impossible, and as a "creative" editor who could take a grabbag of miscellaneous footage and turn it into an entertaining short. At "Omnibus" Boris Kaplan, the film supervisor, had a fondness for odd bits of film, some of which came to him over-the-transom from wayward or would-be cameramen. Marching school bands in New Jersey, traffic cops from all over Europe with their crazy arm motions—he'd screen this material for me and ask if I couldn't make a five-minute "thing" out of it. The attitude seemed to be, "Give it to Rosenblum, he'll put some music to it, turn it into a little ballet, and we'll throw it on the air for some variety." The montages I cut were presented as novelty items and spoofs and not taken seriously by anyone, but audiences always got a kick out of them, and they were a great source of secret satisfaction to me.

"Omnibus" also made endless unreasonable demands, something that seems inevitable in an industry surrounded by hungry peripherals ready to do twenty-four hours of slave labor at a moment's notice. In 1958 Alistair Cooke returned from the Brussels World's Fair with over eight hours of film. The raw footage came out of customs on a Tuesday night: Kaplan screened it for me all day Wednesday, at which point I had just two days to get something assembled for airing the coming Sunday. It was one of those situations in which I said to myself, "What difference does it make? My nerves are shot anyway." I worked through the next two nights, and a twenty-minute film on the World's Fair went to the lab on Friday.

For two seasons I cut the "Guy Lombardo Show," a program that was put together the way airplanes are built. The show consisted of several instrumental and vocal numbers introduced by Lombardo, shots of the band, and shots of dancers in the ballroom.

At the beginning of each thirteen-week segment, the producer, a brusque, beefy character named Herb Sussan, called everyone in for a week of shooting. First the band went into a sound studio to produce the perfect sound track, or "playback" track. From there on the tape recorders were turned off and silent filming commenced. They ran through each number again and again, as first the entire band was shot, then the horns, then the saxophones, then the two pianists, until every group of musicians was filmed playing that one number. This process was repeated for each piece they played and went on day after day for a week. The accumulated film filled an entire rack in my cutting room.

On another rack I'd have several reels of Guy Lombardo doing the introductions. Each take would start with him saying, "Thank you, thank you," to the imaginary applause that I would put in later, and then he would say, "And now the band will play 'Nola.' . . . Thank you, thank you, thank you. And now the band will play 'Boo Hoo,' composed by my brother, Carmen. . . . Thank you, thank you, thank you. And now the vocal trio will sing 'It Had to Be You.' . . . Thank you, thank you, thank you. And now our guest vocalist, Eugenie Baird, will sing 'April in Paris.' . . . Thank you, thank you, thank you. . . ."

A third rack was filled with the dancers. The dancing was all shot in one day. Sussan would put a cameraman on a ballroom dance floor with several hundred extras. Ten minutes of tango, ten minutes of foxtrot, ten minutes of waltz, ten minutes of cha-cha, ten minutes of mambo, ten minutes of polka, a half hour for lunch, and then back to the floor again. At the end of a single week of shooting, I had all the material I needed to assemble the next thirteen shows.

I found the Lombardo show very boring to cut. It was like painting by the numbers. Every time the saxophones played, I had to cut to the saxophones; when the brass played, I cut to the brass. And when the band had been on for X number of minutes, I cut to the dancers. Once I tried to make it just a little more interesting, and instead of cutting to the trumpets when they started playing, I cut in a little sooner, when they were in their seats getting ready to play. One guy was shaking the saliva out of his horn, which brass players always do, and I thought, hey, this livens things up a bit.

I still remember the morning I screened this segment for Sussan. He was leaning against the wall cleaning his pocket comb of a formidable accumulation of wax and hairs, paying about as much attention to gliding the crud out with his thumbnail as he was to the material on the screen. Suddenly we came to my trumpet improvisation, and Sussan straightened up and stopped picking. "Hold it right there," he said. I stopped the projectionist, and he pointed the comb at me: "This is not one of your fuckin' documentaries, kid. I don't want to see a trumpet player spritzing in my living room. Get it? When he starts playing, *that's* when you cut to him."

In fifty-two shows the only number I ever enjoyed cutting was a song by Marion Hutton, who came on once as the guest vocalist. The guests for all thirteen shows were shot in succession, and for these sessions three cameramen were used. Hutton was exciting to look at, and with the advantage of three camera angles, I was able to produce a fantastic cut. But when Sussan saw it at the screening, he told me to go back and re-edit it. "Take out some of those cuts," he said. "You made it too exciting." I was dumbfounded, but he had a point. I had made the band look boring by comparison: "You don't mess with a multi-million-dollar institution, kid."

After MKR disbanded in 1961, I did a few more jobs for TV. One was a group of five pilots that screenwriter-turned-TV-producer Robert Alan Aurthur was preparing for CBS at United Artists Television. The scripts were by a group of unknown authors—Mel Brooks, Woody Allen, Neil Simon, and N. Richard Nash—and the concepts were exceptional. Had even Aurthur's most pessimistic predictions come true, I could have been a TV supervising editor for the rest of the decade. But James Aubrey, then the president of CBS, had his own production company (a secret that later became a scandal) and favored himself with contracts. None of Aurthur's pilots sold.

In 1963 and 1964 I worked as the supervising editor for "The Patty Duke Show." The show started off in a state of panic, with producer-creator William Asher so paralyzed with uncertainty that the first installment didn't come out of the lab until the day it was aired. Panic prevailed throughout the rest of the first season, as we operated without a single show in backlog. Shows like this have a rigid division of labor. Several installments are produced in tandem, with two or three directors working in rotation. Although each show is produced to the same strict formula, the tension level can be overwhelming. The enormous amounts of money involved, the anxiety over ratings, reviews, and the reactions of the sponsors, not to mention the ever looming and irrevocable deadlines, make a weekly television series the most ulcerogenic atmosphere I've ever known.

The supervising editor takes over the director's role in the TV cutting rooms. At "Patty Duke" we also had two associate editors. One would be finishing an installment while another would just be starting, and a third cutter did nothing but synchronize dailies all day long. When each cut was down to thirty minutes, I screened it for the producer (who after the first week was no longer William Asher). With his criticism and suggestions, I brought it back to the cutting room, where it was trimmed down to the standard twenty-six and a third minutes. From there it went down the assembly line to the sound-effects man, the music editor, and finally the lab.

If the network takes a prospective show seriously, the panic can begin even before the pilot is completed. While I was cutting the pilot of "East Side, West Side" for David Susskind, the CBS executives were already approaching their list of cereal companies, car companies, and gasoline companies for sponsorship and pressuring us to finish. As it turned out a cereal company took the show before the pilot was even completed, whereupon Susskind asked me to become supervising editor. I turned him down. I'd had it with TV.

Sidney Meyers ended up supervising that show for one season. He had edited a great deal of television material and a few features since the war, with just an occasional opportunity to direct. The last picture he cut was *Tropic of Cancer* in 1969, the year he died. Sidney and I hadn't really kept in touch, and I couldn't be sure what was going on in his mind. Had he come to hate the business? Hate the cutting room? I didn't know. But one day a couple of years before he died I was in a recording studio somewhere, and there was Sidney, a man listed in Sadoul's *Dictionary of Film Makers* as "a major contributor to the independent, realist school of filmmaking," hunched over a synchronizer winding film. Without thinking, I blurted, "*Jesus,* Sidney, what are you doing over a synchronizer?" He looked at me and didn't say a word, but his look told me everything.

In 1958 Herb Leder, an executive at Benton & Bowles, decided to leave advertising and become a director. He got hold of a gangster property called *Pretty Boy Floyd* and asked me to be the editor. Ever since the early fifties, when I first started meeting feature editors and discovering that they had no more on the ball than I and often considerably less, I'd been aching for a chance like this. I determined to make *Pretty Boy Floyd* the classiest-cut gangster picture in history.

Now, it turned out that *Floyd* was pretty awful in almost every respect. But this did not discourage me. For I was still young and utterly consumed by the specialist's mentality. When I went to the movies with friends who were editors, all we saw were the cuts—the rest of the picture didn't exist. So the fact that *Floyd*'s script was absurd, its staging inept, and its performances wooden was hardly a deterrent. I was going to take all this junk into the cutting room, edit it in a classy way, and make a first-rate picture out of it.

The editing took about three months, and I believed the whole time that I was turning out a masterpiece. It wasn't until the picture hit the theaters that I saw how mistaken I was. I've seen it a couple of times on television since then and it's still an embarrassment. *Pretty Boy Floyd* was terrible when it went into the cutting room, it was terrible when it came out, and it taught me some humility regarding the limits of my trade—for a film to be good, *everything* has to be good. Be that as it may, I had devilish fun cutting it, and believed I was getting close to the big time.

I had now edited one gangster picture. Therefore, in the eyes of the industry, I was a gangster man. In 1959, when Twentieth Century-Fox decided to shoot a picture in New York called *Murder Incorporated* and was fishing about for a local editor, I was the natural choice.

Murder Incorporated was based on actual gangland activities in Brooklyn in the thirties and particularly the famous incident in which a top prosecution witness, sequestered in a hotel room, was thrown umpteen stories to his death while police guards stood outside his door. My experience with *Pretty Boy Floyd* in no way prepared me for this picture. *Floyd* was filmed in a few weeks on a small, independent budget, was composed of scenes that rarely had more than two actors, and was shot in a conventional A-B-C fashion: for each scene I was provided with a long shot of the two actors and close-up of each. It was the simplest and fastest piece of feature cutting imaginable, and, contrary to what I thought, I had barely been introduced to real dramatic editing.

The scenes from *Murder Incorporated* were better written, more intricate, and frequently involved more than two people. They were shot with seven or eight camera angles, and each actor was completely covered whether he was speaking or not. I was thus confronted with a dizzying quantity of film, like nothing I'd seen since *Louisiana Story*. But unlike documentary cutting, dramatic editing is not a matter of piecing together miscellaneous bits of film. It requires the judicious selection of the best takes of each performance and the best angles, decisions regarding whether to focus on the actor who is speaking or play the dialogue over the person listening, and a constant attention to tempo—when necessary by splicing out all the pauses in a conversation to accelerate the pace. I faced subtleties I never knew existed: we could shift the dramatic emphasis from one actor to another or change the entire point of view of a scene. I learned that if scenes were too long, there were ways to shorten them by cutting out dialogue, something I never even considered when editing *Floyd*. Because of my documentary training, once I began to recognize the places where trimming was needed, I didn't think to wait for the director's instructions. I'd search the script for sentences or whole paragraphs that I could safely delete, and begin to devise new transitions to cover the cuts. Burt Balaban, the young director, encouraged my contributions. We worked like buddies, partners, and it never occurred to me that this was anything but the standard practice.

The editing finished, Balaban and I went out to Los Angeles, where the score was recorded. This was my first trip to the West Coast and a major professional event. Despite my cynical attitude toward Hollywood, it was still the Mecca of the movie world. But the trip left me a little deflated about the success I had just achieved.

There are certain things that unsettle nearly every Easterner his first time in Los Angeles, almost as a preparation for any deeper bringdowns the town may have in store for him. In my case the discomfort began with the array of foreign-car dealerships that gilded the roadway in from the airport—an intimidating line-up of Maseratis, Alfa Romeos, Jaguars, Mercedes, Rolls-Royces—that seemed determined to remind me of exactly where I stood in the social order. This was accompanied by an incident that reinforced all the preconceptions that New Yorkers have about Los Angeles. Toward the end of the ride, I spotted a most stunning piece of architecture, a white-domed building that rose up beyond the palms like a Greek temple. "What is that?" I asked the cab driver. "Oh, that?" he said. "That's a funeral parlor."

My feelings of estrangement were further inflamed the next morning. Balaban and I had an eight-thirty appointment with some studio executives, and I got up early and took a stroll down Rodeo Drive. Cars were on the street, people in them going to work, but no one else was out walking at that hour. I later discovered that walking is not a highly rated activity in Beverly Hills. Anyway, as I strolled along, looking at the fabulous window displays in the fancy shops, I noticed a police car inching behind me, stopping when I stopped, moving when I moved. After a couple of blocks, it pulled up next to me, a window came down on the passenger side, and a cop motioned to me. "What are you doing?" he demanded. "Window shopping," I said, "I'm from out of town." He looked at me quizzically, but finally said, "All right," and moved on.

A few hours later I got my tour of the Fox cutting rooms, and the premonitions I'd felt since my arrival in Los Angeles finally developed into full-blown despair. In contrast to the opulent front offices, the cutting rooms were located at the far end of the property in a low, factorylike building. The barren corridors were lined with twenty or thirty cubicles, small windowless rooms, almost like cell blocks. Inside, the furniture and equipment were old and shabby. And in the eyes and smiles of the cutters, the men who had made it to the top of my profession, I saw fear and servility.

It was now fourteen years since I'd left the OWI, and I had spent most of those years hungering to become a feature-film editor. I had no greater ambition. Cutting *Murder Incorporated* had been the biggest event of my life. And now, in a way I only partially understood, everything seemed sullied.

When I got back to New York, the first thing I did was order a carpet for my cutting room.

Sidney Lumet (hat) working with Boris Kaufman (camera).
(Courtesy Museum of Modern Art)

10 ▪ *The Pawnbroker*
Part I: The Re-creation of the Flashback

I n 1961 Ely Landau, an independent New York producer, hired Sidney Lumet to direct Carson McCullers' *The Heart Is a Lonely Hunter,* which was to star Montgomery Clift. Lumet had just completed a dazzling film version of *Long Day's Journey into Night,* Landau's first production, and the galvanized producer was preparing for even bigger things from McCullers' highly acclaimed novel. Meanwhile, running tandem to *The Heart Is a Lonely Hunter* was another Landau production, *The Pawnbroker.* Under the direction of Arthur Hiller (who nine years later scored an enormous hit with *Love Story*) and starring Rod Steiger (chosen from a list of actors that included Burl Ives, Kirk Douglas, and Sir Laurence Olivier), *The Pawnbroker* was a saga of pain, despair, and hopelessness. It was a less prestigious property, an act of homage to the concentration-camp victims and survivors whose lives it portrayed, and Landau accorded it less expectation for success.

As the directors wended their way through the usual preproduction throes of casting and script revision, Landau worked out the final business arrangements, including the acquisition of insurance policies for the two films, insurance being an absolute necessity given the financial disaster that would arise from the death or incapacity of the director or one of the stars. But by early 1962, with a bare three weeks left before shooting was scheduled to begin, an unusual, even incredible, circumstance developed: Landau had yet to find a company willing to insure the erratic Montgomery Clift. With preproduction time on the point of evaporating, Landau made the only decision he could and jettisoned *The Heart Is a Lonely Hunter*; but he held onto his first-choice director by dropping Hiller and moving Lumet over to *The Pawnbroker*.

It thus happened that with his head full of the details and deliberations of another film, Lumet was confronted with a picture that had already been cast and worried over by its intended director, a film that turned out to be one of the grimmest, most challenging, and most memorable of his career.

I first met Sidney Lumet in 1959. I was just back from my disheartening trip to Hollywood when I heard that he was about to film Eugene O'Neill's *Long Day's Journey*, a play that I had worshiped since my early twenties. With three gangster pictures to my credit (*Mad Dog Coll*, a disaster, was my third) and the threat of becoming a gangster editor hanging over me, I decided it was time to promote myself. I went to see Sidney with a reel from a low-budget feature I was cutting, screened it for him, and then pitched for myself in so blatant a way I still get gooseflesh recalling it, not to mention a swoon of wonderment over his decision to hire me. The film turned out to have few editorial challenges, mainly because it had long scenes adapted faithfully from the play (as provided for in an agreement with O'Neill's widow). It was shot in six weeks and cut in eight. Although my contribution was routine, my name was now linked with an acclaimed film, and thenceforth I was perceived as a serious feature editor.

The Pawnbroker was our second film together. Based on a novel by Edward Lewis Wallant, it is the story of Sol Nazerman, a concentration-camp survivor who lost his wife and two children. He now lives in a New York suburb with his sister-in-law's family, works in Harlem as a pawnbroker, and spends time in a city apartment with his girl friend and her dying father, also survivors of the Holocaust.

He's a man with a trudging walk and a dour expression, a man who seems to care about nothing, a "hard man," as his customers call him, or "the walking dead," as his girl friend's father insists. The events of the film all take place within a few days of the twenty-fifth anniversary of his wife's death, during which time he finds himself harassed by horrible memories that he thought no longer had the power to intrude on him.

The success of the film depended on its ability to make the audience identify with Nazerman, one of the most unsympathetic heroes in film history. The memory flashbacks to the Nazi era were clearly the key—if viewers could see what Nazerman had been through, they could understand his crusted condition and maybe even acknowledge that "there but for fortune go I." But by 1962 people had put World War II and its atrocities behind them, and it was questionable whether audiences would be willing to reopen themselves to the stupendous evil that had squeezed the life out of its victims. What tricks of emotional penetration could Lumet perform that went beyond the well-known newsreel images of liberation bulldozers pushing piles of emaciated dead into mass graves? Surely if viewers had hardened themselves to that, they could harden themselves to anything. So another family is ripped out of its daily existence, packed into a crowded freight car, and after losing one or two members along the way is interred in a camp and suffers unspeakable agonies. The information is either too brutal to portray or else simply incapable of reaching us any more. The scriptwriters, Morton Fine and David Friedkin, must have known what they were up against, for in an unusual note to the director they asked that some more graphic way be found of representing memory. They feared the traditional flashback would not have the needed impact.

The time was right for an overhaul of the flashback. In the thirties and forties flashbacks had been very popular and always happened in the same way. A sequence quieted down, Joan Crawford or Bette Davis said, "I remember . . ." or began reminiscing in a dreamy way about her first marriage, the camera moved in on her entranced face, an eerie "time" music saturated the sound track, a shimmering optical effect crept over the screen as if oil were dripping across it, and everyone in the audience knew, "Uh-oh, we're going into memory." And sure enough, during a long, slow "ripple" dissolve, the star's face gradually disappeared, to be replaced by a scene from the past or perhaps the same face looking twenty years younger. Some films started at the end and the rest of the story was told in retrospect. Orson Welles's *Citizen Kane* was told entirely through flashbacks, as a reporter tried to uncover the truth about the dead newspaper magnate by interviewing the men who worked for him. Over the years certain aspects of the flashback technique had been shortened or done away with, but the basic formula prevailed.

Then in 1959, an editor-turned-director named Alain Resnais, after several years as a documentary filmmaker, made his first feature, *Hiroshima Mon Amour*. *Hiroshima* was so innovative that it was inaccessible to most viewers; they found it confusing and disorienting. But it turned out to be an important work in motion-picture history (as well as a direct influence on *The Pawnbroker*) in part because Resnais broke with the established pattern of showing flashbacks.

In the film, a French movie actress, on location in Hiroshima, has an affair with a Japanese man. As they make love, as they talk, elements of the past—her love for a soldier of the occupying German army; the soldier's death; her humiliation after the war when partisans grabbed her along with other women who consorted with the enemy, marched her through town, and publicly shaved her head; the incineration of Hiroshima by the atomic attack; the aftereffects of the bombing—intermingle without warning with the present action. Sometimes we don't even know for sure whether we are in the past or the present, and unlike any previous flashback movie, the pieces of past action—memories that are triggered by certain words, questions, or emotions—erupt on the screen out of chronological order, so that we cannot grasp the story—we're never quite sure that it all holds together—until the end. Here and there Resnais throws in a flash four-frame cut—a mere sixth of a second, too fast for the viewer to pick up the information—to suggest the continual dominance of the remembered events. When I saw the film, I knew it would have a liberating impact on filmmaking. Resnais was extreme, he was ahead of his time in technique, but he was a trailblazer and others would now be free to follow.

In 1960 another French director shook up filmmaking even more. Jean-Luc Godard was one of the leaders of the "New Wave" of French moviemakers. His first film, *Breathless,* had all the elements that characterized the New Wave films—location shooting, hand-held cameras for getting into otherwise inaccessible spots, a bouncy image, a low budget, and a lot of action. Although the film has something of gangster flavor, with Jean-Paul Belmondo playing the hood and Jean Seberg his pretty American girl friend, the greatest and most significant action was in Godard's cuts—he jumped characters from location to location without the slightest concern for the time-honored geography of cutting. In the indirect way that a pioneer work influences everything that comes after it, the jump cuts initiated in *Breathless* allowed Lumet and me additional avenues of freedom in trying to solve the special problems with which *The Pawnbroker* script presented us.

This is not to say that jump cutting was entirely new to film. A jump typically occurred from one scene, say a coffee shop where a group of bandits are plotting a bank robbery, to another, say a bank where the busy tellers are innocently awaiting their fate. A jump also occurred when a scene was clearly ended (the robbers getting shot to ribbons by the police as the getaway car gets away with the bare remnants of the gang) and a new scene, sometime in the future, is beginning (the same characters reunited in the interrogation tank at the police station). In early pictures these transitions were covered with an imaginative array of fades, dissolves, wipes, and irises, but gradually the flat cut became standard.

But unless a scene had come to an end, or a cut was made to simultaneous action elsewhere, or the focus jumped from one character to another within a single scene, editorial geography was carefully followed. This meant that when an actor moved from one location to another, the camera went with him. We saw Bogart's car pull up in front of a building and we saw Bogart glance up at a high window and grimace. We saw him get out, walk up to the entrance, open the door, and pass through. Then we switched perspective to the inside of the building. We saw Bogart enter the lobby and walk toward us, coming to a stop in front of the elevator. We saw him poke the button, wait, mash out his cigarette, grind his teeth. We saw him get inside the elevator, and we saw the doors close around him. Then we switched to the interior of the elevator, a close shot of his tense face as he watched the elevator indicator; then the indicator itself slowly sweeping across the floor numbers and coming to a stop on "17." We cut back to his face as he lowered his vision to watch the door open; cut to a view of the opening elevator from the hallway, Bogart exiting and approaching the camera. We then followed him down the hallway to his destination, saw him knock, put his hands in his pockets, and wait—until Lauren Bacall cracked the door, put her face in the opening, and said, "Yeah, whatta *you* want?" A predictable series of cuts then led us inside her apartment, where the action resumed.

For all of editing's advances, this was the standard procedure for thirty years. To build suspense, the process was lengthened and seemed like an eternity; to evoke an atmosphere of crackling speed, it was abbreviated, with certain elements omitted entirely. When taken to its literal extreme in early television, we saw side views of actors moving from room to room in a way that revealed the absence of a fourth wall and seemed to scream out, "This is only a set!" Stultifying adherence to geographical logic was another example of filmmaking's vestigial dependency on its theatrical heritage.

Like a modern Alexander, Godard undid this awkward connection by recklessly slashing film loose from decades of convention. When he wanted to move Belmondo from his bedroom to the street across town where Jean Seberg is peddling the *Herald Tribune,* he simply cut from the bedroom to the street. He didn't bother to show Belmondo leaving the room; he didn't bother to include an establishing shot of Belmondo's arrival. One moment Belmondo is staring at his pistol in his bed, dreaming of American gangsters, the next moment he is talking to his girl friend about pulling a heist. The film's title is not supposed to mean "thrilling" or "thrilled" (as in "Smirnoff leaves you breathless"), but "out of breath"—and out of breath is how many viewers felt as they clambered along after Godard's cuts, their mental computations working overtime to fill in the geographical gaps the jumps created.

Godard and his editor, Cécile Decugis, were so impatient with film's theatrical heritage that they couldn't even bear to follow a character across the room. If what Belmondo said on the left side of the room was important, and the next useful thing was said on the right side, they just jumped him from one position to the next. Today this technique has become convention, and no one loses any breath following it. On television every evening you can see a cop, awakened in the middle of the night by a telephone call, put down the phone, and—zip!—he's gettting out of his car on the other side of town. Through a painless spin along a well-established mental circuitry you quickly grasp what would have been confusing twenty years ago—that it's only a half hour later and the cop is responding to the tip he got on the phone. You forget that this has followed thirty years of kissing his wife, getting out of bed, pulling on his clothes, walking to the door, and all the other little steps of traditional editorial geography.

In terms of film technique, *The Pawnbroker* is not as radical as either *Hiroshima* or *Breathless*. Adding some important innovations of his own, Lumet successfully assimilated the advances of these two pioneer films and put them to work in a way that was close enough to traditional movie methods to keep the picture within the grasp of the average viewer.

He made his first innovation in the film's opening sequence, which was a setup for the flashbacks that were to follow. Before we see the titles or have any idea what the movie is about, we see two children running happily through a field of high grasses, stirring up butterflies as they go. The writers had asked that this scene be filmed with a heavy grain to give the effect of pointillism, the Postimpressionistic painting style, most often associated with Seurat and his parasol-bearing ladies, in which the picture is created entirely by visible dabs of paint. Instead, Sidney chose to represent the action in silent slow motion, a shrewd decision because it gave the entire scene a cherishing, timeless quality. The characters open their mouths and call to each other, but we cannot hear the words. They are a memory.

We are witnessing a family picnic in another time. We see the mother fetching water from a stream, an elderly couple on a blanket under a tree—the man, an Orthodox Jew with a hat and side curls, occupying himself with a chessboard. Now we see Rod Steiger, a big open-faced man, aglow with the pleasure of the day, waiting as his butterfly-chasing children run to him. In slow motion, he drops his wine bottle and kneels to grasp the boy and the girl as they leap into his arms. With a child's head over each shoulder, he turns and turns and turns, whirling them through the air. The camera moves in on the boy's face as his smile turns to fright. Quickly we glimpse each of the characters as they look up and see something that drains the spirit from their faces. Finally we see Steiger, the slow motion freezing, as, terror-stricken, he lets the children slide slowly down his sides.

The scene changes. We are in the back yard of a suburban home in the present time. The air is full of raucous sounds from an AM radio station, and two teenage kids, one of them a gum-chewing, Jayne Mansfield–type blonde, are pestering each other noisily. There's a bleached, stark, strident quality. On a chaise longue sits a rumpled, balding man of about sixty years reading a paper. By his looks you would never guess that this deadened, unresponsive character is the same Rod Steiger. A woman his age approaches him and says gently, "Sol, I've been thinking. What do you say we take one of those tours to Europe?" As she speaks, as the teenagers fight shrilly in the background, as Steiger grunts his negative responses, we cut from his face to instantaneous glimpses of the opening sequence. At four frames apiece we can barely make out that it is the lovely young mother waving to Steiger at the picnic. "My poor sister Ruth," the woman says. "Do you realize, Sol, it's been twenty-five years?" Now a sixteen-frame cut, plenty of time (two-thirds of a second) to recognize Steiger's wife waving to him in slow motion in the field. The old man's response is curt and bitter: Europe is a stinking graveyard.

We now grasp the essential facts: Steiger is the man from the opening sequence. His wife was killed in a death camp. He is living with his sister-in-law. His heart is dead. And quick flash cuts will be used throughout the movie to represent his memories. The audience is signaled to be on its toes. As we cut to Steiger driving in his car over the Triboro Bridge, paying his toll, and entering Harlem, an unobtrusive series of black script titles present themselves on the screen, and Quincy Jones's mournful, dissonant jazz score howls its opening notes.

The first sequence in the pawnshop establishes Sol Nazerman as a man with little or no sentiment, completely unmoved by the variety of characters who come in to pawn their belongings—each of them by turns charming, touching, or pitiable to the audience. He's a man who doesn't bargain, insult, or otherwise engage his customers. He states his price, a figure that always horrifies them, he sticks to it with bored implacability, and he is utterly cold and even merciless in his refusal to respond. His distance from them is somehow heightened by the paper napkin he's wrapped around the glass of milk he drinks. At lunchtime he's rude to a chirpy, well-meaning social worker (Geraldine Fitzgerald) who comes in collecting for the Little Leagues: "If it's a handout you want, why didn't you say so?" He pulls out his checkbook and asks, "How much?"

At the end of the day the weary Nazerman drags the gates across the front of his shop and begins walking past rows of ashcans down the tenement-lined street. It's very dark, very bleak. A dog is barking. Barking, barking. As Steiger plods along, the dog barking insistently in the background, we see another of those flash cuts. It's just four frames, and we're uncertain of the content. It is followed by three more in rapid succession as Steiger proceeds trancelike down the street. In each of these cuts a dog, a German Shepherd, is running toward the camera with a soldier's legs alongside it, and by the fourth cut the dog's head almost fills the frame, allowing us to register it for the first time. All the while a present-day dog continues to bark relentlessly in the background. Now the camera moves in on Steiger's face as he turns to look at something. Behind a schoolyard fence a group of teenagers is surrounding and beating up a single kid. *Flash back to Steiger's transfixed face, four-frame cut to a haunting face out of the past,* and then the schoolyard again, as the victim runs from the mob and leaps to climb the fence.

The boy on the fence is climbing desperately, beads of sweat gleaming on his black face; *cut to Steiger, cut to another visage from the past.* Then the boy, struggling, his hands gradually losing their grip as he's pulled down from below. We are wondering, What was that second flash, that big shaved head that momentarily filled the screen?

Now we cut to broad daylight: an exhausted man in drab prison woolens, hanging on a barbed-wired fence in a Nazi camp, while on the sound track the yelling mob gives way to the familiar barking. Slowly the weary prisoner loses his grip and slides down the fence. He hits the ground and staggers backward, horribly, like a ragamuffin, bouncing off the wooden poles that scatter the barren landscape. A Nazi soldier stands by, waiting for reinforcements.

We cut to a group of watching prisoners, particularly a big man with a shaved head, trembling with emotion. Is it Steiger? Cut to a nighttime close-up of the pawnbroker in the Harlem street, his stubbly face, his cold, glinty stare piercing the boy on the fence, piercing the playground mob, piercing all of Harlem to his twenty-five-year-old memory. Back to the big shaven head—yes, it must be Steiger. He is observing the mad escape efforts of a fellow prisoner. His face is full of pity and pain, as close as one can get to crying in a place where crying is futile and even despicable.

By now enough of the memory process was revealed to allow an unfolding of the body of memory itself. From the trembling face of Steiger the prisoner we cut to the source of the barking that's been on the sound track through all the memory cuts. It's the attack dog, the German Shepherd, from the first flashes of memory. Then back to Steiger's sad, shaken face, looking down in impotent pain, in sympathetic defeat, realizing the end is near for his friend on the fence. The dazed runaway, back on the fence, trying to lift his chin above the barbed wire. A quick flash to Steiger in the present, which re-establishes that this is his memory. Cuts to the running soldier and dog, the guard at the fence yelling instructions, the dog nearing the prisoner's leg, the beaten man, still hanging, like a bewildered animal, a bundle of blank desperation, his face smudged with dirt and blood. He tries to throw his arm over the barbed wire just to steady himself.

The dog is loosed on the prisoner, who slowly sags down the fence again, the onlookers watching hopelessly. As we switch back and forth in perspective from the gnashing dog to the prisoner's dazed eyes and his disintegrating grip, to the faces of his watching compatriots, we begin to take in more of the details—the Star of David on Steiger's gray, pajamalike uniform, the three men standing behind him. We cut momentarily to Steiger in the present and the contrast between the two Steigers is powerful—one big and caring and tortured, the other shrunken, impenetrable, and ready to turn away.

A last glimpse of the defeated body hanging pitifully on the fence, before the close profile of Steiger in the present time resumes the former action. He turns slowly and starts to walk away. He's walking away from the schoolyard fight and away from the horrible memory of his friend's piteous destruction. He pauses and puts his hand on the hood of his car. He feels ill and covers his mouth with a handkerchief. Another four-frame flash of the crazed ragamuffin on the fence. This memory won't be shut out tonight.

Nazerman struggles to enter the car. The sounds of the fight and a barking dog are still splitting the night. Another strobelike flash of memory as he turns the motor, and, *vroom*, he's off. He's a wreck now, driving to escape, the camera watching from the back seat. We see a pedestrian about to step off the sidewalk and cross the street. Nazerman doesn't see him, doesn't see the red light, and just before impact, there's a final four-frame intrusion from the past. A screech of brakes, and the startled pedestrian jumps back with his hands on the hood. Nazerman sags in his seat and waits. *"What are you a nut or something, you moron!!!"* the near victim screams into the driver's window.

Another close-up of Nazerman as he turns to face the road. He made no attempt to apologize or explain; just waited for the ordeal to pass. A car honks impatiently behind him and he pulls away. Cut to a new scene at his girl friend's apartment, and the first flashback of the movie is ended.

In the course of this flashback a great amount of detail was presented, the most important of it suggesting the process by which a soft man had been twisted almost beyond recognition into a brittle knot. Thanks to abbreviations in technique, the flashback was very quick, although, emotionally, it seemed interminable. From the moment we first saw Steiger dragging the iron gates across his storefront until the final moments of the traffic incident a mere one minute and forty-five seconds of screen time had elapsed. No flashback had ever been done this way before.

In keeping with the screenplay and the original novel, not one of the gross Nazi atrocities was portrayed in this or any of the subsequent flashbacks. There were no ovens or executions or horrid human experiments. The story revealed the destruction of an identity, and in this respect the delicacy of fiction was more overwhelming than the stink of explicit horrors. Once translated successfully into film, largely through the refinement of flashback techniques, *The Pawnbroker* achieved a stupefying impact—even greater for me than the flood of Signal Corps footage from freshly opened concentration camps that numbed the OWI in 1945.

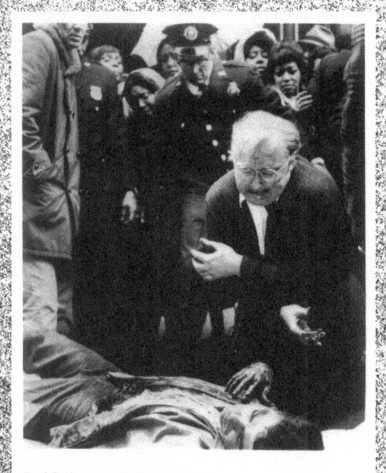

Rod Steiger as Sol Nazerman.
(Courtesy Museum of Modern Art)

11 ▪ *The Pawnbroker*
Part II: X-Rays of the Mind

> Suddenly he had the sensation of being clubbed.
> An image was stamped *behind* his eyes like a bolt of
> pain. For an instant he moved blindly in the rosy
> morning, seeing a floodlit night filled with
> screaming. A groan escaped him, and he stretched
> his eyes wide. There was only the massed detail of a
> .thousand buildings in quiet sunlight. In a minute
> he hardly remembered the hellish vision and sighed
> at just the recollection of a brief ache, his
> glass-covered eyes as bland and aloof as before.
> Another minute and he was allowing himself the
> usual speculation on his surroundings.
> —EDWARD LEWIS WALLANT, *The Pawnbroker*

There are certain young directors today—like Steven Spielberg, who made *The Sugarland Express, Jaws,* and *Close Encounters of the Third Kind* by the time he was thirty-one—who were raised in the age of television and seem to have an intuitive sense of film rhythm and film possibilities. In 1962 Sidney Lumet was the closest thing to this sort of TV-bred talent. When he was four years old, he began acting on the Yiddish stage alongside his father, Baruch Lumet (whom Sidney cast as the dying man in *The Pawnbroker*), and in 1950, when he was twenty-six and already a theater veteran, Lumet joined television as a director. From such popular series shows as "You Are There" and "Danger" he moved on to some 250 teleplays, including *This Property Is Condemned* and *The Iceman Cometh.* By the end of the decade, he had developed a genius for turning theater into television and then into film. His first film, released in 1957, was the unforgettable jury-room drama, *Twelve Angry Men,* and his sixth, released in 1962, was Eugene O'Neill's *Long Day's Journey into Night*, a masterpiece.

The Pawnbroker was the first of Lumet's films to present serious novelistic obstacles. With its frequent scene changes, location shooting on city streets, and the constant intrusion of memory flashbacks, it made the greatest demands on Lumet to break with theatrical styles and move more completely into a cinematic mode. The ease and ingenuity with which he accomplished this in *The Pawnbroker* and the last two films we edited together (*Fail Safe* and *The Group*), not to mention his subsequent pictures (including *Serpico, Dog Day Afternoon, Murder on the Orient Express,* and *Network*), convinced me that Lumet has the greatest ease with film technique of any director I've known.

As a director of live TV shows Sidney had to make fast editorial choices, pushing buttons in his booth to select the best camera angle from those available on his monitor screens. As a filmmaker, the editing impulse has remained. He is the only director I've worked with who could tell me cut-for-cut what he wanted in a scene and even come up with tricks I had never considered. An example arose during the editing of *Long Day's Journey*. I had always cut dialogue scenes by carefully choosing whether to focus on the speaker or the listener. Lumet came up with an alternative approach, "mathematical cutting," in which we cut back and forth from one actor to the other in evenly matched but progressively shorter snippets of film, totally ignoring who was talking and who was listening, and markedly increasing the tension. Clearly, if a picture needed astute editorial consideration, Sidney was the director to handle it.

But despite his mastery of editorial technique, Lumet was respectful of the editor's point of view and contribution; he never rejected something of value simply because he did not originate it. Under Lumet I rarely had an opportunity to work out long stretches of film on my own, and I would have found working with him in recent years unsatisfying for that reason; but we operated as a team, and I always felt well used.

During the months we edited *The Pawnbroker* there was a constant atmosphere of experimentation, with attendant feelings of excitement and doubt. What new film technique could be a more graphic way of representing memory than the traditional flashback? We knew from personal experience that memories, especially unpleasant ones, are not engaged in by a voluntary swan dive into the past. They intrude in flashes. Trained to reject the unpleasant intrusions of memory, a mind can usually keep itself from going into a full-blown reliving of past events. In the novel, Wallant was able to switch time frames through italicized dream sequences. Such novelistic devices have a counterpart in the theatrical monologue. Had the first flashback been transported to the traditional stage, Steiger might have delivered a passionate speech in which he cursed the shame and desperation he felt while impotently watching a fellow sufferer rush headlong into certain suicide; or cried over the nagging sensation of cowardice and humiliation that hovers over him to this day. But film has little room for soliloquies of such dimension. True, the need could be met by sandwiching a flashback between short pieces of explanatory monologue, but Lumet was trying to take the process a step further, to discard all explanations and give the audience a direct experience of what it feels like to be Sol Nazerman. And so he took a stab at suggesting the onslaught of memory by using flash cuts. They would represent the beginnings of a memory voyage, the mind's instantaneous, semiconscious, involuntary association of current and past events. Nazerman's reaction to this unwanted intrusion of the past would say the rest.

The execution of the plan was arduous. How long should an initial flash last in order to suggest the percolation of memory? Eight frames, a third of a second, seemed (incredibly) to linger too long. But four frames were impossible to read. Would viewers become irritated by cuts they couldn't make out, or would they experience just the sense of anticipation we wanted? Back and forth we went from eight frames to six frames to four frames to eight frames, experimenting, screening, recutting, until every shot went through the Moviola in a comprehensive selection of lengths, and the entire flashback seemed to have experienced exhaustive permutations. Even when we had finally settled on our formula, Lumet feared that no one would understand it, and as a precaution he worked out a backup plan for editing the film in a more traditional way—a simple procedure whereby the story would dissolve from the black boy on the school-yard fence to the dazed prisoner on the concentration-camp fence and stay in the past until the memory scene was completed. Only the initial screenings convinced him that the experiment had worked, and worked in an exponential way.

By the end of the first flashback the film has run about thirty of its hundred and fifteen minutes. Sol Nazerman spends a solemn evening with his woman friend, Tessie, and her sick, white-haired father, who raves a lot about the pawnbroker's deadness and inhumanity—in response to which Nazerman quietly shuts the old man's bedroom door. Tessie and her father are more sympathetic than Nazerman but barely more alive, and the scene is awfully gray, all the more so when shots of Sol and Tessie making love are juxtaposed with shots of Nazerman's assistant, an eager young Puerto Rican named Jésus, in bed with his sexy black girl friend. The young couple laugh and talk about the future as wild jazz howls on the sound track. Sol lies on top of Tessie and silently grips the pillow, gazing icily through the headboard as he comes.

From here on there are two major flashbacks and two minor ones. The flashbacks will seem to serve as a counterpoint to the modern-day plot, but actually the plot and most of the supporting characters wither in contrast. The current story serves a number of important functions—to reveal Nazerman's frigid bitterness, to present him with situations that trigger the memories and push him to his limits, and to make certain statements about tragedy and its historical repetition. But the fact that Nazerman is cruel to Tessie when her father dies; that he tries to defy a Harlem crime boss only to be beaten and humiliated; that he makes a stab at friendship with the well-meaning social worker and fails; that his naïve assistant, a sweet engaging lad who cannot bear to be going nowhere in life, decides to rob the pawnshop and is accidentally killed by one of his accomplices while trying to protect Nazerman—much of it, if scrutinized, has the ring of melodrama. Many of the gray issues and subtle character traits explored in Wallant's book turned to black and white when translated into the movie, for there was a great simplification of almost all the material. Fortunately, the weaknesses in characterization and plot do not scream at the viewer, because the real force of the film is the unraveling of Nazerman's mind.

Back at the pawnshop the next morning Nazerman is going through the usual ordeal with the hopheads and petty thieves and pitiful losers who come in off the street. Jésus, who considers Nazerman to be his "teacher" (a ghastly piece of naïveté), says, "You look bad, Mr. Nazerman," but Steiger brushes him off, as he usually does. There's a half-second memory cut of a woman standing before barbed wire that primes us for the coming flashback.

A pregnant waif enters the shop. She can barely open her mouth. To Nazerman's impatient demands, she responds haltingly, "My diamond engagement ring . . ." She pulls it off. *Nazerman's face, another flash cut.* "I want to borrow," she stutters, and then looks down in shame. "It's glass," he says, handing back the ring. Third flash—it seemed to be a row of trembling hands.

"Glass?" she says despairingly. Nazerman again—he's lost; a fourth flash. The waif: "He said it was real." Nazerman is silent; a fifth flash; he's staring past the counter into the floor as she backs away. He's remembering a scene from the camp. A long line of prisoners are stretching their hands over a barbed wire fence as a helmeted soldier plucks off their rings. It's a devastating second and a half of film, and suddenly we're back in the shop. As the pregnant girl leaves, Marilyn Birchfield, the good-hearted, chirpy social worker, comes forward pressing Nazerman to accept her invitation for lunch. She believes that his coldness conceals a lonely man in need of a friend. As she begins to speak, we glimpse his blank face and then return to the flashback. The soldier moves down the line of quivering fingers, collecting the wedding rings of the Jewish women, as Miss Birchfield speaks in voice-over: "Wednesday or Thursday?" The pawnbroker, lost in reverie: "What?" The dreary camp scene again, the ragged female hands seemingly eager to give up their precious jewelry, and again Marilyn's cheery superimposed response: "Lunch in the *park*," she reminds him. "*Wednesday* is better for me." We cut away from the camp and return to Nazerman's face. He speaks vacantly: "Wednesday, Thursday, whatever you like." There's a last instantaneous glimpse of the human gold mining before Marilyn says, "All right, I'll see you then," and exits. Nazerman had no idea a conversation had taken place.

Before we come to the next flashback, the pawnbroker misses lunch with Miss Birchfield and tells her where to take her petty loneliness and sorrows. Jésus forces him to state something about his beliefs, and Nazerman exclaims angrily, "Money is the whole thing!" after which Jésus reconsiders stealing the five thousand dollars that Nazerman recently locked in his safe. This upsets Jésus's girl friend, however, a prostitute named Mabel who happens to work for the same crime kingpin who uses Nazerman's pawnshop as a front to launder money. Trying to divert Jésus from a life of crime, Mabel decides to raise some money herself, beginning by pawning her necklace and turning a trick with the pawnbroker.

She arrives as Nazerman is closing up for the day and coaxes him back inside. He offers her twenty dollars for the "One hundred percent gold" necklace she presents to him ("*Plate,*" he says), and they haggle a bit. She gets to the point: "You have it in your power to make me a beat-up old woman." "What makes you say that?" Nazerman asks. "If my boss finds out I've been messing around in private, he don't stand still for nothing like that. If it was to get out to him, he'd make me old before my time."

The phone rings. It's Tessie calling to tell Sol that her father has died. "Papa is dead, what am I going to do?" she pleads, but is unable to get any support from him. "Have him buried. There's nothing else to do. Nothing. Nothing." She accuses him of being inhuman; he says he can't leave the store, and when she complains, he reminds her that the store is where her rent comes from. Again she whimpers, "Papa is dead." Nazerman snaps, "Well, that's what you wanted, isn't it?" and she hangs up.

By this time Mabel is engrossed in the bewitching rituals of her profession. "I'm good, pawnbroker, *good,*" she says. "I'll do things you haven't never even dreamed of before." Nazerman is so overcome with tedium, he sits on a crate in back of the shop and puts his hand to his forehead, completely unmindful of her offer. "Just twenty dollars more and I'll make you happy like you never known." She gently drops the necklace beside him. "I'll show you how pretty I am," she says. She looks over her shoulder and hurriedly shifts the suits hanging on an overhead rack to block the view of any passerby. She's brimming with sexual energy, pulling down her panties from under her dress as she speaks: "You say nothing about this, you hear?" She's still fearful of what the boss, Rodriguez, would do if he caught her moonlighting. Nazerman still hasn't raised his eyes. "*Don't tell Rodriguez nothing,*" she says emphatically, "*nothing.*"

"Rodriguez," says Nazerman blankly, and then a flash: it's Steiger in the camp with a German soldier. "*Rodriguez,* the big man, the boss, the biggest in Harlem," she says defiantly. Nazerman looks up, his eyes wide, realizing something for the first time. She puts her hand behind her back to reach for her zipper. "Wait a minute," he says. *Flash to his wife, Ruth, in the camp.* "You work for *Rodriguez?*" He had no idea Rodriguez dealt in prostitution.

She, sassy, unzipping: "Oh, yeah, he gots lots of irons in the fire." *The pawnbroker, another glimpse of the camp.* "He's a powerful man, so it's better if you don't tell him a thing." Again Nazerman's astonished face, awakened to a new thought, and another flash of memory—it seems to be a prisoner and a German officer. "I got to get me some *money,*" she says, and with that the front of her dress falls. She has a fabulous body, trim to the ribs and sharply curved, with full, flawless breasts. She stands proud, her fingers at her waist, waiting for his response. "*Look,*" she says.

A flurry: the old pawnbroker. The soldier and the prisoner. Ruth's withered gaze. Mabel: "Look," she insists. "That's *better.*" Ruth again, sitting on a cot. A close-up of her face. Sol in the pawnshop, his eyes wide, his lips curdling. Several successive glimpses of Mabel saying "Look!" her face full of plucky confidence, alternating with Nazerman lost in another world. "Look!" Mabel says, this time with a tinge of disappointment, and her word is echoed by a German expression uttered in flashback. "*Willst du wa sehen?*" says the laughing officer to the young Steiger. A long shot of Ruth elsewhere in the camp, sitting impassively, naked from the waist, awaiting her fate.

The cutting flurry ends on Nazerman's face as he sits in the shop, overcome by the past. He is racked with emotion, his lower lip drawn in, as he shrinks into the corner of the screen. We now return to the camp. It's a rainy, dreary day, and soldiers are herding a line of male prisoners alongside a barracks. Behind a fence, trucks are arriving, and gradually we realize that the trucks are unloading women, who are being taken into a nearby building. Steiger reaches the foreground in his gray woolens, the Star of David on his chest. His familiar shaved head, like a large wounded Teddy bear's, fills the screen. He hugs himself to keep warm and lets the other prisoners pass as he watches jeepfuls of laughing German officers enter the same building as the women prisoners. An officer comes up behind him and says, "*Willst du wa sehen?*" ("Do you want to see?"). As Steiger stares at the building, the officer repeats himself more aggressively. Steiger, looking like a confused child, fails to respond. The officer, incensed by the lack of response, grabs him viciously by the chest, twists his arm behind his back, and, in a feverish rage, drags him through the mud to the nearby building, the big man scurrying to keep pace as best he can. The officer is cursing furiously as he pushes Steiger toward the camera and finally bursts the gentle giant's head through a pane of glass, from which it emerges in wincing, pathetic close-up.

The twisted old pawnbroker sitting in the shop, paralyzed in his darkness. Steiger the prisoner slowly raising his eyes, shattered glass in the edges of the wooden frame, to see what the officer was so intent on showing him. A naked woman is being scrubbed down beneath a shower spigot in a small cubicle. Another cut to Nazerman in the shop, his desolation mounting. In the camp, the camera pans along a row of cubicles. Another naked, defeated woman is lying face down on a bare mattress. Mabel's soft voice-over: "Look!" Mabel, her magnificent chest, her faltering plea. Nazerman, trembling. "Don't cost you nothing to look," she says, her words superimposed on the continuous flashback of women in cubicles, lying on dingy cots. In one room an officer is stretched out beside a naked prisoner, chatting with confident charm and loosening his tie. "Look!" exhorts the sound track.

And there's the lovely Ruth, sitting up on the cot, as we saw her in an earlier flash, her breasts bare, just like the Harlem whore. Her face is drawn, her eyes lost. The pawnbroker, closer to crying than we've ever seen him. Ruth, as we move in for a close-up, and then Steiger's big pitiful head in the window, watching helplessly as a Nazi officer enters Ruth's cubicle and stands before her arms akimbo and legs outstretched, his black silhouette filling the frame and blotting her out.

Nazerman rises, fidgeting blindly, reaching about the shop for something—*anything*. The naked Mabel, disbelieving and dismayed, finally realizing that he is beyond her powers. The pawnbroker's pleading distorted countenance, every molecule in him—from his clenched fists to his rabid eyes—begging, begging for it not to be so. In the midst of his distraction, he finds Mabel's raincoat and places it over her chest. She looks down, almost ready to weep. Still uninvolved with her, he places a roll of bills in her hand and turns away. The camera moves in on his desolate features, his face contorting horribly and finally emitting an agonized roar. A cut to the lavish home of Rodriguez, an enormous black man played by Brock Peters, and the scene is over.

We've been watching Sol Nazerman for over an hour now. Events have been moving so fast, with such unexpected twists and such riveting revelations, we've barely had time to recollect. If we ever hoped for Nazerman's reform, wished that the man who had suffered such injustice might turn out more appealing, more redeemed in the end, we have abandoned such expectations as trivial. His experiences were so damaging, we suspend our right to judgment. We are torn and unsettled, but too absorbed to think about it. The Steiger of the camp scenes is innocent, with a mournful animal dignity; he is able to arouse our caring. Steiger the pawnbroker is still a revolting man. But we no longer dare to imagine him any different. We just watch, stunned, as he is, by his memories.

Now in the final third of the picture, as he tries to alter something about his life, we hang on in disbelief, for he is stepping out beyond any threshold of pain we have imagined. We see him telling Rodriguez off, we see him trying to get help from Marilyn Birchfield, we see him abandoning his strict utilitarian code—and we see each effort to rise out of his pit leaving him sealed in at a deeper level. By the climactic end, we understand what it means to be a prisoner, serving a life sentence in one's own skin.

Brock Peters' Rodriguez is a menacing giant who can terrify an audience with a single flare of his huge nostrils. As he plucks cubes from an ice bucket, he calls Nazerman "Professor," and in sinister tones tells him what a rare pleasure his visit affords. But when Nazerman says he won't launder Rodriguez's money any more if it comes from prostitution, the white-robed Goliath tongue-lashes him, threatens him, manhandles him, and humiliates him, sending him out in worse shape than when he came in.

We cut from Rodriguez's apartment to a grouping of strange lights that look like shifting UFOs. Dazed and disheveled, Nazerman enters the frame from the left, crossing in front of the lights in full profile. As Quincy Jones's haunting cello plays a distorted variation of the Jewish liturgical prayer, Kol Nidre, Steiger seems as close as one can be to the walking dead, a soul lost in limbo. As he trudges across the frame, filling the screen from his chest to his head, the camera focus shifts to the background, and the UFOs now take their natural shape as the oncoming headlights of cars on One Hundred Twenty-fifth Street. It was an important moment in the film, all the more so because a jump cut was used from the apartment to the street, and three intermediary "geographical" shots that Lumet originally intended to use were omitted at my urging.

Sol Nazerman now begins the all-night walk that eventually takes him to the Lincoln Towers apartment where Marilyn Birchfield lives, and where he finally expresses the words that define him. In the predawn morning, they sit on her terrace and she invites him to talk.

> SOL (subdued, searching):   There were *memories*, that I well, I thought, thought that I had pushed far away from me—and now they keep rushing in. And then there are words, words

that I thought that I had kept myself from hearing. And, now, now, they flood my mind. . . . Yah, today is an anniversary.

MARILYN: What happened?

SOL: What happened?

MARILYN: Yes.

SOL: It's been a long time since I've felt . . .

MARILYN: *Anything.*

SOL: . . . *fear.* Fear. Fear, that's what I felt. And then I called you, and . . .

MARILYN: I'm sorry you are so alone.

SOL: No, no, you don't understand.

MARILYN: What happened?

SOL (in close profile, Con Edison smokestacks in the distance): I didn't die. Everything I loved was taken away from me and *I did not die.* There was nothing I could do. Strange, I could do nothing. No, there was nothing I could do.

Inside again, she offers her hand. There is a long pause. He doesn't take it. He walks to the door, and as it shuts behind him the blur of a speeding train fills the screen.

This is now the beginning of the third major flashback, the one that audiences responded to most profoundly. The blur slows and reveals a train stopping in a noisy subway station. Nazerman gets on. Shaken, unshaven, unkempt, he looks deranged and on the run. He suspiciously studies another passenger, a Jewish man about his own age. The man eyes him back. Nazerman is so disturbed by this, he moves off down the car, looking back a couple of times as he goes. Finally he stands in the center of the car, and the camera scans the other passengers, simulating the sweep of his eyes. Each new set of eyes is staring right back at the camera, at Nazerman, curious about him in some way. Intercut with this panning-camera survey of the subway car are instantaneous memory shots. By now we automatically associate these flashes with Nazerman's mental processes. And this time they seem to suggest dissolution.

Nazerman is leaning against a pole in the center of the car. Again, he looks at the other passengers, and as the camera sweeps their faces, we again intercut flashback segments. The flashback material ultimately reveals a packed Nazi freight car bearing camp-bound Jewish families, but the initial flashes are so brief that the content is not immediately clear. And because the memory film is sweeping the Nazi freight car at a speed and angle that suggests a continuation of the subway pan, we are disturbed for a moment without knowing why—a factor that contributed to the unsettling power of this scene.

The passengers are staring back inquisitively at Nazerman. The first flash is four frames, and each one is progressively longer—growing to eight, twelve, sixteen, twenty, twenty-four, and finally twenty-eight frames, always returning to the searching eyes of the New York subway riders. The last memory cut—one and one-sixth seconds—seems to linger for a long time, enough to make out the suffering faces of the herded, hungry, exhausted people being transported for extermination. When at last we cut back to Nazerman paranoically clinging to his pole, we feel as if we ourselves have been jolted out of a reverie.

Nazerman turns and flees, anxious to escape this haunted car. We see him through the window of the adjoining car coming our way, staggering and frantic. As he opens the exit door of his car, the train noise increases. He reaches desperately for the second door, opens it, and looks up into the next car. Horror comes over his face—he's right in the midst of the Nazi freight train again, only this time the camera is not panning and the cut is not a brief one; a full flashback is upon him. Sound editor Jack Fitzstephens charged the onset of horror with the combined shriek of a baby's cry and a piercing European train whistle.

The freight car was a three-sided wooden box so packed with extras it could only be photographed from above. Lumet mounted the box on two rocking devices and crew members kept the whole contraption in motion throughout the shooting. We see various shots of the people inside the train, beaten, bedraggled German-Jewish townspeople of the thirties, with their tattered old cloth coats and hats, so suffocatingly close they have to hold their heads up to breathe. Eyes are closed, mouths open; people hanging in place like ghosts. Some of them are the same extras that were in the subway car, although we cannot know this except subliminally. The young Sol Nazerman, exhausted, his head leaning on his chest, a child over his back. Across the car, over the train noise, Ruth screams "Sol!" as she notices the boy slipping off

Steiger's shoulder. He tries to regain his grip on the child, howling in anguish as the boy finally slips to the floor, irretrievable amidst the densely packed, quickly shifting feet.

We cut to the subway train pulling into a station and Nazerman getting off. The sound track is still laden with haunting screams from the freight train, and he covers his ears to block them out. Intercut are contrasting shots of the boy from the slow-motion picnic and the boy dead on the floor of the train. (Lumet tried to give the impression that the child was trampled to death, but this didn't work. Instead you assume that he died for some other, unstated reason.)

The last flashback occurs just before the climax of the movie, and it completes the backward odyssey. Nazerman is in the pawnshop again after his sleepless night. He's become somewhat unhinged, offering ridiculous sums for the pathetic items his customers bring in to pawn. Rodriguez and a henchman show up and give him a beating for refusing to sign some papers. The only thing that saves him from getting killed is Rodriguez's awareness that killing is just what he wants. When the big boss pinches Steiger's face in his powerful black hand, the pawnbroker seems like a pathetic child.

Shortly afterward, a sweet, bespectacled black man enters the shop, talking gently about the value of the butterfly collection he wishes to pawn. Nazerman isn't looking or listening, but suddenly he bolts up and puts a large-denomination bill on the table. A four-frame cut of the glass-encased butterflies, a quick close-up of Nazerman, and then a long (four-second) dissolve that brings us back to the opening scene of the movie, Steiger and his family at the picnic. The old-fashioned memory device seemed appropriate for this last reverie. We are too emotionally exhausted now to go the other route, and the dissolve suggests the coming end. The music, too, sets us up for the resolution of the story.

Steiger's children are running in slow motion through the field of high grasses, reaching for butterflies. Intercut with glimpses of the other members of the family is a new element, German soldiers arriving on two motorcycles with a sidecar. Pieces of the silent picnic scene flit by punctuated regularly by an ominous DING! on the sound track. A momentary flash to the drained and beaten pawnbroker before the young Sol puts the children behind his back in a frightened, protective gesture. A last close-up of the German soldiers looking down on their prey gives way to Jésus's three hoody friends entering the pawnshop to steal the five thousand dollars that Nazerman recently took in for laundering.

Jésus organized this heist after he became convinced that the man he thought was his mentor had no special feelings for him. (Jésus: "I'm a student to you." Nazerman: "You're *nothing* to me.") Now Jésus waits on the sidelines, pretending to be uninvolved, until he sees that one of the punks, ignoring his instructions, has a gun and is pointing it between Nazerman's eyeballs, trying to force the intransigent old man to open the safe. Dashing forward to protect his boss, Jésus is shot. As the others flee, he wriggles into the street, clutching his gut.

Nazerman emerges from his stupor, runs out to the sidewalk, and pushes through the crowd to reach the dying boy. He holds Jésus's bloody hand as Jésus mutters, "I told them no shooting," and then expires. Hovering over Jésus's body, Nazerman puts fierce fingers to his ravaged face and tries to howl. Three brass notes fill his silent scream.

The pawnbroker plunges back into his shop. Slowly he impales his hand on a receipt spindle, trying to reach some answer through the self-inflicted pain, and as he does, he's visited by a reprise of memory cuts of the last two days, many of them calling forth the customers he's dismissed as pitiable "creatures." (The reprise montage was a tame device at this point, too tame to have much impact.) As Jésus is taken away in an ambulance, his mother wailing, and crowds milling in the eternal Harlem day, Nazerman runs hysterically out of his shop and down the street, a man who has finally been forced to feel, but to no advantage.

In the spring of 1963, I took the workprint of *The Pawnbroker* to Los Angeles to screen it for a high-level Hollywood committee consisting of actor Gene Kelly, director Fred Zinnemann, and screenwriter Ernest Lehman, who were responsible for selecting the American entry for the Berlin Film Festival. The screening was set for 3:00 P.M. at the Directors Guild Theatre. At three-forty-five the three men arrived, offered apologies for being late, and additional apologies for the pressing five o'clock appointments that would force them to leave before the end of the film. Inasmuch as I was screening an obscure, privately produced New York film without titles or music, their courteous attention for seventy-five minutes was about as much as I had the right to expect. Nonetheless, when the lights came on in the huge auditorium one hundred and fifteen minutes later, all three were still seated. They were traumatized. *The Pawnbroker* was selected to go to Berlin, and later that year it won the first prize.

I discovered when I returned to New York that Lumet planned to hire John Lewis, the leader of the Modern Jazz Quartet, to write the score. I protested that Lewis's music was too cerebral for this picture and I suggested Quincy Jones, the former trumpeter for Count Basie who was now leading his own band. Lumet invited Jones to a screening from which he emerged (as he later said) "covered with goose pimples." He had written notes to himself on a matchbook cover. Among his notations were the words "Kol Nidre," the lamentful Yom Kippur liturgy. Both Lumet and I sensed at once that the right man had been chosen. His score evolved into a mournful blending of Jewish themes and jazz rhythms, rhythms that were so complex he asked his friend Dizzy Gillespie to come to the recording session and tap out the beat for the band. The score was a masterful first-time achievement. Afterward, Jones moved to California, left the record business, stopped arranging for jazz bands, and devoted himself to scoring films. *In Cold Blood, Bob and Carol and Ted and Alice,* and *The Anderson Tapes* are among the more than two dozen films he has since scored.

Despite the Berlin award, *The Pawnbroker* was quickly mired in serious problems that held up its distribution for two years. Trouble began when the Legion of Decency (the national Catholic censorship board) condemned the picture for frontal nudity. Immediately thereafter, the Motion Picture Association of America (MPAA) refused their seal of approval. Ely Landau, the producer, was enraged; he protested the ruling and ultimately took the association to court. To quell the growing tempest, the entire forty-member MPAA Board was convened, an emergency procedure that had been invoked only twice before in the association's forty-three-year history. With the help of proponents like the director Joseph Mankiewicz, the seal was granted.

But all this took time, and Landau was impatient. None of the major companies seemed willing to touch the picture, with or without MPAA approval. Even before the Legion of Decency stigma, distributors recoiled at the heavy content of the film. With the court suit stirring publicity, Landau decided to seize the initiative by establishing a private firm to distribute the picture, and in the end that was how it got into the theaters.

Landau's importance cannot be overemphasized. Considering how thoroughly movies have become identified with their directors, it would be easy to overlook the work of such a tenacious and farsighted producer—not to mention the screenwriters, the cinematographer (Boris Kaufman), and Rod Steiger, who turned in a volcanic performance. Without minimizing Sidney Lumet's daring and expertise, we should note that *The Pawnbroker* was preceded by a distinguished novel, that all its characters and themes originated there, and that Ely Landau found the book, optioned it, and hired two men to write the script before the director ever came on the scene. None of this can be fairly omitted from the story of the film's success.

When it was finally released in 1965, *The Pawnbroker* was enthusiastically reviewed, and it has remained a favorite—except for some critics, like Dwight Macdonald and Pauline Kael, who were repelled by the degree of triteness and melodrama. (Kael acknowledged being wrenched by the film, but she was unable to say why.) It was a moderate financial success, as well, although Landau believes it would have done three or four times better had a major company handled it.

Audiences for the most part were devastated. From the very first screenings the response was emotionally calamitous. I still recall an early screening at which a middle-aged woman began weeping uncontrollably and struggled to get out of the room. She was a psychiatrist and the wife of one of the backers. I helped her into the lobby where she waited, sobbing, for the film to end. I believe the effect was so profound because once again an advance in film technique had made something more real. The flashback had gone beyond a convenient plot device and even beyond a backward voyage into an anguished man's past. It had become, for the first time, an X-ray vision of the anguish itself.

Within a few years all the devices Lumet had pioneered in this picture made their way into film, television, and advertising. The most obnoxious result has been the myriad of hair preparation, deodorant, and sanitary-napkin ads that depict lovers running toward one another in whisper-of-eternity slow motion. The most significant has been a loosening and broadening of film's ability to suggest the hidden workings of the mind, one of the slowest and most laborious searches in filmmaking history. *The Pawnbroker* succeeded in penetrating the surface without words; it achieved in cinematic terms what Wallant had done in the novel. And it did so in a way that was accessible to viewers: the movie did not have the confusing tone of an experimental film; Lumet built on convention and took a significant step forward. Fifteen years later, already many of the film's achievements have become routine. And perhaps in another decade everything we did will seem as archaic as Griffith's first innovative efforts to banish the dream balloon.

Herb Gardner and Ralph Rosenblum during the cutting of A THOUSAND CLOWNS.

12 ■ *A Thousand Clowns*

Part I: Flouting Convention

The movie by my measurement is much more
than the play. . . . It's no mere happenstance
that author Gardner and Ralph Rosenblum,
named as the associate producers,
spent ten months on the editing alone.
—PHILIP K. SCHEUER, reviewing
A Thousand Clowns in *The Los Angeles Times*,
December 19, 1965

I n 1964 I turned forty years old. In many respects I had achieved
the goal I set for myself at least a dozen years earlier when I
determined that I wanted nothing so much as to rise to the top of the
editing profession. I had now cut eleven features—the three gangster
flicks, five forgotten films called *Country Music Holiday, Jacktown, Two
Tickets to Paris, Gone Are the Days!,* and *The Fool Killer,* and three major
releases by Sidney Lumet, the last of which, *Fail Safe,* was completed
in 1964. The Lumet films had established me as one of the top two or
three feature editors in New York, but to satisfy a more personal
ambition, I still felt the need to work with a director who would allow
me greater editorial independence.

As the year began I was midway through my second season as the
supervising editor of "The Patty Duke Show." I was still working at
the old MKR offices in the Movielab Building on Fifty-fourth Street

near Twelfth Avenue, and even though Milford and Katz had long since departed, I kept the MKR name. My offices consisted of four rooms overlooking the West Side Highway and the ramshackle docks on the Hudson River. In the two rooms at either end of the suite, the six editors and assistants I hired to do the actual cutting of "Patty Duke" worked on their separate installments, while the two center rooms I reserved for my current feature work, which at this time was *A Thousand Clowns*, a filmed remake of a play that had just run for over a year on Broadway.

Nineteen sixty-five was an exciting time to be working in film. The French New Wave directors had shaken many of the premises about how films should be composed, with the result that there was an air of experimentation and daring that showed up in films like Antonioni's *L'Avventura* (1960), Fellini's *8½* (1963), Tony Richardson's *Tom Jones* (1963), and Stanley Kubrick's *Dr. Strangelove* (1964). In the summer of 1964 Richard Lester released his first Beatle picture, *A Hard Day's Night,* with its dizzying editorial flamboyance and unabashed reliance on fast motion, reverse motion, stop motion, and other cutting-room tricks. In the spring and summer of 1965 Lester came out with *The Knack* and *Help!* which further flouted convention.

But it was not yet clear what all this fermentation meant or where it was going. No one knew exactly which rules were being broken, and certainly no one had come up with the new set of guidelines to encompass what we have come to think of as modern film style. The biggest film of 1965 was a very old-fashioned picture called *The Sound of Music* (still one of the top profit-makers of all times), and other hits of the period included *Doctor Zhivago* (1965), *Cleopatra* (1963), *The Bible* (1966), and *My Fair Lady* (1964), all extremely conventional in technique. The people who were making changes in the cutting rooms of New York, Paris, London, Tokyo, and other major production centers were groping in the dark, sometimes vaguely influencing one another but more often coming to similar solutions out of a shared awareness that the conventional way of making films had come to seem stiff and old-fashioned.

Although I knew that I was living in a period of exploration and change, I had no thought when I came in each morning to piece together the rough cut of *A Thousand Clowns* that I was stepping into the front lines of the revolution. I had no idea that this would be my chance to really command the editing of an important picture. And the last thing I anticipated was that the film would be hung up in the cutting room for an almost unheard-of eleven months. In those days you either cut a traditional commercial film, a textbook enterprise with a predictable four-to-six-month gestation period, or you cut an avant-garde film, a process that allowed more invention but did not necessarily demand more time. Only an exceptional filmmaker, like Stanley Kubrick, tried to do both by making a serious stab at the time-consuming task of bridging the gap between the traditional film language audiences expected and the new opportunities for expression that were then emerging.

There was no Kubrick in charge of *A Thousand Clowns*. Rather, we had an unusual combination of personalities—a fanatical young author with a head full of visions, a paternalistic and easygoing director, an experienced and perfectionist editor—that, when stirred together in a woebegone turmoil of enthusiasm, hysteria, and despair, brought forth a transformation that shocked them all.

The script was the work of an illustrator and cartoonist named Herb Gardner who had written the play from which the film was adapted when he was twenty-five and whose only previous popular achievement was inventing the squushy little plastic figure known as the "Nebbish." For two and a half years Gardner lugged his play from producer to producer, each failure heightening his obsession over what to this day is still the masterwork of his career. "Some producers said it was too funny to be sad," remembers Herb, "some said it was too sad to be funny, and others said it was too philosophical for a Broadway comedy." But through Anne Bancroft and her husband, Mel Brooks, Herb was introduced to director Fred Coe, who loved the play, agreed to direct it, saw it through major financial obstacles, and gave tremendous strength to the greenhorn playwright. "My idea of a good production," says Herb, who probably attended half of the play's several hundred performances, "was they talk loud and don't bump into each other. I still remember the opening night in Boston. I saw people actually getting a ticket to go and watch—I was so excited!" Herb went on to write a voluminous screenplay for the film version, and Coe faithfully produced and directed it, taking along many of the Broadway players.

Now neither of these men knew much about the fine points of filmmaking. Fred Coe had produced *The Miracle Worker* and *The Lefthanded Gun*, but *Clowns* was his directorial debut. Herb's script moved a number of scenes outdoors, allowed for some intercutting between simultaneous pieces of action, and generally attempted to free itself of a stagebound quality. But it was still the most traditional sort of dialogue movie, something that became plain to me when I began the first assembly. I spent a few weeks with the dailies, put them together in a standard, workmanly way, and produced a rough cut that flowed nicely and expertly followed all the nuances of film composition. It wasn't a very stylish film, but it had some of the funniest material I'd ever seen or heard.

It took me a few weeks to realize, with somewhat wounded pride, that Herb was mortified by what he saw. "I felt responsible as the screenwriter," he recalls. "They shot what I wrote, but I saw no life in it. It was still too much like a play." Herb revealed his dissatisfaction to Fred Coe, and thereby initiated the first of a string of peculiar developments that characterized the cutting of this film. Fred, who was enormously fond of Herb, never very possessive about the picture, and not much inclined toward spending painstaking months in the cutting room, agreed to hand over the entire project to the younger man. And that was the last we saw of Fred Coe.

When Herb came to tell me that Fred had moved on to other things, that he, Herb, would be hanging out in the cutting room with me for a while, and that he was hoping to make a few "change-a-roonies" here and there, I thought he meant we'd fool around for a couple of weeks, do a little face-lifting, and soon be on to other things ourselves. He said he wanted to do some more outdoor shooting, that some of the dialogue scenes were too long.

The first thing Herb wanted to do was to look at all the film. "I had never seen a Moviola," says Herb, "I didn't know about cutting. I mean nothing. I was a screenwriter, a new screenwriter on top of it, functioning with the authority of the director. I had a lot of feelings and instincts about what I should do, but no vocabulary to translate it. I felt I was in a strange country. I didn't quite know what an editor did. I remember I said, 'Which is the machine you put the film on?' "

For a long time neither Herb nor I had any idea what he was after. But gradually I realized he had no intention of bothering himself with my first cut. He was looking at all the dailies as if a first cut had never been made. More than looking at the dailies, he seemed to be trying to merge with them. The experienced director or the experienced editor looks at the raw material once or twice, selects a shot or an angle, and he's through. But Herb sat there for hours viewing the same material, often for a dozen times or more, and without any sense of conclusion. For days nothing would happen, except that Herb would run the film.

After weeks of examining the dailies and making little stabs at reworking the opening scene, Herb began bringing in his favorite record albums and asking me to transfer them onto tape—march music, circus music, Dixieland music, Handel's *Messiah*, the ragtime piano music of Eubie Blake. Then he went into a recording studio with Jason Robards, the leading man in both the Broadway and the film production and by now a buddy of Gardner's, and he recorded him for about two hours playing the ukelele and singing and humming the theme song, "Yessir, That's My Baby."

"I was trying to start all over again with a blank canvas," says Herb. "I thought I'd take the character and try to find music for him. So I got all this marching music, Jason singing, and I labeled it—Jason Soft, Jason Romantic, Jason Whatever. He wasn't really a singer, he didn't play the ukelele that great, and his voice cracked and whistled a little, but it was intimate. I'd listen to the tapes over and over, and poor Ralph didn't know what was going on."

In fact, nothing in my professional career had prepared me for this dungareed writer who never wore a watch. My major influences were people like Helen van Dongen, who was quick, precise, and efficient, and Sidney Lumet, who was famous for coming in ahead of schedule. Certainly Sidney never sat around staring at a single scene for hours or listening to taped transfers of his favorite records, waiting for an inspiration. We cut *Long Day's Journey* in about two and a half months, *The Pawnbroker* in about five months, and *Fail Safe* in just over four months. At the end of two full months in the cutting room with Herb Gardner, we had about five minutes of usable film and the promise of eternity hanging over our uneasy marriage. At times I'd look at Herb sculpted before one of the Moviolas and I'd feel like a prisoner in a shaggy-dog joke. I'd want to feed him to the trim bin.

But it was impossible to stay angry at Herb for long. He was always funny and never stopped making me laugh. He'd pay me the most ingratiating attention. If he sensed I was getting testy, he put on a servile Southern accent and began calling me "Mr. Ralph," with a ludicrous accompaniment of bowing and scraping. If that didn't work, he'd do his Prussian imitations. Via the latter routines he'd spout what as far as I could tell was the sum total of his film knowledge—hysterical German-accented declarations such as, "Eisenstein warned: *'Watch out, the movie shouldn't go into the toilet!'*"

Time meant nothing to Herb. I still remember a moment in a Mexican restaurant when he tried futilely to understand what was making me disconsolate. He joked that with all the big pictures being made United Artists had probably forgotten all about our little black and white production off by the river and that they'd continue to pay for the editing for years before the executives caught on. A lovable madman, I thought. A nutty incompetent that United Artists will one day have to cart away in a straitjacket in order to salvage their investment. Herb's recollection of me: "Mr. Rosenblum here was a much older man at the time."

The conventions that had gradually accumulated and come to rule feature-film editing were not so much laws as guidelines and assumptions, many of which were first developed by Griffith, Eisenstein, and Pudovkin and later codified for film students by Karel Reisz in his 1953 book, *The Technique of Film Editing*. They concerned such issues as the proper way of making a smooth cut, the right dramatic length for a piece of film, how the interplay of cuts creates the desired rhythm and tempo, and how the selection of the appropriate perspective and camera angle can generate a specific emotional tone—suspense, terror, grotesqueness, or humor—based on what the editor chooses to focus on and· what he leaves out of the viewer's vision. These guidelines were sensible and appropriate and left considerable leeway for individual choice and invention, but their very existence was symbolic of ossification. The potential for editorial play in feature films was not nearly what it had been in the silent era when stories were told through clever juxtapositions or even in current documentary, which in some quarters was still freewheeling and uninhibited (Bert Stern's and Aram Avakian's 1960 film, *Jazz on a Summer's Day*, being an exhilarating example). By and large, feature editing had become focused on the small issues.

Making the film smooth was the major preoccupation, and certain elementary principles had become sacred. You had to be sure the background and lighting stayed the same when you cut from a long shot to a close-up. If there is a cat on the mantelpiece in the first shot, he should still be there in the second, along with all the predominant shadows and highlights. You had to know the exact moment to make the cut. You don't wait until James Cagney's hand has almost reached the revolver on the table to cut in for a close-up of the grasp. Rather, you change angles the moment after his eyes glance downward and he realizes that the gun's within reach. The second choice is smoother and more dramatic.

Smooth continuity is similarly enhanced by preserving a sense of direction. Since Griffith's day characters, armies, battleships always moved in the same direction across the screen from long shot to middle shot to close shot. Griffith also used direction as an ongoing means of identification: In *The Birth of a Nation* Union soldiers always emanated from the right side of the screen and Rebels from the left. And, of course, directional flow was applied to completely unrelated pieces of action—a man falling from a twenty-two-story window giving way to a toy parachute falling into a boy's hands—as a useful tool for making transitions.

Other rules governed subtler questions. If a young lady being assaulted in her houseboat by Robert Mitchum suddenly grasps that her life as well as her chastity is endangered, the editor may want to cut to a close shot of her face to accent her panic. But the close-up must be complete; just a slight enlarging of her image would be jarring in its lack of resolution. On the other hand, if the woman shows no panic at all, and in response to Mitchum's lustful aggression asks coolly, "What was the food like in San Quentin?" using a close-up would be ludicrous in this context, creating an unintended joke.

At the beginning of new scenes, editors traditionally chose to stand back as far as possible to give a sense of place and situation. Thus we see an isolated houseboat hidden on the wooded shore of the Cape Fear River, cut inside to a long shot of Mitchum with his leading lady pinned to the kitchen sink, than a medium shot in which the actors fill the screen, and finally a close shot of Mitchum's hand moving menacingly across her half-bare chest. An alternative approach, popularized on television in the fifties, was to begin the scene with the detail and only gradually move back to reveal the context of which the detail is a part. The opening of *Louisiana Story*, in which the first thing we see is a dew-covered lotus leaf, is a perfect example of this alternative. Recent instances of the more traditional style are *Pretty Baby, Doña Flor and Her Two Husbands,* and *A Special Day,* all three of which begin with aerial views of the locale where the stories take place.

All of these editing conventions—to which Reisz was able to devote over 250 pages—served the essential task of enabling the editor to do justice to the script and the shot material. They were like a writer's grammar, and as such are still crucial to the making of any film. In the sixties they would be not so much abandoned as diminished in importance as directors and editors saw opportunities to move cutting away from simple subservience to the script and use it as a major vehicle for molding the film. In the process they discovered that some of the old commandments were not as immutable as they had thought. The rules had only seemed sacred—because, after decades of seeing armies moving obediently from right to left, audiences had become conditioned to expect it. They could be deconditioned.

The intended title sequence for *A Thousand Clowns* was a scene from "Chuckles the Chipmunk," a ghastly television kid show. The camera moves back to reveal a TV in the apartment of the main characters—Murray, played by Jason Robards, a TV gag writer who quit the "Chuckles" show in order to lead the free (unemployed) life, and his all-but-adopted twelve-year-old nephew Nick, played by Barry Gordon, a less liberated individual who would like his uncle to get a job. Nick comments on how awful the show has become since Murray quit, and Murray, anguished by the false sounds of childish cheer, tries to bury his head under a pillow.

After the titles role by, the scene switches to a junkyard, one of Murray's favorite haunts, where Nick, who has cut school, tries to talk his uncle into looking for work. He explains that the child-welfare people have discovered his unwholesome living conditions and may try to relocate him in a foster home if Murray doesn't improve their circumstances. We follow them around for a good part of the day, first in the junkyard, then the South Street Seaport area, Liberty Island, the Liberty Island Ferry, and finally the Battery Park waterfront. Herb and I fiddled with the editing of this very funny but cinematically staid material for quite some time before he was struck with an inspiration.

Herb got hold of cameraman Joe Coffey (Arthur Ornitz had done all the original photography), went out early one weekday morning, and shot crowds going to work. Since Murray spoke with mortification about the horrible spectacle of regimented, workbound urban-ites, Herb thought, why not really show it, make it vivid? Certainly that would be less like a play. The results encouraged him. "This was just like movies now!" says Herb. "This is what Murray talked about—going to work, what it feels like, what it can look like with those long early morning shadows, with every New York face looking like they're about to be executed, like there's their stop and then there's Auschwitz. And now we're seeing it. So I came in with this pile of stuff, and I sat down with Ralph, and I said, This is going to be our new title scene."

The shots of people going to work *were* good. The bleary-eyed New Yorkers moved in unison, like troops in permanent retreat. Hundreds of thousands of semiawake people, following their well-worn paths to work, obeying the WALK and DON'T WALK signs as if they were all powered by the same remote-control device. The signal changes and they rumble toward us across the intersection. Cut to an overhead shot as scores of feet step forward in obedient formation. Cut to the crowd filing across the screen, another group emerging from the subway, each angle amplifying the grim procession.

Then Herb had another inspiration. He took one of those reels of taped march music and began playing it over the marching New Yorkers. "It was a breakthrough," says Herb, "in Ralph's relationship with me, in finding a style for the movie, in realizing we could make a film together. Because I took the march music and started running a couple of overhead shots of people going to work—and *they started walking to the music*. And I'll always remember, Ralph turns to me with a happy smile on his face, and he says, 'I think we got something here.' "

From now on Herb began to listen to his music for a mood or a spirit that suggested where to go next, and then we'd begin to shape the movie in that direction. When the new going-to-work title scene was completed, Herb presented it to United Artists, and they were impressed enough to extend his budget for additional shooting.

Bypassing the rest of the film's first hour, Herb now set his sights on a moment in reel six. With cameraman Coffey he went out and shot additional footage of Robards and his leading lady, Barbara Harris—the social worker who falls in love with him—riding around the city on a bicycle-built-for-two. In the play, the screenplay, and the initial cut of the film, their first love scene consisted of mutual declarations of love followed by several minutes of tender, self-revealing dialogue. We eliminated all the talk and replaced it with a bicycle-riding montage.

Herb Gardner: "I wanted to show they loved each other and that there was life to their connection. In the opening two lines of the scene she says, 'I've thought about it and I probably love you.' And he says, 'That's very romantic—I probably love you, too.' It then proceeds to three pages of dialogue. It was a pretty decent scene that always worked well in the play. What we ended up with in the movie were those two lines and the most exuberant of the bicycle-riding shots."

It was the sort of transition that violated the conventions on continuity as they had been applied to feature films. But as Herb points out, it was *emotionally* correct and the audience could grasp its meaning.

"You don't have to say, 'I'm going to ride a bicycle,' or finish the scene, or anything. The next thing is they're riding a bicycle and a full brass band is playing the 'Stars and Stripes Forever.' The brass band and the two of them riding this bicycle-built-for-two is a celebration of they-love-each-other. What would have been a three-minute love scene inside was now a three-minute love scene done with a brass band and eventually Jason humming in his cracked, intimate, very rough, and deeply believable sound, humming and playing, 'Yes, Sir, That's My Baby.' "

Antony Gibbs, one of the all-time top British editors (*Tom Jones, The Knack, A Bridge Too Far*), once said that the greatest influence on the development of his editing skills was his relationship with director Tony Richardson. Because Richardson was a novice who knew almost nothing of editing technique, "He pushed me," said Gibbs, "further away from convention than I would have dared go alone." Watching Herb Gardner use music to lead him toward the feeling he wanted to create was having a similar effect on me. This was simply not the way feature films were made. Not only was the music traditionally added at the end of a film, it was never used to alter or adjust the message on the screen, but only to amplify it. Whole music libraries existed for just this purpose with thousands of one- and two-minute recordings for "tragic closings," "romantic background," "street scene," "approaching monster," "wild ride," "conquering hero," "longing," "treachery," "uplift finale," and so forth, and original scores tended to serve the same limited and predictable purpose. Rather than using music as background or amplification, Herb was using it as counterpoint to the material on the screen, a new, independent, juxtaposed element that was every bit as important as words. For the first time in my feature-film experience music became a part of the editorial composition of the film. It was only one of many jolts I would receive in the coming months, jolts that would stimulate my own inventive resources and permanently influence my cutting-room technique.

"When we used up all of our most dramatic bicycle shots, I said, 'We should end this now.' And Ralph said, 'Why?' And I said, 'Well, the rest of the shots don't look like much.' He said, 'We'll put them all together.' I said, 'What do you mean?' He said, 'We'll put them on top of each other.' So he took a bunch of ordinary shots, like they were colors, and put them all together. There are times when there are five images of Jason and Barbara riding bicycles, floating through each other and past each other. There was one deeply, deeply boring shot—I thought it would be romantic—of them riding by the fountain in Central Park. Ralph took stock footage of the Central Park South skyline, with the Essex House and all those buildings, and a fairly close shot of the two faces riding through on the bicycle, plus the fountain shot, and blended them together. And we added to it the soft voice of Jason roughly singing, and it looks as if they're riding on top of the buildings of New York. It makes you remember for the whole next hour of the movie that these people care for each other, and that there's a tenderness between them. It was as if you were seeing a soft romantic deck being shuffled properly together. It was a madhouse from then on. We were willing to try anything."

Director Fred Coe, Betty Todd (script supervisor),
Jason Robards, and Ralph Rosenblum at the Moviola.

13 ▪ *A Thousand Clowns*
Part II: A Style Arrived
At by Repair

It's one thing to take some routine footage of high-school marching bands or some bizarre shots of European traffic cops and, just for the fun of it, cut them into bits, set the montage to some improbable music, and after several hours of spare time come up with a lively three-minute short for "Omnibus." But to go through that process with a feature film, to maintain that rhythm and sparkle for 118 minutes, to perform that kind of transformation was a new proposition to me. Lumet's pictures were edited with tremendous rhythm and pace—catch *Fail Safe* on TV some night, and you'll see that it never stops; it pulls you along like a rapids. But Lumet and I never edited against the intentions of the script or the raw footage; *Fail Safe* was an action movie and we gave it superaction cutting. With *A Thousand Clowns* Gardner and I were attempting through the addition of some extra film, an idiosyncratic use of music, and the abandonment of the script to create a movie that simply wasn't there before.

True, the initial alterations in *A Thousand Clowns* were encouraging. But at least three months were gone now, and I had to face certain things. Our new inventions represented only a few minutes of razzmatazz in a film that was otherwise extremely stagebound. The contrast between the two styles was so apparent it suggested a black and white movie with one or two color sequences. To make this picture conform to the stylistic excitement of the title scene and the bicycle-riding montage, it would have to be handcrafted inch by inch. Nothing could be left alone any more; every scene would have to sing somehow, would have to come to color. It was a long time before I had any reason to believe that I wasn't digging myself deeper and deeper into blunder and illusion.

Herb Gardner: "I think Ralph and I went through every kind of emotion you can have—from love to absolute outright hate. Petulance, fondness, excitement, despair, boredom. Even paranoia. Ralph had every reason to believe that I was on a cutting jag. He figures I'm crazy. I figure he's resisting me. We were involved in the most extraordinary, intimate circumstances, exposing to each other on a daily basis such joy followed by such disappointment. Ralph would become morose—and boy, can he do a morose for you. It's Greek. You see a man, looks like a nice Jewish fellow, works as an editor—suddenly he's got three pillars behind him and I'm in *Medea*. So I would change my voice, do a German accent, and Ralph would start to laugh."

Our first major obstacle was right there in the opening scene of the film, in which Nick follows Murray to his favorite haunts, trying to read to him from the want ads and to convince him that "for me as an actual child the way you live in our house and we live is a dangerous thing for my later life when I become an actual person." It was all outdoor material, but it felt like a stage set. Something had to be done.

Gardner: "Suddenly I thought, it doesn't have to be a day. It could be all the days they've ever talked about this. Maybe it's many days. Maybe Nick asks him a question on a pier and Murray answers him in front of the Statue of Liberty. Who knows what time it is? Time is whatever you feel it is."

We then proceeded to create what for that period was a very unusual scene for any kind of film—one that completely ignored the old rules of continuity. We cut together a single continuous piece of dialogue from the conversations that were recorded between Murray and Nick at the four original locations. We placed the dialogue over a visual montage that shows them at the junk dealer's, walking with a parade, at Lincoln Center, on a dock seeing off a ship, at a fishing pier, back at the junkyard, on the Liberty Island Ferry, on Liberty Island, walking along Park Avenue (with Murray pulling a kite and Nick trying to read aloud from the help-wanted columns), in Central Park, in front of a store window, at a parade again, and so forth. Without the slightest break in the dialogue, the locale keeps shifting. They're in Central Park when Nick says, "You know, Murray, you don't *want* a job is the whole thing." A close-up of Murray: "Would you just concentrate on being a child. Because I find"—cut to Murray and Nick on the ferry boat—"your imitation of an adult hopelessly inadequate."

The raw material we had with which to construct this scene was not always cooperative. Frequently, in order to make it work, we had to choose pieces of film from the original scenes in which the character who was speaking was looking away from the camera, so that we could put the desired dialogue in without the interference of his original mouthings. Some of the conversation is played over silent footage of Murray and Nick that Herb shot with Joe Coffey on one of their outings. To work that material into the montage we had to select long shots or angles that didn't reveal the speaker's face. We were thus able to maintain the illusion that the actor is indeed saying the words on the sound track. Into this fraudulence we had to work enough synch-sound sentences coming from genuine moving lips to avoid abandoning all contact with reality. To this end, we several times slowed the flurry down and allowed the conversation to continue for several moments at one location.

But because we had much bigger issues to worry about, we totally ignored such matters as whether Murray and Nick moved in the same direction from cut to cut or whether the same person stood on the right or the left. This was a different sort of film action, one in which the real continuity was on the sound track, while the visuals offered a kaleidoscopic view of the World of Murray Burns. It was a style arrived at by desperation and repair.

It is difficult for an outsider to imagine how tedious cutting a scene, especially a complex one like this, can be, and how boring it is to observe. Visitors who've come to watch me work invariably depart with awkward apologies after just a few minutes. When *New Yorker* critic Pauline Kael was preparing a major article on the making of *The Group,* the last picture I cut for Lumet, she put aside four hours to sit in on the editing. She lasted twenty minutes. Few have lasted longer.

Even fast movies rarely proceed at more than a few minutes a week, but *Clowns* was not fast. It was especially trying because we never knew for certain if we were on a wild-goose chase. Whole weeks were spent in fruitless exploration. Once, an entire month was lost composing what amounted to an eight-minute satirical short on the lunchtime habits of New York business people. Everyone loved it, but it didn't fit in the film. The constant agony over wasted effort can be very disheartening and, as much as anything else, accounts for some of the extreme feelings that sometimes emerge in the cutting of a motion picture.

The title scene of people going to work, the new opening scene with Murray and Nick, and the bicycle montage were our three stylistic guides that would now rule the editing of the remainder of the film. As Murray and Nick complete their wanderings and return to their Brooklyn apartment, they are met by two social workers, and the movie settles down for its first dramatic episode.

The pair of social workers who arrive at the Burns residence this morning have their own barely concealed problems. Albert Amundson is impersonal and priggishly professional ("not one of the warm people" he later admits), whereas his fiancée and junior partner, Sandra Markowitz (Barbara Harris), is a much more emotional individual who, one way or another, tends to become overly involved in her cases ("I hate Raymond Ledbetter," she cries, "and he's only nine years old!"). Sandra tries to live up to her co-worker's standards, but faced with Murray Burns and his diversionary tactics, even Albert begins to show signs of disarray.

Murray immediately throws the two off guard with his lighthearted responses to their solemn questions. He freely admits that he has been unemployed for five months, that Nick has been living with him for seven years, that the question of the "little bastard's" real father is a *who* question not a *where* question, that Nick's mother communicates with her brother Murray "almost entirely by rumor," that "Nick" is not the boy's official name, but merely his current infatuation. "He went through a long period of dog names when he was little," Murray explains. "He received his library card last year in the name of Raphael Sabatini. His Cub Scout membership lists him as Dr. Morris Fishbein."

If Murray's aggressive nonconformity flusters the social-work instincts, they re-emerge in an aroused condition when Nick produces his "favorite plaything," Bubbles, a twenty-four-inch bare-chested hula girl whose electronic breasts blink on and off in spectacular fashion. None of Nick's efforts to add sobriety to the image of the Burns household ("We play many wholesome and constructive games together") can dampen the excitement that Bubbles has created: "Nick, tell me," says Sandra, "do you like best the fact that the chest of the lady lights up?" Nick: "Well, you got to admit, you don't see boobies like that every day. You want to see the effect when the lights are out, when the room is dark?" Sandra (oozing social-work sanctimony): "Tell me, Nick, is *that* what you like best about it, that you can be alone in the dark with it?" Nick (unaffected): "Well, I don't know. But in the dark they really knock your eye out."

As Sandra tries to probe for Nick's fixation, asking if the statue reminds him of his mother in any way, her punctilious partner can no longer contain his discomfort and requests that Bubbles be turned off. At this point, Murray loses his patience and informs Sandra that Nick's mother's chest did not light up and that Nick "is no more abnormally interested in your bust than Mr. Amundson is." This throws Albert into a high state of anxiety and defensiveness, and much to her own anguish, Sandra cannot contain her mirth. The crumbling team argues privately in the corner (as Murray watches with binoculars), and finally Albert leaves in a huff.

Sandra now emerges as the leading lady in the film, the woman who falls in love with Murray and hopes to steer him toward the responsible behavior that will satisfy the Child Welfare Board and thus allow him to keep Nick—a project that proves to be almost beyond her powers. Meanwhile Herb Gardner and I will struggle to break up their dramatic scenes with cinematic activity, to keep anything from staying in one place too long.

Alone in the apartment with Murray, Sandra, who realizes she has lost both her boy friend and her job, begins to weep, lamenting all her limitations as she does ("I cry all the time and laugh in the wrong places in the movies"). Robards offers her a pastrami sandwich, assures her she's well rid of both Albert and her job, and proposes a trip to the Empire State Building.

We leave the apartment for about three minutes to follow Robards and Harris on a Murray Burns Manhattan Outing that includes seeing off an ocean liner, visiting the Statue of Liberty, strolling down deserted after-hours Wall Street, and running across the Brooklyn Bridge. When we return home, it's the next day and the pair are facing an awkward morning. This was meant to be another long dramatic sequence, but within moments Murray and Sandra profess their love for one another and Herb and I were able to insert our beloved bicycle montage—which had by now been sitting on the shelf for over four months.

Though the bicycle-riding sequence seems to take place over the course of building an entire relationship, the next scene brings us back to the apartment on the same morning. Albert comes by to inform Murray of the Child Welfare Board's decision to relocate Nick. He also inquires about "Miss Markowitz," who didn't show up at her mother's house in Queens last night. (She's hiding in the closet.) Eventually Murray confesses to Sandra that he doesn't want Nick taken away, and the scene is set for Murray's great afternoon job hunt.

At this point the script required that two simultaneous elements be intercut: Murray going on the emergency job appointments that his brother Arnold (who is also Murray's agent and the voice of responsibility) has set up for him; and Sandra first trying to explain herself on the phone to her mother and then redecorating Murray's apartment in a style he later derides as "Fun Gothic." Herb and I saw this as an opportunity to get things flying again by quickening the intercutting and giving the whole afternoon a whirlwind energy.

We started off with a bang: intercut with Murray making his way through midtown Manhattan to his luncheon appointment, we see a stock shot of a hand with a gun. The sound track bursts forth with a gun blast, then a drum roll, as a flurry of cuts go by depicting the lunch life of a great city—highlighted by sandwiches revolving into view in the Automat (to sound track peals of "Hallelujah!") and climaxing with a trainer throwing a hunk of meat to a hungry lion. From here on we see Murray entering and leaving his business meetings faster and faster, each of his appearances getting more and more abbreviated, while Sandra's moments on the screen—putting up curtains, stuffing Murray's treasured junk into cartons, phoning her mother to say she's happy and in love—become longer and longer. The sequence ends with Murray meeting her on the street outside his tenement, Sandra laden with grocery bags and Murray laden with guilt over having turned down all the jobs. Avoiding her questions, Murray goes into a song and dance about a unique experiment he engaged in today of apologizing to strangers in the street ("And seventy-five percent of them forgave me!"). At first amused, Sandra gradually realizes what he's doing. We eliminated a chunk of dialogue here and intercut her fading expression with memory flashes of their courtship around Manhattan. This use of flashbacks, one that I would later employ in almost identical fashion at the end of the wedding scene in *Goodbye Columbus*, replaces her verbal evaluation of the inadequacy of life with Murray Burns.

As we passed into the second half of the film, Herb and I succumbed to a growing anxiety over whether what we were doing would mean anything to an outside observer. As Herb recalls, "There were those moments of terror when you realize, this may only be for us. What reason would an audience have for responding to it?" We began arranging screenings for friends every Friday evening, and we were soon living and working for their laughter and approval.

"They responded more than I imagined," says Herb. "People crying, laughing, and I remember Ralph sitting next to me, and in those few seconds we both would feel, it's all worth it. You remember how you got into this line of work. Your motive is to tell a story from the most personal source. We made this to *show* to people—and that's what we're doing. And they're getting the idea of it. It looks like it was meant to be. Yes, that's where the close-up goes, and that's where that line goes, and that's where we cut out that look on his face, and that's where we didn't say the extra two lines—because *it was meant to be*. The audience doesn't see the cuts, they don't see the machinery. It's just this ribbon of emotions running out in front of them."

To the very end Herb and I had difficulties over the dialogue. A typical problem concerned the scene in which Martin Balsam (playing Murray's brother Arnold) confronts Murray in the abandoned Chinese restaurant beneath the apartment. We added only one piece of editorial effects: as Murray tells his brother about his dread of being among the walking dead going to work each morning, we introduced a series of shots from the title scene of the marching New Yorkers. It had been funny with the march music, but now with just Murray's voice at a rare level of seriousness, it was appropriately and effectively grim. Other than that their confrontation stood on its own.

But Herb wasn't satisfied with Balsam's delivery. Typical of most writers, he was fanatical about every nuance in the dialogue and anxious about an actor's ad-lib alterations that subtly shifted the emotional tone. In each of his takes, Balsam had left out little words or phrases—the absence of which drove Herb crazy—and added others that prematurely revealed that a major character shift was about to take place. Herb spent hours leaning over the Moviola, obsessed with finding the snippets of each reading that passed his judgment. Balsam's soliloquy, in which a beaten and compromised man emerges with a dynamic personal statement, is one of the many self-justification speeches that inhabit this work and give it its charm. He tells Murray that he prefers to deal with the available world, that he has a talent for surrender, that he takes pride in being "the best possible Arnold Burns." At every screening audiences broke into spontaneous applause over this performance, and a year later, the author's profound misgivings notwithstanding, it won Balsam an Academy Award.

Balsam was not the only actor who made Herb fret. Like Balsam, Barbara Harris had not appeared in the Broadway production and thus did not have each precious word down absolutely pat. Chunks of her first major monologue were bowdlerized because of Herb's dissatisfaction, but, again, not before days of agonized uncertainty. It's a special disease of author-filmmakers, one that I would encounter again with Woody Allen.

Herb responded to frustration with hours of pacing, often spilling forth dialect jokes and wisecracks instead of the anger and impatience I know he felt. Sometimes he went into the hallway and followed it around the city block the building occupied. He refused to answer phone calls, promising to call back and not doing so for weeks. Or he'd decide to take a call and stay on for hours. Trying to relax, he began to cover the walls of my office with his cartoons, mostly Magic Marker Nebbishes, which I still regret having left behind when I moved. At the time, all this was infuriating.

Gardner: "There were awful times. I could see Ralph's disappointment. And he was everything to me at that point—the audience, the editor, son, daddy. And I could see his face falling, blending into the shoulders, drifting down toward his knees—and I'd want to kill him. There was a bench outside the screening room, several doors down from where we were cutting. I'd go sit on that bench so he wouldn't hear me scream."

Now there was one place where Herb's disappointment over the acting seemed justified to me. Gene Saks, who played Chuckles the Chipmunk on Broadway, was unavailable when the picture was shot, and Paul Richards, who'd played Chuckles on the road, was hired instead. Chuckles is an hysterical egomaniac who caroms wildly from obsessive self-promotion (he presents Nick with a life-sized cardboard cutout statue of himself in full Chuckles regalia) to obsequious exclamations of glee ("*Murray*, there he is! There's the old monkey! There's the old joker!") to gruesome self-pity ("O.K. the kid hates me. I didn't go over very well with him. I pushed a little too hard") to acknowledgments of professional failure ("*Oh*, have I been bombing out on the show every morning!") to fury at Nick's failure to laugh at one of his hideous routines ("Forget it, kid, I just happen to know that that bit is *very* funny. Fun, funny, funniest!") and back to self-deprecation ("Oh, my God! Did you ever see anything so *immodest!* I bring a big statue of myself as a gift for the child! I mean, the pure *ego* of it. I'm ashamed. Murray, please, could you throw a sheet over it or something?").

Paul Richards' Chuckles was full of the frenzy and madness that was crucial to the part, but there was something a little scary about him, a little dark, a little brooding. You feared that at any moment he might pull a hand grenade from his pocket. By the time we reached this point in the film, United Artists was satisfied with the legitimacy of the transformation that was going on, and UA executive David Picker, a sympathetic supporter throughout, was able to arrange for the extra funds Herb needed to reshoot the Chuckles scenes with Gene Saks, who was now available. Saks gave a tour-de-force performance, creating one of the most memorable moments in a film full of memorable moments, and Richards' performance was discarded.

When we finished the picture, Herb and I had a completed score on our hands, a very unusual, if not unique, event in the making of a feature film. It was only a "scratch" score, though, and to make a proper sound track United Artists had two options: lay out enormous sums for the rights to the recordings we'd pirated—which by this time included Eubie Blake, Dave Brubeck, marching music by various circus bands, and the Mormon Tabernacle Choir—any one of which might have cost twenty thousand dollars. Or simply pay for the rights to the music and hire an orchestrator to rerecord all the material, using studio musicians. Except for the Eubie Blake material and a main title theme written by Gerry Mulligan, the latter course was chosen. Herb asked Don Walker, a well-known Broadway composer and orchestrator and a friend of the everhelpful Fred Coe, if he would take the job. Walker, reluctant at first to handle a strictly routine and mechanical assignment, finally succumbed to Herb's pleas. The Academy Awards committee nominated him that year for the best original score.

A Thousand Clowns was the first turning point in my career since *Long Day's Journey*. I was now known as an important contributor to the films I cut. Norman Lear invited me to relocate to California and become a part of his operation—a proposition I refused because of my feelings about the factory atmosphere in Hollywood—and I began receiving my first offers to direct, which at the time I was emotionally unprepared to accept. But most important, *A Thousand Clowns* was the basic training for the kind of editing that has become my trademark. Since 1965 I've put a scratch score to every film I've cut in order to establish the rhythm. I've stopped looking at scripts, which I had once kept nearby like a Bible, and have assumed the right to follow the raw material into the stronger or more appropriate story patterns it often suggests. Above all, I was forced out of my old conceptions and prejudices about how a feature should be cut. I let my documentary training come into play; and my youthful sensation that anything was possible in the editing room was now relevant to every motion picture. This growth would serve me well three years hence when I was left holding the disastrous first cut of *The Night They Raided Minsky's*.

The finished film, shown publicly for the first time at a preview in Fresh Meadows, was certainly one of the most editorially liberated films of its day. With its constant interweaving of scenes, experimental flourishes, startling use of music, energetic overlapping of action, it had no trace of its former stage-bound quality. But there was so much patching in the workprint shown in Fresh Meadows that night that Herb, who delivered the cans of film with the associate editor, Eddie Beyer, had to sit in the projection booth with his thumb on the projector gate to keep the film from bouncing and giving the entire audience a subconscious sense of discomfort. Isolated from the crowd, Herb had no idea how they were receiving his cherished work until just before the end when he sneaked out and heard the clamorous applause. In the lobby moments later, anxiety turned to ecstasy as eight or ten overjoyed United Artists executives congratulated Herb, me, and Fred Coe. They then got into their black limousines and drove back to Manhattan. I got into my car and drove home to New Rochelle. And at midnight in a deserted Fresh Meadows, lugging twelve cans of film, Herb Gardner, who had somehow been forgotten in the shuffle, stood by the Long Island Expressway and tried to find a cab.

A Thousand Clowns made Herb one of the hottest new writers in the industry, and the picture itself has gone on to attract new generations of admirers, becoming one of that special class of films that are always playing somewhere. It is still the most popular picture in my New School course in film editing, and I am no longer surprised to find people who say they've seen it a dozen or more times.

For my part, I was still unprepared to believe that the picture was going to be a hit based on the response of one audience. I allowed my optimism to solidify only during the series of private screenings United Artists arranged before *Clowns* was released in December 1965. I remember one screening in particular because I invited my mother to attend, and because until that moment I still was not convinced that our fancy editorial footwork wouldn't confuse a traditional viewer. I therefore noted with particular interest that except for some initial grunts of approval upon seeing my name in the credits, my mother gave no sign of amusement, not even a chuckle throughout the entire film. Not until the very end, when Murray has finally agreed to take back his old job with Chuckles the Chipmunk; when, wearing a hat and suit and carrying an attaché case, he is frozen on the screen running to catch a bus with the other commuters; when the rest of the audience was wistfully absorbing his moment of surrender, did my mother finally react: "*Well,*" she said triumphantly, "it's about time!"

Mel Brooks and producer Sidney Glazier.

14 ■ *The Producers*
Not Just Another Funny Picture

The myth that the director is the sole creator of his film is a burden on almost everyone in the movie business, including the director, who frequently becomes weighed down by the excess responsibility, incapable of generating a team spirit, afraid to delegate authority, or unable to graciously accept the contributions of the expert collaborators he has summoned to his side.

With a first-time director the pressure of this myth is magnified, especially if he has no film experience, as is often the case. Ashamed to expose his ignorance, he may resist asking the cameraman to "shoot it the way Altman did in *Nashville*" and instead insist on numerous and frustrating retakes in which no one understands his dissatisfaction. If he is insecure and defensive about the degree of dependence he feels on all the experienced professionals around him, and if the production manager, the cameraman, the set director, the editor, or one of the stars is inclined to counter his defensive behavior by subtly making an issue of his dependency, the scene is set for flashes of paranoia, or what the industry gingerly refers to as "psychotic episodes."

Mel Brooks's first film, *The Producers,* is the story of Max Bialystock (Zero Mostel) and Leo Bloom (Gene Wilder), one a seedy, corrupt, over-the-hill Broadway producer who seduces old ladies in order to get them to invest in his awful productions, the other a whimpering, neurotic accountant who falls under his sway. Together they conspire to produce "the worst play ever written," overfinance it by 25,000 percent, and then pocket the excess investments when the play closes. The scheme depends on a sure-fire flop that will fold in one night, and after a laborious search the pair settles on a play by a fanatical Nazi called *Springtime for Hitler: A Gay Romp with Adolf and Eva at Berchtesgaden.* When the timorous Bloom becomes antsy about the project, Bialystock bellows at him, calls him a "white mouse," and insists that he has "taken steps to make sure that *Springtime for Hitler* will be a total disaster" by hiring Roger De Bris, "the worst director that ever lived."

De Bris turns out to be a flaming transvestite with a snippish, catty male "private secretary" named Carmen Giya. Bialystock asks De Bris if he's had a chance to read the play, and De Bris responds "Remarkable! A stunning piece of work. . . . I, for one, never realized that the Third Reich meant Germany! I mean it's drenched with historical goodies like that!" Disaster is further courted by casting Lorenzo Saint DuBois (L.S.D.), a mind-blown acid-head straight out of Sing-Sing who never stops blathering about love and flower power, to play a hip Hitler who dances his way to oblivion. On opening night Bialystock gleefully drives the "last nail in the coffin" by wrapping a hundred-dollar bill around the complimentary tickets he gives to the outraged critic from *The New York Times.*

At first aghast at the production—which includes a chorus line of busty blond storm troopers who kick their legs and sing, "Don't be shtupid, be a shmarty, come and join the Nazi Party!"—the audience gradually begins to chuckle, then to laugh uproariously, as they interpret the whole play as a gigantic farce. Desperate at the prospect of imminent success, Bialystock and Bloom dynamite the theater, but are apprehended in the act, found "incredibly guilty" by an indignant jury, and sent to the state penitentiary, where they launch "Prisoners of Love," a musical production financed by the investments of the prisoners and the warden—and shamelessly oversubscribed.

From the first page to the last, Brooks's script was loaded with enough hilarious material to keep a reader laughing aloud almost continuously. It was an extraordinary screenplay, and two years later it won an Oscar—although the film itself was so crudely shot and edited that, seen today, it looks almost prehistoric.

Better known as a writer, Brooks was himself a natural performer who would grab almost any opportunity to go into an impromptu act. Those of us who were meeting him for the first time found him a very funny, very eager man, someone we knew by reputation for his work on Sid Caesar's "Your Show of Shows" and for his "2000-Year-Old Man" records, who was now full of nervous energy about directing his first script.

"He came to my office, a small guy who looked very nervous, and started to tell jokes, some of which weren't too funny, and I was a little uncomfortable," remembers producer Sidney Glazier. "But finally he told me he had an idea, and I subsequently learned that he had been trying to get it sold for three years and nobody would give him an opportunity to direct. It was called *Springtime for Hitler*—and if it had remained *Springtime for Hitler*, it would have made several million dollars—but we had a Jewish distributor by the name of Joseph Levine who insisted that the Jews would be up in arms, so we reluctantly changed the title to a banal thing called *The Producers*. In any case, Mel stood in front of my desk and did the movie. I was drinking coffee in a paper cup and I began to laugh. I began to choke. He did the movie from beginning to end. He acted every part—he did the fag, everything—and my sides hurt when he finished. You know how Mel is when he's really on. And I said, *I'll do it*. I didn't know where the hell I was going to get the money, but I said I'll do it, I'll do it, and that's how it began."

Cameraman Joe Coffey was invited to Glazier's office to meet Mel by production manager Jack Grossberg. "I was very impressed by his friendliness and warmth," says Coffey. "We discussed the possibility of me doing the film and he gave me the script and I went home to read it. He told me he had seen *Up the Down Staircase* and that he was very impressed with how I had photographed it. I became very enthusiastic, and Mel was very up, asking me all kinds of questions about what I'd done, how I'd done certain things, and so forth. And then there ensued a series of meetings with the design director, Chuck Rosen. Chuck made a series of drawings based on every set from every point of view. He drew in the furniture and the doorways and the windows, and we pondered them and we said, we'll put the camera here, and we'll move it over here when Bialystock says this, and we'll move it here when the old lady kisses him, and Mel was just wildly enthusiastic. He fired my enthusiasm and Chuck's, and as usual, I fell in love with the director. My wife keeps telling me every time I have a disaster in a relationship with somebody in the film business, *you schmuck,* you must stop falling in love with these people, they're all hideous killers! But Mel exhibited such marvelous enthusiasm for my ideas, and he was so receptive to Chuck's contribution. . . . Well, at any rate, this love feast went on for, I don't know, five or six weeks. We would meet and talk about how we were going to make the world's greatest comedy, and I would go home and tell Arlene, 'Oh, Mel is so terrific, he's so receptive.' And meanwhile my ego was becoming more and more inflated—more than usual."

Production day was one month off when Jack Grossberg summoned me to Glazier's office for my first meeting with Mel. Mel was very serious. He spoke at length about the contribution I had made to *A Thousand Clowns,* and he said he wanted a relationship with me similar to the one I had had with Gardner. He touched just the right note when he suggested a collaboration of equals, and like Joe Coffey, I was immediately impressed and optimistic.

By the end of the first morning on the set, Mel was already becoming jittery. His only previous production experience had been in live television where everything proceeded at a much faster, more hectic pace. Each installment started on Tuesday; the writers, directors, producers, and stars polished, rehearsed, rewrote, and rearranged as they went along; and the whole thing climaxed on Saturday with a dress rehearsal and then The Air. Was Mel prepared for the differences between TV and film? Did he know that in movies you can only shoot about five minutes of usable film a day? That most of the time on the set is spent waiting and preparing? That, as the director, he would be faced with an avalanche of demands from subordinates responsible for all the intricate aspects of production?

The film director is like a general advancing an army along a broad front. There are ten to fifteen people working on a scene that will be shot tomorrow, or perhaps next Thursday, when production will move outside for location work. The director has to approve their plans so they can proceed. The set director comes in with a sample of wallpaper or a piece of drapery for Friday's scene. The production manager has a money problem that needs immediate attention. Someone else has a logistical question of some kind, perhaps regarding a city regulation on shooting at a certain location. Whatever his expectations, these time-consuming demands weighed heavily on Mel. He couldn't stand the pestering and he couldn't stand the waiting. And because he resisted delegating authority, the demands increased and the delays lengthened.

His inclination was to spend most of his time working with the actors. He would rehearse Mostel and Wilder to the point where he had them doing exactly what he wanted, and then he would turn around, ready to shoot. Joe Coffey, who'd been standing by doing nothing all this time, would say, "Mel, where do you want the camera?" Suddenly Mel realized that he should have conferred with Coffey an hour and a half ago, before he began rehearsing. Now he will have to watch the clock while the electricians slowly arrange all the lights, his actors get cold, and an inner voice whispers that he's falling rapidly behind schedule, that people are resisting him, and that Levine is going to take away his "points" in the picture, or maybe even the picture itself.

"On the second day of shooting, right after lunch, Mel came up to me and said, 'Joe, I'm very worried.' I said, 'What are you worried about?' He said, 'Well, everything seems to be taking so much time.' I said, 'What do you mean?' He said, 'Well, you put the camera *here*, and then it takes time, you put it over *here*, and then you're turning lights on, and then you're having the guys turn lights off, and they're putting those sticks up and those little black flags—and this is taking so much time. I'm really worried, we're a half a day behind already.' This was the middle of the second day. Of a ten-week schedule. We're a half a day behind! So I said, 'Well, Mel, you know it takes time to make movies. You got to move furniture, you got to move walls.' 'Yeah,' he said, 'you're pulling these walls out and you're putting those walls back again—what is all that about? Why don't you do it like we do it in television? When you're shooting in that direction, you just turn on all the lights that are going that way. Then when you're shooting in this direction, you turn those off and you turn on the lights that're going in this direction?' What could I say? I said, 'I'll go as fast as I can.' But early on in the making of the film I realized that there was a sudden abrupt change from the receptive, outgoing, fun-and-loving kind of experience that we'd had in the preparation stage."

Mel's impatience quickly extended to the cast, and he soon found himself in a head-on conflict with the mountainous Mostel. The first time Zero couldn't perform with just the inflection Mel wanted, Mel saw the entire project slipping from his grasp. After several faulty takes, he started to shout, "*Goddam it*, why can't you . . ." but Mostel turned his head like a roving artillery gun and barked, "One more tone like that and I'm leaving."

By the end of the first week, Brooks and Mostel headed two enemy camps. On one side was the enormous booming actor with a presence, a range, and an inclination to go overboard with semicomic ad-lib insult that could wither an innocent recipient to his ankles. On the other, a short, sinewy, panther-eyed director whose operating temperature was each day rising closer and closer to his flash point. "Is that fat pig ready yet?" Mel would sputter. "The director?" said Zero. "What director? There's a director here? *That's* a director?"

The tense mood soon enveloped every aspect of the production. The actors found the overwrought director repeatedly dissatisfied with their performances. He began to insult and batter them, and sometimes his impatience became merciless. He seemed to feel that the crew, who inevitably had many idle moments, were malingering, and this aroused their resentment. He nearly blew an interview with a reporter from the *Times:* "What the fuck do *you* want!" he asked the astonished woman, as Sidney Glazier, eager for the publicity, sank into despair. At lunchtime when the gofer wrote down the orders, Mel rushed over to supervise: the roast beef gets the Russian dressing, don't forget the mustard on the side, make sure they're the new pickles, not the old, the half-sour pickles, two sugars for every coffee, remember Glazier gets the lean brisket. . . .

In a Viennese-style café called the Blue Gypsy Max Bialystock charms one of the love-starved old ladies who invest in his productions. He whispers in her ear and she draws back giggling: "You're incorrigible, Bialy!" They raise their champagne glasses. She: "Here's to the success of your new play." Bialystock: "*Our* play, my love." They entwine their arms in a disastrously executed toast that ends with her spilling the champagne down his vest. She: "Oh, Bialy, I'm so sorry. Did I wet you?" Bialystock: "Think nothing of it, my dear. A mere trifle, a mere trifle. Did you bring the checkee?" She: "Oh, yes. I have it right here in my purse, and I made it out just as you told me—to

'Cash.' That's a funny name for a play," she adds as she takes out the check.

Suddenly Mel bursts in making gestures as if to pull his hair out. Fourteen times they've gone this far and fourteen times he's cut the action. It's something about the way she says "Cash" or the way she clutches the check to her bosom after kissing it. Involuntary flickers of desperation are twitching on her face now, but Mel can only see the dollar signs floating by. Every day costs twenty thousand dollars. That's twenty-five hundred an hour. How many delays can he endure before the investors muscle in? A fifteenth take and the actress is in tears.

"Oh, yes. I have it right here in my purse, and I made it out just as you told me—to 'Cash.' That's a funny name for a play." "Think nothing of it, my dear," says the implacable Mostel, but before he can get the check from her, the roving violinist reaches their table and serenades the old buzzard. Angered by the intrusion, Bialystock refills his glass with champagne and dispenses the rest of the bottle's contents by pouring it down the violinist's trousers. Carried away by his own performance, the minstrel is slow to realize his predicament, but when he does, his rapt expression sours and he slinks away from the table. As the victorious Bialystock seizes the check from the old lady's breast, Mel again rushes in boiling with disapproval. For the umpteenth time the violinist failed to achieve the perfect reaction of anguish and surprise when he realized his pants were wet. The initial amusement of the observers on the set had by now turned to dismay and embarrassment, for none of us could understand the director's displeasure. Zero had to empty some twenty bottles down the poor man's groin before Brooks relented.

"I think Mel probably suffered more than anyone else in the making of that movie," says producer Glazier, who spent many hours with Brooks after work, sometimes till early in the morning because Mel had difficulty sleeping. "At the end of the day his face would turn gray from fatigue."

In the mornings at eight-thirty we viewed the dailies from the day before, and Glazier, himself a hothead and the one person in a position to criticize Mel and remind him of the financial imperative to keep moving, learned during the first week to refrain from mentioning any flaws he saw in the material. "There were certain things you just couldn't say to him," says Glazier, who survived the film with an affection for Brooks that lasts to this day. "Mike Hertzberg"—the assistant director—"said more to him than anybody, because Mike worked for him. Mike was his boy, his assistant, and more often than not Mel would listen to him. But everybody else was a threat. Everybody else was the enemy. There was always a moment when you felt he would kill you. His face would turn white, his jaw would come out—and it was not so much a question of physical fear; how could you fear him? He was a little guy. But he terrified me, because I always felt he was going to do something that would blow the picture."

One day as Mel was about to launch yet another of his tormented takes, he walked over to Sidney, who was biting his lip on the sidelines, and told him he could not endure his presence on the set. Glazier's first reaction was to say, "I'm the producer, I'm *staying*." But he thought better of antagonizing Mel, and left the set for good.

While Glazier learned patience, many of Mel's subordinates became more alienated. When Mel displayed his insecurity or his ignorance, as first-time directors often do, it had a way of eliciting the very sort of sneering superiority that first-time directors fear. Joe Coffey, who had occasionally gotten into trouble with directors who had interpreted his enthusiasm as an affront to their leadership, was unable to play the diplomat. "There was one instance early in the film where Zero had to make an entrance into his office and sit down at his desk. So I said, 'Why don't we take the camera near the door, so that when the door swings open, there'll be a nice big close-up of that incredible head and face. And as he moves toward us, we'll dolly back and pull into this alcove and pan him over to the desk.' So Mel thought about it for a minute, and he said, 'He's going to be speaking when he's walking.' I said, 'Yeah, right.' So he said, 'But the camera will be moving when he's speaking.' And I said, 'Yeah, you know, we'll start on a tight head, and we'll get wider and wider and we'll pan. . . .' He said, 'But you can't have the camera moving while he's speaking— they won't pay any attention to the words.' I didn't quite know how to answer that. I said, 'But you don't understand, he'll be close to the camera, and he'll be talking, and it'll only get to be a wide shot as he goes by in the middle of the room, and then we'll pan to the desk.' He said, 'But the camera will be moving while he's talking.' I said, 'Absolutely.' And he said, 'No, we can't have that, they won't pay any attention to the words.' So I said, 'What do you want to do? How should we bring him into the room?' He said, 'Let's put the camera back in that alcove where you were going to dolly into and we'll just make a little bit of a pan as he goes by.' I said, 'You'll lose all the impact of that great face in a close-up!' "

Back and forth they argued, with Mel growing firmer and firmer in his determination to start the scene with a long shot and a stationary camera and apparently more and more certain that Coffey's disagreement represented not a desire to make his best contribution to the picture but an effort to enhance the photography at the expense of the script. Incensed at Mel's arbitrary rule, Coffey finally blew up. "There must've been fifty to sixty people. And I don't use words like this very often, because I think it's really kind of pretentious, but I screamed out, 'You can't do that, *it's not cinematic*!' And that was the end of our romance."

From then on the tone of their conversations worsened, and their relationship ground to a standoff. "I did my job," says Coffey, "I lit the sets. But my heart wasn't in it."

By the second week we had become aware of two Mels. There was the Mel who did five minutes of ad-lib routines in the morning for the grips and electricians until fifteen people had put their coffees down for fear of spilling them. The Mel who would jump out of the car in the middle of a traffic jam on the way to a location shoot, run over to a stranger's car, knock on the window, point to himself and say, "*Mel Brooks. The Two-Thousand-Year-Old Man. Recognize Me?*" The Mel who on the way to the studio in the morning with a carful of technicians, cameramen, and assistants would take everybody's order with a pencil and paper, and then, with the car double-parked outside the Chock Full O' Nuts at Eighth Avenue and Fifty-seventh Street, run inside, say good morning to the last person on line—"Do you recognize me? I'm Mel Brooks. The Two-Thousand-Year-Old Man, famous comedian, Hollywood director"—and, as the crew watched in hysteria, make his way, one by one, to the front of the line, telling the secretaries, the Con Ed men, the store clerks about his schedule and his budget, his distributor and his points, his men waiting outside, and emerge with a giant bagful of breakfast. And then there was the other Mel, the Mel who seemed to feel he was being ganged up on by the pros, who felt exposed and isolated, who with barely a transition would become angry and tyrannical, whose neck would stretch and tighten and eyes bulge until, as Sidney Glazier remembers, you were sure he would attack you.

■

We were close to the end of the second week when I realized I was wasting my time on the set. There's a widespread belief that the editor serves a function on the set, but I've always found this untrue—my only contribution during the shooting of the film comes during the dailies, and I'd prefer to look at them with a fresh mind, unencumbered and unprejudiced by the high spirits or conflicts that dominated the shooting. Until now I had witnessed all the tirades, but none of them had involved me, so I was still relatively balanced when I said, "Mel, don't you think I should be putting some film together?" He quickly agreed, and I spent the next two weeks assembling a rough cut of the first twenty minutes of the picture. Since this was a very primitive film in which everything depended on the words and acting, the editing was very basic and uncomplicated. Choices were few; in most cases the scene was funniest with full shots of both characters, and I think almost any editor would have cut it the same way. Indeed, when the movie was finished, 90 percent of the first two reels remained just as I'd put them together in the initial assembly.

I screened the segment for Mel and Sidney at the Movielab screening room. For the first time in Mel's directorial career, he was about to see a fantasy of his in somewhat finished form. For most directors this is a difficult moment because what they see on the screen after the editor has assembled it almost never lives up to their dreams. I realize now that this was a major factor in Helen van Dongen's frustrations with Robert Flaherty, who stalled and stalled and sometimes even took the uncut film away from her. In addition to revealing the inherent shortcomings of the picture, the first rough cut lacks the refinements—the sound editing, the opticals, the finishing touches—that do so much to make a movie come alive. And if just one line doesn't work, if just one transition is weak, it weighs the picture down, deadening everything for the next four or five minutes. But for the beginning director, watching this first assembly is even more painful, because he can't allow for the enormous difference that the refinements will make—he's never had the experience of transforming a dragging first cut into a dazzling finished film.

When the screening was over, Mel stomped to the front of the room to make a statement. I was about eight rows back and Glazier was somewhere behind me. "*You just listen to me,*" he growled. He was furious. He was pointing his finger at me with hideous intensity. "I don't want you to touch this fuckin' film again! You understand? I just finished with Coffey this afternoon—I told him I don't need his help, and I don't need your help either! I'll do it all myself! Don't you touch this film—you hear!—don't *touch* it, until I finish shooting!"

I was very shaken. No one had ever spoken to me like that. I trembled with anger most of the way home, which at this time consisted of a drive to New Rochelle. I gave a lift to Glazier, who was certain he'd never see me again. All the way he shook his head and mumbled, "I don't know why Mel has to do this. Why does he have to make it so difficult?" To Glazier's disbelief, I didn't quit. Quitting never occurred to me. I stayed on like everyone else. And like everyone else, I harbored a thickening knot of resentment.

For several weeks I sulked. I stayed off the set and only appeared for the dailies. And even after I began feeling even again, I had no work to do. I hung around, watched Mel lose his temper, chew out Wilder, chew out Coffey, saw the cast and the crew looking and behaving more and more like whipped dogs, and had plenty of time to imagine what our weeks in the cutting room would be like.

On the first day of editing, Mel arrived in the cutting room at about nine-thirty, a quarter to ten, preceded by an enormous white bag full of coffee, crullers, and doughnuts, and began a ritual that was repeated every day thereafter. With my two assistants and me seated at our benches, Mel pulled out coffees and sugars, napkins and stirrers, and bustled about the room serving us. Each day he brought twenty or thirty extra packets of sugar, which he forbade us to throw out. He stuffed them into all accessible drawers, and there they accumulated until the picture was completed and I had some two hundred pounds of sugar to dispose of.

The mornings were slow because Mel had a hard time waking up. As he worked on his two cups of coffee, he'd free-associate, improvise little skits, tell jokes, do word games, and generally carry on. An intuitive and compulsive entertainer, he would come alive before an audience of three hundred or just three. He'd put on his hilarious Russian Jewish accent—"Did you maybe hear da vone about . . ."—and we'd start to smile, anticipating the antics to come. His eyes would twinkle, he'd cock his head, he'd look like a dirty old man with suspect candy. He'd become manic, fly around the room with his arms waving and eyes bulging, suddenly become a little old man again, a vendor on Orchard Street, a weaseling schemer, a pontificating rabbi, a sleazy seducer, or Super-Jew with a J on his pajamas. He would carry on this way for about an hour, and, as far as I could tell, he had no memory whatever of the tongue-lashing he'd given me two months earlier. The only thing that would spoil his show would be an unexpected intrusion, a messenger or someone from the lab, at which point he would draw back, looking a bit disturbed and mistrustful.

Once he paused in the middle of one of his routines and looked intensely at the ashtray sitting beside him on an end table. I was at my desk, drinking my coffee and expecting another funny line. Suddenly Mel's hand tightened around the ashtray, his face got very tense, and he looked up and screamed, "Next time it's going to be *my* ashtray, goddam it! It's going to be *my* desk, *my* telephone, *my* couch, *my* Moviola, *my* equipment, *my* supplies! Next time you're going to be in *my* office GODDAMN IT!" Then his face relaxed, he glanced casually about the room, and went back to drinking his coffee and thinking up jokes.

By eleven o'clock Mel would be ready to look at some film. But not with the cold eye of an experienced director. This was his first movie, the project he'd been pampering for three years, and he could not find the proper distance. He was unable to look at the film he'd shot as the new given, the material out of which he would now create his movie. Instead he griped about how Joe Coffey screwed him here by taking too damn long, or how Zero never did get that line right, or why didn't he think to do it this way with that actor. This would go on for a couple of hours and then we'd go to lunch. No film was ever cut in the morning.

My cutting rooms were now on Eighth Avenue and Fifty-fourth Street, so we'd usually end up going to the nearby Carnegie Delicatessen to eat. There, on the average day, you can bump into Marshall Brickman or Paddy Chayevsky or Herb Gardner, any number of show-business writers and entertainers that Mel knew and with whom he'd schmooze and exchange bits. He threw funny lines at the waiter, fooled around with a new waitress, and let everybody know he'd arrived. He was really on now, bursting with playfulness, competitiveness, aggression, and a lusty satisfaction at being recognized by one and all. During one of the early lunches, he ordered a whitefish salad, nudged the waiter, and said confidentially, "Tell 'em it's for Mel Brooks."

We usually returned from the Carnegie by two o'clock, and now Mel was fully awake. Awake enough to know he had frittered away the morning. Awake enough to feel the dissatisfaction over all the flaws that were going to keep this film from looking like a major-league production. Awake enough to realize that he had some very boring hours and weeks of work ahead, moving at the torpid cutting-room pace that was anathema to him. Awake enough to remember and resent his dependence on me. In any case, the fun and games were over. He was ready to "kill."

Mel hated to be told that he could cut directly from A to C and do without B altogether. He couldn't stand the thought that a line, a glance, or, worse, an entire scene was superfluous. Statements of this sort were a direct attack, a suggestion that he'd been a fool to shoot the way he'd shot in the first place. Perhaps he really did not know that every director goes through this process in the editing stage, that material that once seemed essential was trimmed away like so much fat, that favored lines or moments often proved pointless or redundant. In any case, he became angry, raucous, combative. Although his belligerence was rarely aimed directly at me, I felt sullied by it and withdrew into a tighter, colder, more severe professional stance that could only have increased his resentment. It was not in me to say, "You're right, Mel, Zero really did screw you there." I refused to behave like a servant, to give in to his extreme emotional demands. The very thought of moving in that direction brought forth all the secret professional hurts I harbored. I felt I was being invited to play the time-honored role of the editor as the director's valet. In defense, I became impatient with Mel's ignorance and hesitance, and, I imagine, Mel saw in this all the arrogance that embittered him against the veteran pros.

Bialystock and Bloom spot Franz Liebkind on the roof of his tenement talking to his pigeons. Liebkind is the author of *Springtime for Hitler*, the play that the partners are convinced is their "guaranteed-to-close-in-one-night beauty."

> BLOOM (quietly to Bialystock): He's wearing a German helmet.
>
> BIALYSTOCK: Shhh. Don't say anything to offend him. We need the play. . . . Franz Liebkind?
>
> LIEBKIND (startled, cringing against his pigeon coop): I vas never a member of the Nazi Party. I am not responsible. I only followed orders. Who are you? Vhy do you persecute me? My papers are in order. I luf my adopted country! (He salutes and starts to sing.) Oh beautiful, for spacious skies, for amber vaves of grain . . . Vat do you vant?

BIALYSTOCK: Relax, relax, Mr. Liebkind. We're not from the government. We came here to talk to you about your play.

LIEBKIND: My play? You mean *Springtime for You-Know-Who?*

Bialystock tells him that the play is a masterpiece and that he wants to produce it on Broadway. Liebkind screams, "Oh joy of joys!" and rushes to tell the birds: "Otto, Bertz, Heintz, Hans, Volfgang, do you hear? Ve are going to clear the Führer's name!" He then begins singing "Deutschland Über Alles" very boisterously until Bloom reminds him that people may be listening, whereupon he switches abruptly to "I'm a Yankee Doodle Dandy." The trio then repair to Liebkind's apartment to celebrate the occasion with a Schnapps.

LIEBKIND (as he passes Bloom and Bialystock their drinks): Gentlemen, with your permission, I would like to propose a toast to the greatest man that ever lived. Let us say his name quietly to ourselves. The walls have ears. (He whispers) Adolf Hitler. (He downs his drink.)

BLOOM (whispers): Sigmund Freud. (He downs his drink.)

BIALYSTOCK (whispers):   Max Bialystock. (He downs his drink.)

LIEBKIND: I vas vit him a great deal, you know.

BIALYSTOCK: With whom?

LIEBKIND (astonished by the question): Vit the Fuhrer, of course. He liked me. Out of all the household staff at Berchtesgaden, I vas his favorite. I vas the only one allowed into his chambers at bedtime.

BIALYSTOCK: No kidding?

LIEBKIND: Oh, sure. I used to take him his hot milk and his opium. Achhh, those ver the days. Vat good times ve had. Dinner parties vit lovely ladies and gentlemen, singing and dancing. You know, not many people knew about it, but the Führer vas a terrific dancer.

Rosenblum (approximately): *That's* your opening line, Mel. You bring them from the roof into the apartment and right to Liebkind telling them what a wonderful dancer the Führer was.

Brooks (approximately): Those goddamned sons of bitches. They ruined it. That fat pig! He had to play it *his* way. If I ever get ahold of him I'll kick his head in!

The material shot in Liebkind's apartment worked magnificently on paper, but, for whatever reason, turned out flat on film. It killed Mel to lose a word. And here he lost over a hundred.

Liebkind goes into a tirade about Allied propaganda, reaching a crescendo on the subject of the disgusting adulation it paid to Winston Churchill.

> LIEBKIND: But let me tell you this, and you're getting it straight from da horse. Hitler vas better looking dan Churchill. He vas a better dresser dan Churchill, had more hair, he told funnier jokes, and could dance the pants off Churchill!

> BIALYSTOCK: Yes, yes. (Mock snarl) Churchill! That's exactly why we want to do this play. To show the world the true Hitler, the Hitler you knew, the Hitler you loved, the Hitler with a song in his heart!

Liebkind is so touched by Bialystock's speech, he begins to sing. The partners join in as Bialystock pulls out a contract and Bloom a pen.

> BIALYSTOCK: Here, Franz Liebkind, sign here and make your dream a reality.

Rosenblum (approximately): That's where you want to cut, Mel. We'll drop the Siegfried oath, the Wagner music, the blood-ritual, and go straight to Mostel and Wilder on the sidewalk gloating over the contract.

Brooks (approximately): But that's half the scene. You're talking about half the fuckin' scene!

Mel could not stop thinking about the wonderful laughs the Siegfried oath had always gotten when *he* performed it. About Liebkind, Bialystock, and Bloom in their outlandish Wagnerian helmets, complete with horns, horns that no one would ever see now. No matter what portion of the film had to come out—and ultimately everything that needed to came out—he was neither appreciative nor cooperative, but behaved as if he were losing a relative, like an hysterical aunt at a Jewish funeral who throws herself onto the coffin as it's going into the hole. His clutching and resistance stretched an eight-week editing job into six months.

Once I came up with a transition that transported Mostel and Wilder from Bialystock's office into the street and on their way to lunch, a transition that eliminated some unnecessary geography and created a piece of visual humor in its place. Mel was placated for only a moment. Only until it registered that someone was taking his film away, that he was losing control. When he found his response—"Who wants a joke by a fuckin' editor?"—he said it as if he wished to see the whole editing profession exterminated.

When he became frustrated, when he saw something in the acting he didn't like, when he recalled an affront by Joe Coffey or Zero Mostel, or when he became upset with his own little failures, he abandoned himself to anger with no apparent thought of the effect he was having on those around him. He always seemed ready to explode, and we never knew what would ignite him or what form the explosion would take. Once he erupted by throwing every object within reach across my two rooms—grease pencils, film cannisters, tape dispensers, the ashtray that would one day be his ashtray—as my burly assistant, an angry young man who used to speak with glee about the sensual pleasure he took in axing down doors during his weekend stints as a volunteer fireman on Long Island, hid behind the draperies at the window.

Only once did I shout back at Mel and reprimand him for his behavior. Mel calmed right down, looked a little contrite, and then went back to whatever he was doing, as if nothing had happened. I realized then that while shouting matches left me debilitated for hours or days, to Mel they were an accepted everyday phenomenon. He could demean, insult, or threaten you one moment—or suffer the same sort of treatment himself—and return to business as usual the next. This awareness did me little good, however, for I felt violated by his rancor and moodiness until the last day of cutting.

A midnight preview of *The Producers* was held in the fall of 1967 at what is now the Playboy Theatre on Fifty-seventh Street. Hundreds of people attended, including scores of Mel's show-business friends and Joseph E. Levine with his entourage from Embassy Pictures. For fifteen minutes Mel stood in front of the crowded room and performed. The audience was in a state of utter comic delight before the film ever began.

An hour and a half later Mel stood in back of the theater as all his friends shook his hand, kissed him, and congratulated him. He spotted me coming up the aisle with Davida. It was a month since we'd been in the cutting room and I had already begun work on *Minsky's*. My distaste for him was still strong, though, and I had no intention to stop and chat. Mel shook himself loose from the crowd and came over to us. He said something pleasant to Davida, then put his arm around me and led me away. He walked me out into the early morning street, down the block toward Sixth Avenue, and away from the stragglers. "Thanks for making it look professional," he whispered. And that was the last I ever saw of him.

Ali MacGraw, Jack Klugman, Richard Benjamin, and
Monroe Arnold as Uncle Leo in the wedding scene
from GOODBYE COLUMBUS.
(Courtesy Paramount Pictures)

15 ■ *Goodbye Columbus*
The Face on the Cutting-Room Floor

> The more an actor knows about films, the more he
> realizes his helplessness, the more he therefore will
> seek to control the selection of story, director, and
> cameraman, as well as that process of
> ultimate demolition known as editing.
> —JOSEF VON STERNBERG

In 1927 Stalin banished arch-rival Leon Trotsky from the Soviet Union and thus helped initiate a new and unhappy twist in the editing of films. Sergei Eisenstein, who had just completed the final cut of *Ten Days That Shook the World*, a picture about the Bolshevik rise to power in which Trotsky figured heavily, was now compelled to re-edit the film for the sole purpose of purging every trace of the vanquished Soviet hero. An ordeal for Eisenstein and an affront to history, it was the sorriest cut of all for the luckless actor who played the young Leon Trotsky. He no doubt realized, as many actors have learned since, that in film as in revolutions even a star performance is a very vulnerable thing.

In recent years, as directors have relied more heavily on editing as the means of determining the shape and substance of their pictures, an increasing number of actors have suffered Trotsky's fate—seeing their contributions slashed, distorted, or entirely discarded during the ever lengthening periods that modern films spend in the cutting room. Paul Richards' disappearance as Chuckles the Chipmunk from *A Thousand Clowns* is an extreme but not altogether unique occurrence. During the editing of John Frankenheimer's 1968 film, *The Fixer*, the director made a late revision in the script that eliminated one of the key male characters, and supporting actor Jack Gilford saw several months' labor hit the cutting-room floor. In both *Godfather* films major performances by Diane Keaton (as Al Pacino's wife) were whittled down to insignificance. While in *Annie Hall*, the film that finally made Keaton a star, a half dozen other performances—including Colleen Dewhurst's biggest scene—were decimated or lost completely as the plot changed in the editing.

On the face of it, film offers great advantages to actors. It permanently records their work, making their best efforts available for generations. It can spread a single tour-de-force performance before millions, thereby generating immediate recognition or stardom. Never have so many actors been so well known to so many people. And yet, largely because of the power of editing, the actor's importance to the over-all production—compared to what it has been in the theater—is greatly diminished in film. His heightened vulnerability and dependency never struck me so profoundly as in the cutting of *Goodbye Columbus*.

Monroe Arnold is a mid-sized, jowly Jewish actor with an eager generosity and a loquaciousness that, once in high gear, vibrates through his cheeks, achieving at peak moments an urgent, rheumy inflection. In 1969, when he was thirty-six years old and plodding up through the ranks of minor character actors in television, theater, and film, he ran into Larry Peerce, with whom he had recently worked on a "Dick Tracy" TV pilot. Peerce reported that he was about to direct a film version of Philip Roth's popular novella, *Goodbye Columbus*. "I said *terrific*," recalls Monroe, "and I said, 'I may as well ask you the question now so we can have a normal conversation: Is there a part in it for me?' "

Peerce was noncommittal, but he had an idea that his friend might be right for the part of Uncle Leo. Uncle Leo is a secondary but important character. He appears only in the wedding scene, about two-thirds of the way through the story, but he dominates that scene and is highly memorable.

Peerce believed that Uncle Leo was a man full of suppressed rage, and he thought Monroe Arnold had enough anger in him to do that rage justice. But he had doubts—would the studio insist on a name actor? should he cast someone who would give the part a funnier edge?—and because of these doubts he was reluctant to put up a fight when his producer, Stanley Jaffe, also expressed reservations. "I want you to stay and work with me until I can smooth the whole thing out with Stanley," is what Monroe remembers Peerce saying. And so, until a date was set for his own tryout, he worked with Peerce, helping him cast the other actors and hoping that through his physical presence he would become an inevitability. "I had never met Stanley Jaffe," says Monroe. "I was told he was very young and a heavyweight business kind of guy, and this made me very nervous. So I asked Larry, 'What am I supposed to do?' And Larry said, 'Make him laugh, get him upset, and then make him laugh again.' And I said, 'O.K., I'll do it.' "

Monroe was received for his tryout like any other actor. Jack Weston, a successful, rotund character actor who had played in the TV series "The Hathaways," as well as a half dozen movies—usually as a bumbling penny-ante gangster—was in the waiting room when Monroe arrived. "I thought to myself, 'Oh my God, if this guy is here, and that's the caliber of the people they're calling, how am I going to get the part? What the hell are they doing to me?' And all the other paranoid thoughts that jump into your mind."

After Weston left, Monroe rose to go in, reminding himself of Peerce's instructions. "There were a couple of steps down as you entered the office, so I threw myself down those steps and landed flat." Stretched out near Jaffe's and Peerce's feet, he looked up and, brimming with Donald Duckish earnestness, said, "Oh, hello, Mr. Jaffe!" Jaffe was amused. "God, I can't control my feet I'm so nervous!" squeaked Monroe, and this slapstick absurdity burst the otherwise tense moment; Peerce and Jaffe looked at each other and started to laugh.

"Then I jumped up and sat down on the couch and said, 'Let's be dead serious. How much are you going to pay me for this part?' At that Stanley's face got very long, and he mumbled and grumbled and said, 'Discuss money with me, mumble, mutter,' and I said, 'Sure I'm going to discuss money with you. If you think I'm going to take this goddam part without being paid . . .' and so on and so forth." Then, says Monroe, as Jaffe looked on in astonishment, "I gasped and clutched at my heart, and said, 'Oh my God! . . . Oh! . . . Ah! . . .

Oh!' and fell off the couch." The young producer became very agitated. "What's the matter?" he said. "Nothing!" said the triumphant actor with Romper Room glee. "I *fooled* you! I *fooled* you!" Jaffe started laughing again and said, "You son of a bitch, you got the part!"

Goodbye Columbus is the story of Neil Klugman, a sensitive but aimless college dropout (played by Richard Benjamin) whose wisecracking obscures an uncertain idealism. Neil, who works in a library and comes from a poor Jewish family in a working class section of the Bronx (Newark in the book), falls in love with Brenda Patimkin (played by Ali MacGraw), a perky, self-confident beauty of the suburban Jewish *nouveau riche*. They have a summer love affair, much to the chagrin of her status-conscious parents; he spends two weeks as a houseguest at the Patimkin's manorlike home during which he and Brenda secretly make love every night; he accompanies her to her brother's wedding, where he overhears her boozed father pledge his everlasting love and support for his princess; and they break up in the fall after Brenda allows her mother to discover her diaphragm in her bureau drawer. It was a love powered by an enormous lust and passion, a love that flickered and then died in an instant.

The emotional turning point is the opulent wedding scene in which Neil gets a failed-life speech from the rapidly deteriorating Uncle Leo. Leo is crushed by the disparity between his station in life and that of his brother, Brenda's father. Reading the story or the script, one senses that Leo, whose financial status is not that distant from Neil's, is an ugly reminder to the younger man of the threat that Brenda poses to his identity. Embracing Brenda and her comfortable world may seduce Neil into denying his own background and values. Perhaps, in some unseen way, the process has already begun.

Like a cryptic, ancient seer clothed in rags and covered with sores, Leo attaches himself to Neil and, with great self-serving pathos, unloads his disappointment and pain. Arnold Schulman's dialogue (with additions by Monroe Arnold) was adapted almost verbatim from Roth.

> LEO: You're Brenda's boy friend, huh? (He nudges Neil confidentially.) You got a good deal there, boy, don't louse it up.
>
> NEIL: She's very beautiful.

LEO: Beautiful, not beautiful, what's the difference? You're Aly Khan you worry about movie stars. I'm a practical man. On the bottom, you got to be.

Leo is a traveling salesman who makes less than a cabby and doesn't even own a car. "*His* brother, and I don't even own an automobile." He tells Neil that only two good things have ever happened to him, one being a low-rent apartment his mother-in-law found for him in Queens after the war and the other the oral-genital affections of Hannah Schreiber, a schoolteacher "with long, slim Christian legs and a Jewish bust," whom he met one night while still in the army. At one point, for no apparent reason, he blurts, "I'm the only guy I know who wears out three pairs of rubbers every winter. Most guys get new ones when they lose the old ones. I wear them out like shoes." With all his woes, he naturally likes to stop after work for a couple of martinis, but his wife complains of the expense. "I spend all day on the road. I don't want to come home and drink a martini from a jelly glass."

The one-sided dialogue continues as Leo, drinking sloppily, follows his reluctant listener about the ballroom. The script carefully follows the novella: men and women are dancing, eating, and carrying on everywhere. One fat relative puts his hands over his wife's breasts as the photographer walks by and calls out, "Hey, how about a picture of this!" Gradually, people start leaving or passing out on the sidelines. Brenda's father (Jack Klugman), on the verge of stupor, stops for a moment and offers Neil a ride home, then teases his brother, calling him "Bigshot." Afterward, Leo traps Neil again and resumes his obnoxious rambling, much of it concerning Leo's observations that Neil is "nobody's sucker," that he's a "smart boy," that he'll "play it safe," that "next time I see you it'll be your wedding."

LEO: The son of a bitch who invented the fluorescent bulb should drop dead! They never wear out, those things, you know that? They last for years. Look at me. I sell a good light bulb. What does it get me? Who needs a guy like me any more? Salesmen—you spit on them. . . . I got more brains in my pinky than my brother Ben has in his whole head. Why is he at the top and me at the bottom? Why?

The soliloquy continues in this fashion, with minor interruptions, for several pages.

"I felt that Leo was the pivotal character in the film," says Monroe. "I read the script, and I read the book a number of times, and I realized why Philip Roth devoted so much time to Leo—because he gives you the other side. One side is wonderful, the big wedding, the brouhaha, the upper middle class—and Leo represents the underbelly of that whole way of life. I felt that in order to play Leo, you had to play him hard on the outside and soft on the inside, and the softness on the inside would bleed through until eventually Leo would break down."

Although Monroe worked constantly with Peerce in various informal capacities during the casting and production, he remained anxious about his part almost until the day of his performance. "As far as I could ascertain, there seemed to be some doubt about me, about my range, and whether I could handle the part. I had a constant dread that inevitably somehow I would be fired from what I considered to be my big break."

The wedding scene was shot in the Delmonico Hotel on Park Avenue. Peerce, who is Jewish himself and at least as alienated as Roth from the garish behavior for which some suburban Jews are easily satirized, filmed the wedding in full parvenu splendor, with some two hundred extras (who were simply told to "behave as you would at a Jewish wedding"), three cameramen (including one on roller skates), and a heavy concentration of gorging, goosing, and other sorts of mildly grotesque behavior.

Monroe was used intermittently throughout the wedding scene, but his major monologue came at the end, when almost everyone has left but him, Richard Benjamin—who is seated at a long table covered with pieces of food, crumpled napkins, and half-empty bottles and glasses—and the two extras who played Leo's wife and daughter, asleep on the other side of the now deserted ballroom, their heads flopped down on another slop-covered table. The scene was shot just before midnight, and among those who remained to watch Monroe's performance were Peerce's wife and mother, Jaffe's wife, and Ali MacGraw, all of whom were to be deeply affected by what they saw.

"I decided to play Leo Patimkin with a cigar," says Monroe, "which I kept in my hand and at some points put in my mouth and talked through. I played as if I were the other Patimkin—as if *I* had the money, as if *I* had the power. The drinking that I did while going around the table was very helpful, too, because I suddenly started to play him slightly drunk, and it was the slightly drunk that allowed me to play the breakdown, the disintegration of Leo Patimkin."

Every actor lives for the experience of feeling completely at one with the character he's playing, and as Monroe rounded the ravaged dinner table, drinking champagne out of a bottle and spilling it out of his mouth and down the front of his shirt, his command of Leo Patimkin was so thorough that the mixture of repulsiveness and pain that oozed out of him was frightening to watch.

"I played it coarse, but gradually I began to soften the character, and when I got to the very end, they pulled the camera down so that it was pointing up to my face. I looked up and I said, 'Those fluorescent fixtures, they never wear out, those things,' and it was at that point that I started to break down and cry. I finished that section in tears."

The camera momentarily focused on Richard Benjamin's reaction and then returned to Monroe, as the observers on the sidelines watched with mounting involvement. "And that's where I gave him the warning, the one place where I was neither rude, crass, gross, or maudlin. I just looked at him and said very straight, don't make the same mistake I did—marry the girl. Then I crossed the ballroom.

"I was totally self-involved now, and it was easy for me to mobilize any feelings I wanted—they were all on tap. The camera picked me up walking toward the table where my wife and child were seated, and again I made a change of character. I thought to myself, how would this kind of man act toward his wife and kid? What does he got to be with them? A *prick*—what else could he be? How does he justify his existence? So when I reached the table—all this was done on impulse—I took the cigar and put it in my mouth and with all the rage I could muster, I smashed the table. I said, all right, wake up, it's time to go home. And the two people jumped up. I hit the table so hard, that regardless of whether they were sleeping or not they would have jumped. I looked at them and hustled them out, and that basically was the end of the scene."

When Monroe finished his ten-minute performance, he immediately sensed the spell he'd cast over everyone in the room. "I can't explain how I was feeling. It was wonderful. When you're really acting, it's like being high. I was twenty feet tall. Because I knew I had done something. I kept saying to myself, 'You did it! You son of a bitch, you did it, you finally did it! And you did it where it counts, in front of the camera.' MacGraw was standing there and she said, 'Man, you're something else!' Stanley Jaffe came over to me and he said his wife had to leave the room, because she was hysterical. She had an uncle like that and she couldn't stand it. Larry's wife, who up to that point hadn't liked me very much, said, 'I thought Larry gave you the part because he was your friend, but actually you're a friend to him.' And then Larry came over to me and put his arms around me and kissed me and said, 'You're absolutely magnificent.' Jaffe was delighted, he was beside himself. 'I never would have believed it,' he said. 'It's one of the best performances I've ever seen.' There was a feeling in the room that I still remember vividly—that they were in the presence of some kind of special person. I had never thought of acting that way; I never conceived of 'movie stardom' and all that. But all in all, it was a wonderful, wonderful moment for me.

"The next day Jaffe called me into his office and from what had been a very cool relationship, he greeted me like a long-lost brother. Friendly, warm, he said, 'Monroe, how would you like to be nominated for an Academy Award?' I didn't know what the machinations of that kind of thing were, but I took it as a tremendous compliment to my work. I had been acting ever since I was a kid. I never went to school, I was just an actor. I went away and joined the Merchant Marine—I was a galley boy—and when I came back I started acting. I started at the Y in the Bronx, and I continued through the amateurs, the professionals, and finally got to Broadway. I felt without a question this performance would've put me in the category of actors like Rod Steiger, like Edward Arnold, like Edward G. Robinson. I have the energy—I don't act any more at all now—but I have the energy, and I have the intelligence, and I have the sensitivity, and a lot of experience. Certainly, in regard to my career this was the big break."

Watching the "dailies," or "rushes"—interchangeable words referring to the accumulated film from each day's shooting—usually takes no more than a twenty- to fifty-minute bite out of each evening during the making of a movie. Actors are not generally welcome at the screening of the dailies, which partly accounts for the fact that Monroe Arnold has never seen the single most stirring performance of his career. Those who do come—the producer, the director, the editor, the cinematographer, the makeup man, the sound man, the electrician, the set director, the script supervisor—are present not out of desire but necessity, to make sure that each aspect of production is operating smoothly. Because he is in the best position to be objective and neutral about the raw footage, the editor often makes his first important contribution during these sessions. As Peerce says, "The editor may see a piece of film that I hate because I hate the actor, or I hate what I had to do with the actor, or what the actor did to me that day. And if he remains divorced from those feelings, it's a tremendous help." Dailies are screened before or after work hours, customarily around six-thirty in the evening, and after the first few weeks, even required attendance slips off.

Watching dailies is nothing like watching a finished film. It consists mainly of viewing the same action over and over again from different angles. "Scene 40" may be a "master shot" of Richard Benjamin and Ali MacGraw having their initial conversation outside the Briarpath Hills Tennis Club. Scene 40-A: a re-enactment of that conversation with the camera focused solely on Benjamin. Scene 40-B: the same action with the camera in close-up on MacGraw. Then there may be an additional take or two from one or more of these angles. Each scene—which in film can be anything from a three-second establishing shot of Neil's arrival outside the Patimkin home to a several-minute dinnertime fiasco around the Patimkin family table—begins with the clap of the clapstick and the voice of an assistant cameraman saying, "Scene two hundred one-H, take two." The name of the film, the director and other principals, as well as the number and take of the scene, are all chalked on the clapstick's surface. The assistant holds it in front of the camera and smacks down the black and white diagonally striped arm that is hinged to the top of the board. The moment of impact is used by the editing assistants to align the separate audio and visual reels on the synchronizer, a job they must perform each day before the dailies can be screened.

The rushes from *Goodbye Columbus* were a routine affair until we came to the wedding scene and Monroe's performance. Then for over ten minutes we forgot that we were working and became transfixed by the action on the screen. I had no doubt that this was the tour-de-force performance of the picture. No one did. It was electrifying.

As it happened, the wedding scene also initiated the first problems in the cutting room. All through the summer of 1968 Peerce and I edited the film with almost uncanny ease, and a rather snappy, fast-paced movie was evolving. But the wedding scene was very complex. Before Monroe comes on for the melodramatic conclusion, we are introduced to a handful of minor characters and hundreds of extras. The plot continues in skeletal fashion, but the hectic atmosphere of comic excess had to be pieced together like a mosaic.

When I came to the wedding material, I knew what I was expected to do. Larry had shot a lot of film of people eating. In particular, there were two little fat girls who were told to dance and then run to a table and eat. He shot a number of takes of these little girls—who, I had to assume, were cast because they were fat, not because they were good dancers—approaching and ingesting the food. Larry and I never discussed our attitudes and prejudices, but the way he photographed the wedding revealed a degree of disgust toward certain aspects of his Jewish background. Of course, with all the raw material I had, I could have produced anything from a Roman Circus to a polite if somewhat exuberant affair. But as Eisenstein said, the filmed material leads you, and with all those shots of people eating, I had little doubt where I was being led—especially since my own background and prejudices were similar to Peerce's and eager to spur me on in case I hesitated or lost the way.

It thus developed that when I cut the wedding scene, I brought the two girls to the table and let them eat, cut to people dancing on the ballroom floor, cut back to the kids eating, cut away to other episodes in the crowd, and cut back a third time to those two girls eating. Although it was all done with the same piece of film, the impression I created was that the little fatties were gorging themselves. Peerce fully concurred with my approach in this and numerous other instances, and we were both somewhat pleased with the hilarious demolition job we were pulling off on the offensive relatives that had at one time or another made us ashamed to be Jewish. But our pleasure was mitigated by guilt, and though we never openly shared our uncertainties, we found ourselves taking longer and longer lunch breaks until the editing of the wedding scene consumed as much time as the rest of the picture combined.

By the time we finished we were so overcome by guilt that the sight of the final cut made our stomachs rise into our throats. "My God!" we thought. "What have we done? This is treason. We've got to put some clothes on this thing!" And in a few days of panic-fast revision we had the whole thing cleaned up. We took the workprint of *Goodbye Columbus* to the Paramount offices in Hollywood, feeling like good Jewish boys again, and much relieved that we had retrieved our pranksterish bomb before it exploded.

Bob Evans, then the production chief at Paramount and a man who prided himself on seeing all the dailies of all the films that were being produced for the company, viewed our print and immediately squawked, "*You've left out all the ethnic stuff!*" Evans also prided himself on being a master of editing, and his favorite word, one of his own coinage, was "rejuxta." "All you have to do is *rejuxta* this and *rejuxta* that . . ." and, in short, *put back* all the ethnic stuff.

Chastising ourselves for having allowed wide swings of emotion to lead us into unprofessional editing decisions, and convinced that we had lost the tone that Roth intended, Peerce and I returned to New York and immediately put back the repeat shots of the stuffing chubkins, put back the extra in the bright red dress who crammed food into her mouth with both hands, put back the goosing and guffawing. In the final version the wedding scene opens with a close shot of an object that looks like a chicken. It turns out to be a chicken-shaped chopped-liver mold. A hand comes into the frame wielding a butter knife, lops off the bird's head, and spreads it on a Ritz Cracker. The camera pulls back to reveal a long table full of food surrounded by noisy, reaching, chomping celebrants, and cut after cut expands on the raucous irreverence. Many critics singled out the wedding scene for poor taste. Stanley Kauffmann in *The New Republic* charged that we dwelled on ethnic characteristics that Roth had handled in stride: "The producer and director and screenwriter" (he mislabeled the villains, a typical problem in film criticism) "are feeling so courageous at making a noncomplimentary picture about Jews that they can't restrain their courage." Offended Jews asked, "Do we have to hang our dirty wash in public?"

With all the hullabulloo about the ethnic pungency of the wedding scene, only a handful of people knew of the drama that had taken place over the performance of a single pudgy, drunken character who came and went during that scene with barely a notice. The drama concerned Uncle Leo, whose final speech, as magnificent as it was, seemed to drag the picture down like a giant weight.

"Everybody wanted to take it out," recalls Peerce, "except Ralph and me. We both made a very emotional connection to the character. But it was an extremely painful performance to watch. Monroe showed so much pain, so much anger—it was so raw and so naked in the middle of this film about people who are living a pretense—it was really almost too much to handle. It was so agonizing that after a while I would close my eyes when we came to it. Anyway, the fight started very quickly—*take it out, take it out, you don't need it.*"

Jaffe and Evans were the main antagonists, but the decision was still Peerce's. We were both very ambivalent. My own feeling all along had been that *Goodbye Columbus* was an airy and insignificant film, and that Monroe's speech was the only thing in it of real substance. But like Larry, I slowly realized that instead of giving the picture validity, a ten-minute soliloquy by a newly introduced character at the tail end of the movie seemed to tip the whole thing over, as if it had sprouted a large malignant bud.

For weeks we jerked with the speech, trying to work it in. Since Larry had shot it from only one angle, making it impossible to break the performance down into bits and pieces and re-create it, we found ourselves lopping off more and more of Monroe's opening lines. From over ten minutes it went to nine and from nine to eight and from eight to six; and each time we hoped that we had chipped away enough so that it wouldn't stick out so blatantly. The more we fiddled the further it went. From six minutes to four, and after another screening, to two, but none of these versions worked properly and we kept returning to the old choice—the whole performance or nothing. It was a choice we couldn't face.

From almost the first day of editing Monroe showed up regularly, asking to see his performance, and Peerce kept putting him off. I had no objection to setting him up in a corner with a Moviola and his reel of film, as I had done during the editing of *Murder Incorporated* for Peter Falk, who was very anxious about his first major role. But Larry, knowing what might happen and afraid to give his friend false hopes, refused. "Whenever I was in the cutting room," Monroe recalls, "they were always cutting something else. I would say, 'Could I please see the film,' and Ralph would say, 'Show it to him,' and Larry would say, 'oh, no, no, no. You'll be surprised. It's wonderful. You'll see it when it's all cut." Finally one day when Peerce wasn't around, I let Monroe hear himself on the sound track.

Knowing that all or most of Monroe's performance was in jeopardy, I began seeking some alternative means of introducing a negative element into the film—some off-note that would reveal Neil's subconscious disturbance over his courtship of Brenda. Influenced by my experience with *The Pawnbroker* and *A Thousand Clowns*, I settled on the use of flash cuts, which I tied to the end of Monroe's speech: we see the sloshed and miserable Uncle Leo warning Neil not to repeat his mistakes, to grab opportunity and marry the girl. From Monroe I cut to Neil sitting alone at a table. He has a long, thoughtful face as he watches Uncle Leo leave the room, and alternating with his gaze I intercut a series of eight-frame reprise shots from successively earlier portions of the film to represent his reflections. The reprise lasted only seconds, but with Richard Benjamin's forlorn expression and the flute music on the sound track, it injected a profound note of doubt, one that could, if necessary, serve as cinematic substitute to Monroe Arnold's performance.

When Peerce went to California late in 1968 to screen a final cut of *Goodbye Columbus*, Uncle Leo's appearance remained almost intact, but Peerce's commitment to it had grown very weak. Again he was pressured to remove the scene, and finally on the airplane back to New York, he made the decision. "It came out just like cream," says Peerce, "whomp! There was no problem, no mixing, not even a pop." In the final cut all that was left of Monroe's monologue were the few lines that introduced the flashbacks. From over ten minutes he had been cut to less than forty-five seconds.

Goodbye Columbus premiered before some six hundred people at the Loews Tower East in New York City in the spring of 1969. As Monroe Arnold approached the theater, dressed up like the rest of us for the big event, he was more confident than ever of imminent success. As luck would have it, a critic from the *Daily Variety* had attended the West Coast preview that contained Monroe's complete performance and had written a review that singled him out for praise. The review was all Monroe had to go on, for Peerce had been too frightened to give him the bad news. For my part, I had finished working on the film several months earlier and knew nothing of what had occurred between Peerce and Arnold in the interim. But when Davida and I caught sight of the Arnolds in the theater lobby, I had a terrible feeling that Monroe had not been warned.

"I walked into the theater without any foreknowledge of what was going on," Monroe remembers. "I did notice, peculiarly enough, that Jaffe and Peerce and their wives, all the very top executives, did kind of sidle away from me, but I figured they're into their own things, never dreaming their behavior was in any way connected with me. I was terribly nervous, because my wife and I were about to see this performance for the first time, which was to be the launching of a real career for me on another level.

"I'd already seen a lot of the picture in the cutting room, and I was waiting for myself to come on, so I said, yeah, it's good and everything, it works, but I didn't pay too much attention—I was all tensed up waiting for my scene to come. Now there were a number of little scenes at the wedding that I was in that preceded my big scene, and most of them had been cut. That was the first big shock. I said, 'Where the hell are those scenes? Where the hell are those scenes?' They were all relevant; they all had to do with my attitudes toward my brother, ass kissing, telling him it's quite a wedding you're throwing here, all of which was relevant to the final build. And I started to wither, to sink in my chair. I felt as if somebody'd kicked me in the balls. I just kept sinking in my chair, until I went down under the seat, because I couldn't look at the screen any more. Because from what I had done there was practically nothing left.

"Why did I stop acting? Although I never really admitted it to anybody, I think that this had a lot to do with it. I never understood before the true meaning of power. I wanted to be an actor, I worked very hard, I became an actor, I was given parts. And if somebody could take it away from me with a scissors, that which I had worked so hard to do, then I wanted to be in the position of the man with the scissors, with the power, and I began to develop an interest in directing and writing. I felt my life had been taken from me, and in a certain sense my future. And I suppose the shock was too much for me. I couldn't absorb the shock. And I didn't want to open myself up to that kind of thing again." Shortly after the film's release, Monroe co-starred with the aging Betty Grable in a tour of *Born Yesterday* and then gradually withdrew from acting for good.

Goodbye Columbus was on the screen for just a few minutes before I sensed—by the silences and the general atmospheric response— that the audience was moving with it and that it was going to be a big hit. The picture took off at once, and there were lines around Loews Tower East for the rest of that spring and summer. And then some peculiar things happened to the people who rode the film to the top.

Stanley Jaffe, the twenty-eight-year-old producer, was soon made the president of Paramount, a position he held for only a year before quitting to become an independent producer again. In 1972 I cut his next film, called *Bad Company*, a Western without action that died a quick death. Thereafter he was relatively inactive, finally returning to the charts with *The Bad News Bears* in 1976.

Ali MacGraw, who had mainly been a fashion model before *Goodbye Columbus*, was instantly one of the most talked-about actresses in Hollywood—all the more so after her (very brief) marriage to Bob Evans. Her next film, *Love Story*, was one of the all-time top grossers. But after marrying Steve McQueen and co-starring with him in *The Getaway*, she found herself overwhelmed by publicity and negative reviews, and emotionally incapacitated, she withdrew altogether from acting for the next five years.

Richard Benjamin, who turned in an immaculate performance in *Columbus* and has had plenty of work since, has yet to fulfill any of the great prophecies that were made about his career. Indeed, he has never been better known than he was in 1969.

Larry Peerce continued to use my cutting room as his office for a number of months, and during that time he received offers by the cartonload. At one point we were going to do *Love Story* together, but then he changed his mind. He said he didn't want to do any more "romantic light stuff." He continued to turn down offers and put off making a choice, and finally, over a year later, he came to me and said, "I've got a script for you to read." It was called *The Sporting Club*, based on a novel by Thomas McGuane. I read the script, knowing that Larry could write his own ticket based on the twelve million *Goodbye Columbus* had made, and I said to myself, *this guy has lost his mind.* Far from being romantic light stuff, the script seemed nothing short of a maniacal rap at all the institutions of the country. I tried to talk to him. But I ran into a scary sort of resistance, typical of what sometimes arises in this business. He said he was definitely going to make this picture, that he wanted me to cut it, and that he was testing five actors for the leading role.

Shortly thereafter he took five actors into a small West Side studio and had each of them read a portion of the script. The next day, Peerce, the producer Lee Rich, and I screened the dailies, and Larry said, "What do you think?" The part was that of a crazy rich charmer who was going to blow up a sporting club. One actor obviously had a feel for it and played it with just the right psychotic edge. He was sensational. A second actor was adequate. Two others were homosexual, and that came through in their performances, which made them all wrong. Last was Larry's friend Bob Fields, a very good actor, but totally inappropriate for this part. That's what I told Larry, and Lee Rich seconded my analysis. Said Peerce, "I'm going to go with Bob Fields." He said he was going to reach in, shove his hand down Fields' throat, and pull the performance out of him. Again, I figured, *this guy has lost his mind.*

I was just finishing a picture with Hal Prince late in 1970 called *Something for Everyone,* when Larry's dailies started coming back from Arkansas. Instead of the normal three thousand feet a day (about thirty minutes), he was shipping ten thousand feet. It was coming in torrents, and it was awful.

In February 1971, just before Larry was due back from location, I went to Washington with my wife and my son, Paul, for a short Lincoln's Birthday vacation. On Saturday morning, while in the shower at our motel, I dared to ask myself for the first time in my career whether I would continue with a film to which I was already committed and for which I had already begun an initial assembly. The internal response was thunderous: *I cannot do this picture. This picture is going to kill me. I'm going to lose my mind.* I imagined it lasting a year in the cutting room and being remorselessly depressing. The one-two-three punch of *A Thousand Clowns, The Producers,* and *The Night They Raided Minsky's* still hung over me like a warning cloud, and I feared that another year of desperate cutting would sink me. Worst of all, I didn't think this picture could be saved.

When I returned to New York, I did something I'd never done before and about which I still get a twinge of guilt. I called Avco Embassy and told the executives that by doctor's orders—because of high blood pressure or some such thing—I had to beg off. I agreed to serve as supervising editor, but someone else would have to cut the film.

The picture was in my cutting room for thirteen months. It was edited and re-edited right down to the wire in an ever-expanding atmosphere of panic. In the end, eighteen people, including sound-effects editors, assistant sound-effect editors, apprentice and assistant cutters, worked in four teams to patch and repatch, mix and remix the constantly changing final touches.

In 1972 *The Sporting Club* opened in New York and played for less than a week, during which it was demolished by the critics. Pauline Kael said, the "film is loathsome, a word I don't think I've ever before applied to a movie." Later that year Avco Embassy pulled it out of release and gave the finished film together with all the unused rushes to an editor in California to see if it could be saved. After several months of examining some 250,000 feet of film, he sealed it all back up—nothing could be done.

Peerce went on to make two more commercial disappointments, *A Separate Peace* and *Ash Wednesday*, before seeking some made-for-TV work to regain his footing. He then came back with a solid Middle America hit, *The Other Side of the Mountain* (about twenty-five million in profits), and a sequel that was also a financial success. As of this writing, he is again considered a major commercial director, having just completed his tenth feature, Sylvia Plath's *The Bell Jar*. Monroe Arnold, who in the decade since *Columbus* has struggled to rechannel his talents into writing, directing, and the managerial side of filmmaking, is listed as the associate executive producer.

"The rest of it stinks."

16 ■ My Problem with Directors

Artists were too happy, so God invented film.
—SIDNEY MEYERS

When you've worked in one field for most of your life, a time comes, I suppose, when you have to take a stand if you're going to continue to live with yourself. Although I've held long-smoldering opinions about the attitude and behavior of movie directors, I've only spoken heatedly on the subject on four occasions. Each time it was to a director, and each time I lost my temper, a relationship improved: Mel Brooks piped down; Billy Friedkin bought me a gift; William Asher invited me to work with him in California; Howie Morris wept. On many other occasions I've suffered silently, mistakenly choosing discretion in situations that badly wanted valor. In any case, I now have over three decades of observations and feelings about what I consider a serious problem in filmmaking, and I would like to express them before I go on to explain the circumstances that led me to work the last five years almost exclusively on Woody Allen's films.

Because filmmaking has become the foremost popular art form, its practitioners have become the cultural heroes of the twentieth century. First we had the age of the producer, then the age of the actor, and now, thanks to the achievements of a few extraordinary people and the critics who championed them, the age of the director.

Great filmmakers, like Renoir, Fellini, Hitchcock, and Bergman—the men who made the word "director" stand out in the list of movie credits—frequently write their own material, envision it almost cut for cut, and carry out their vision with a technique acquired through years of immersion. Because of their almost total control, they go beyond the position of a theater director, who is recognized mainly for his ability to interpret an author's work, and are seen as authors in their own right. Some, like Chaplin and Allen, also star in their films and on occasion even write the scores. None can get by without the help of talented associates—Eisenstein's work was deeply affected by the photography of Edouard Tissé and Bergman's by Sven Nykvist, while other directors have depended on a close association with an editor or a screenwriter or an actor. But in an art form that is otherwise essentially collaborative, a handful of directors approach the independent stature of a great writer or painter, which is a remarkable achievement.

Most movies have nothing in common with the masterpieces for which the title director has won its awesome respect. In the sixties some six thousand feature-length films were released in this country, most of them bearing titles and credits of well-deserved obscurity. Of those that made a brief or lasting impression on the public consciousness, only a handful owe their strength to consummate direction.

Since 1945 I have worked with close to two hundred directors in advertising, television, and feature films. Some had been agents before they became directors, others had been writers, still others businessmen or actors. Some lacked the talent to direct and disappeared after one or two tries; others had just enough ability to get by in the field, and either stuck to minor projects in advertising or TV or consistently aimed too high with disappointing results; still others developed undeserved reputations and were carried by the talents of their associates. As in any other field, only a few are worth remembering or writing about. If I were a producer I would give almost none of them the right to "final cut." But whether they made one-minute television commercials or pulp assembly-line thrillers, almost all directors I've known identified themselves with the giants of their trade, assumed that the shared title accorded them equivalent stature, and, in the case of feature directors, immediately began demanding the right to control the final cut of the film, not because their ability or their body of work justified it but because their swollen sense of self-importance coveted it.

In 1969, a time when the concept of the Star Director was surging through the trend-addicted world of film, the old-time Hollywood director Edward Dmytryk (*The Caine Mutiny, Murder My Sweet, The Young Lions*), who had been an editor himself during the thirties, commented on the unwarranted egotism that was spreading among his colleagues: "In our own guild," he wrote in the Directors Guild magazine, "the annual meetings invariably erupt with cries of, 'Let's fight for the right to control the cutting of our pictures.' It's been interesting to note that these cries almost always come from our youngest, least experienced members, men who would probably strangle in their own trims if they were placed at the bench and told, 'There, go ahead, cut!' "

By and large there is little harm done if a writer who works for a popular magazine imagines himself to be Tolstoy. But a director is fundamentally a leader, and such grandiosity stifles the contributions of subordinates, who are crucial to a film's success. A director's prideful resistance to any idea that is not his own—or not shrewdly planted in a way that allows him to believe it's his own—is symbolic of the handicaps under which films have been made for the last twenty years. Another aspect of the problem, one that is rarely discussed, is the inclination of innumerable directors, infatuated with the excessive attention they receive, to conclude that their immense gifts acquit them of the courtesy and decency that would be required of almost any other human being. The subservience and kowtowing they demand and get from the artists and skilled technicians with whom they work is a disgrace to the whole profession.

Mel Brooks terrorizing people on the set of *The Producers* was symptomatic of distortions that the director mystique has inflicted on the business of making films. And yet Mel's behavior, extreme as it was, is representative of the way the title director goes to men's heads. I have seen countless numbers of accomplished adults, highly respected in their fields, dressed down unmercifully by a vainglorious director, and each time my opposition and distaste hardens. Waiting for an elevator at Columbia Pictures, I was embittered to have to witness a distinguished director browbeating a man who had worked for him for years and, sadly, was also someone I knew. But unfortunately it has become common for a director to bawl out a sound man, or a makeup man, or a set designer and pile humiliation upon humiliation by doing it in front of the cast and the crew and anyone who happens to be passing by.

Year after year I've had to face these men, many of whom are drawn to directing mainly because of the power and prestige the position has accumulated, and spend huge portions of my working and nonworking hours racking my mind for a nonrebellious way to deal with their arrogance. Bill Asher, the man who conceived "The Patty Duke Show," whose indecision almost destroyed it, and who was finally bought out and replaced as the producer/director a week before the first installment was aired, was, as I experienced it, so insulting that nothing but a direct challenge could possibly salvage one's dignity. It was an ugly, violent fight, my first real confrontation, and afterwards I harbored the irrational hope that it would never need to happen again.

I spent only four or five weeks working with Billy Friedkin, but he was the sort of man who let you know he was in charge before he finished his first sentence, and, like Asher, he was unmoved by polite protests. You expect, perhaps, if you work with an Ingmar Bergman that you may have to put up with some moodiness, but you try to take it in stride because you're getting so much in return. But in someone who had barely directed a film before, the temper and rudeness seemed premature.

I well remember, in the middle of the second week, parking my car two blocks from the studio and starting the argument with Friedkin as I walked to work. As so often happens in cases like this, all my carefully rehearsed objections spurted out in a single indiscreet sentence: "If you don't change your attitude, you can take this film and shove it up your ass!" Friedkin was even more taken aback by this outburst than I was, making it obvious to me in retrospect that no one had ever stood up to him. Hollywood was in its down-on-your-knees-to-youth phase at this time. The studio executives had billed Billy as a prodigy—who could be surprised if he behaved as if he were on an altar?

The role of The Director has become so intoxicating that, inevitably, along with the egocentric behavior there has been a great deal of mediocrity dressed up in modern adaptations of the Emperor's

Clothes. So many directors I've worked with, or met at parties, or seen on TV talk shows have perfected the swagger, the dress, the jargon, and the attitude of the Autonomous Film Creator. Putting their work alongside their images, one could easily conclude that in the contemporary list of ingredients required for becoming a great director the only noncompulsory item is talent. The contrast was made amusingly vivid for me in 1963 when I was working on *Gone Are the Days,* from the play *Purlie Victorious.* One day as the director, Nick Webster, pontificated to one of the actors, the producer leaned over to me and said, "When this picture is over, I'm going to tell Nick what it's about."

As a career editor, I have been very fortunate in many respects, particularly because I had chosen to work in New York, where one is more likely than in Hollywood to find a Sidney Lumet, a Herb Gardner, a Larry Peerce, or a Woody Allen. Having to deal with prima donnas with explosive tempers is an unfortunate inevitability in an ego-drenched business, and, all told, I probably had fewer than my share. But by the late sixties and early seventies I was beginning to perceive another problem. I was old enough by this time to have lost the thrill of merely being able to work on feature films and sure enough of my own skills to be disappointed when a director blocked my attempts to use them. Although few directors I worked with were dramatically unpleasant, even fewer demonstrated a desire or willingness to make the best of their collaborator's talents. I understood, of course, that directors had to command the creative input on their films, and I never objected to taking orders. But when directors put their images and insecurities ahead of the quality of the work, I found it necessary to subordinate not only my feelings to the director's ego but my productivity as well. As this issue became more and more pronounced in my mind, for the first time in my career I felt rankled by the film editor's anonymity. If I could have freely contributed to the common cause, been allowed the pleasure of a job well done, the lack of recognition would have remained a personal problem but not a rankling problem. But under the growing class of imperial directors, this work without acknowledgment, this crucial work that often figures significantly in the critical assessment of the director himself—a dependency that many directors keenly resent and therefore try all the more to deny—had begun to feel like slavery.

I was developing a reputation around this time as an editor who cut directors' first films, and already a surprising percentage of my credits were debut efforts for the directors who made them. It was my way of trying to circumvent the director mystique and all its paralyzing ramifications. In some cases my collaboration with inexperienced filmmakers worked admirably. Herb Gardner, Woody Allen, and Joan Silver—for whom I cut *Bernice Bobs Her Hair*, a 1976 TV special from the F. Scott Fitzgerald story—all welcomed and respected my expertise. I had met Joan when one of my ex-assistants, Kathy Wenning, cut her first feature, *Hester Street*, and I was called in to help with some particularly difficult passages. I gladly did it without credit, because in the atmosphere of openness and mutual respect that Silver encouraged such informal support is natural and gratifying.

But the pressure to live up to the image discourages many unsteady beginners from making the most of their co-workers' skills, with the result that my solution of working with newcomers often amounted to little more than an exploration of the varieties of insecure behavior. And my career as an editor seemed to be approaching a dead end.

Shortly after Woody Allen's first picture, *Take the Money and Run*, was released, the producers asked me to edit the film version of Allen's play, *Don't Drink the Water*, which had just finished a successful Broadway run. The director was Howie Morris, the "pipsqueak" star of Sid Caesar's "Your Show of Shows," who in recent years has been employed mainly doing cartoon voice-overs with occasional appearances on TV and in films. The producers had hired him after their first four choices proved unavailable, and, worried about how Morris would handle the assignment, they asked me to spend some time on location in Florida to keep an eye on production.

Morris's comment to me in his introductory phone call—"Hi, Ralph, I understand you're the guy who saves directors"—indicated that Role Anxiety was going to be the theme of this production. Once in Florida, I quickly assessed that Morris seemed more intent on playing director than in producing a good film. Regardless of how small the issue, he insisted on having his way, and always in a style that was calculated to remind every one of his co-workers that he was his subordinate. He behaved as if any fresh idea or interpretation or inspiration that didn't come from him was an accusation of his inadequacy. Big problems arose the moment we began cutting. Morris lacked the expertise to supervise the job himself and yet he rejected every one of my suggestions out of hand. I finally abandoned all efforts at collaborating and simply followed his orders. And in the end, when the people at Avco Embassy saw his cut, they ordered him to let me recut it my way.

Two incidents dominate my memory of this picture. Once during the editing of a particular sequence I stopped and asked my assistant what he thought of the results. Morris turned a sour expression over this and moments later, in an imperious voice, said, "Ralph, step outside please, I want to speak to you." Once in the hallway, he informed me that "in California we don't even allow assistants to *talk*," such was his anxiety over rank.

About two days before the fateful screening for the producers, Morris and I were examining the film alone when he pulled rank on me over a trivial matter that sent me into one of my rare bouts of rage. For several minutes I bombarded him with all the terrible thoughts I'd had about him since filming began, while the projectionist, who'd known me for years, looked on in shock. Morris began to quiver and pale and finally broke down, revealing the enormous pressure that living up to the image of the director had placed on him. He told me he was frightened and that he felt his whole career was at stake. It was something I'd never fully appreciated or understood before, and I did what I could for the next few hours to talk with him and stem his occasional tears.

In 1970 I cut Hal Prince's first movie, *Something for Everyone*, a picture that I liked, but to my surprise hardly made a stir. Prince is royalty on Broadway, where he has spent most of his career. Although he was very professional and pleasant to work with, the problem for me was his lack of film sense. The way he shot the film, it was apparent that he expected very little from the editing process, and the way he reacted to my advice, it was clear that he expected just as little from the editor. If I suggested a subtle change or a cut that would heighten someone's performance, he was enormously grateful, as if I were making a contribution way beyond the call of duty. He saw the editor as a mechanic who, by whatever magic, cleaned up certain problems that arose in the shooting or assembling of scenes. And so the best I could do on *Something for Everyone* was a technically proficient job.

The opposite problem arose the next year in a picture I cut for Ivan Passer called *Born to Win*. Passer was one of a group of Czech directors discovered by American cinéastes in the late sixties. His reputation seemed to have been built on a very poetic seventy-one-minute film called *Intimate Lighting* (which I had heard had put David Picker to sleep when he screened it at United Artist). *Born to Win*, a low-budget, offbeat comedy written by David Scott Milton and starring George Segal and Karen Black, was his fourth film and his first American feature.

I met Passer, a clerkish, medium-sized man of about forty, for a feeling-out session over dinner at the Duck Joint, a Czech restaurant on First Avenue. The first words he spoke to me were, "I want this picture to look as if an American had directed it." I smiled, unaware of the insecurity responsible for that remark. The picture was shot on schedule, the dailies looked interesting, the performances were solid. Then, during the editing, Passer would arrive at the cutting room and each of us would wait for the other to make a move.

The waiting game was a frustrating, emotionally intricate ritual that lasted for days. Passer was so slow-moving and soft-spoken I wondered how he got the picture shot on schedule. He didn't want to talk about the film. The big decision of the morning, which arose around eleven o'clock, was where we would go for lunch—and being a Middle European, he was accustomed to making lunch the major meal of the day, a two-hour affair at least. All the while, I was waiting for him to give me some idea of where he wanted to go with the film; but he said nothing. I probably understood on some level that he was waiting for me to take charge of the thing and make an "American" movie out of it, but I wanted his participation.

After a couple of weeks of this, the frustration overwhelmed me, and I began to cut the picture myself and to put a scratch score to it. Passer sat by in the same nonchalant manner, occasionally looking rather pensive, but never making an effort to get involved. One day, as I worked, he mused out loud that the ideal way to make a movie was to spend five years on it, mold it into a major work of art, and then burn it. This seemed a maniacal statement to me, engrossed as I was in fitting his film together, but I realize now that such way-out thinking was a reflection of his inner conflicts. Part of him must have craved to take over the picture and yet he was too frightened to do so. I can only guess at the helplessness he felt over not being able to express an opinion, to give me the smallest suggestion, to participate in the work in the slightest way. And I resented him for it. Not because he was destructive, but because there was something fundamentally false going on: I was carrying him, and he was behaving as if it were business-as-usual. If this picture were to succeed, this man, who impressed me mainly for his helplessness during the time we worked together, would be hailed as a new discovery. The truth of my contribution would never be acknowledged, not even between us.

Years earlier I'd had a comparable experience cutting *Two Tickets to Paris*, a film that was created as a vehicle for Joey Dee, a rock singer whose hit, "The Peppermint Twist," was making him and his group, The Starlighters, a hot item in New York in the early sixties. The film was directed by Greg Garrison, who has since become very big in television, producing and directing the Dean Martin shows and other big variety specials. Garrison was a slicko, cool, macho dude, sueded and silvered from hat to shoes, a director who could write the book on how to look the part. During the screening of the first day's dailies, when everyone is traditionally laboring under crushing anxiety, Mr. Cool leaned over to me, pointed up to the chorus girls on the screen, and said something like "You see the second one from the left? She's terrific—any time you want her, she's yours."

As far as I could tell, Garrison spread no sweat on his suede during the remainder of the shooting either, and when it was all done, he took me aside and laid it on the line: "Look, I've heard a lot about you. You know what you're doing. I'm taking off for California for a few weeks, and when I come back, you'll show me what you've put together."

I had a magnificent time cutting that picture. True, I was younger and easier to please, but the difference between Garrison and Passer was that Garrison knew where things stood and had enough character to be explicit about it. And the results were quite dazzling from the editorial point of view, even though the picture was otherwise strictly from hunger. True to his word, Garrison blew in from the coast about a month later, spent most of our time telling me about a great Italian shoe store on Broadway, looked at what I had done, said it was "terrific" and that I should continue in the same vein, and then blew on out of the way again.

The Sporting Club was the beginning of my disillusionment with editing. It was the first picture I had ever backed away from and the first time I considered abandoning the cutting room. It was an extreme situation, because Larry Peerce, whom I like very much and rate as one of the finest collaborators I've ever had, was in the midst of personal turmoil and displaying an intense insularity. To know that a picture was a disaster from the start and to be unable to get the director, who in this case was a friend, to shift off his fixed idea long enough to read my distress signals, was so disturbing that I finally began to wonder whether the lack of authority inherent in the editor's position made it the wrong profession for me.

Then in 1972 came Stanley Jaffe's first production since *Goodbye Columbus, Bad Company*. The project started out pleasantly. Jaffe, whom I'd liked and was happy to see again, introduced me to the two screenwriters, David Newman and Robert Benton, whose work—including *Bonnie and Clyde*—I knew and respected. Benton, a gentle, professorial man with a slight build, a salt-and-pepper beard, and a slow-burning cigar, was directing. I thought the screenplay for *Bad Company* was good, perhaps too stylized, but nowhere near as stylized as what Benton soon shot. I was disappointed when I saw the first dailies coming back from Kansas, and I think Jaffe was nervous, too, for he sent me out to the cornfields for added insurance. I spent a few days trying to discuss with Benton the photographic coverage we'd need for an adequate assembly, but I found myself engaged instead in a conversation about aesthetics, lighting, composition, and other fine points of photography—all the things that I generally consider the secondary aspects of filmmaking. Benton was all fired up about film theory and art and rather uninvolved with questions of drama and action and whether the picture would actually engage an audience.

When it came time to edit, I found that Benton was completely unwilling to entertain any ideas about the over-all feeling of the film. I remember in particular a very long dolly shot in an early scene that must have lasted about seven minutes. Viewers were bound to have trouble understanding the two main characters because they are so far away, and I automatically began intercutting some of the close material. It was important that they be clearly visible because they were just being introduced. Benton objected. He said he wanted to maintain the "purity of the camera move," a phrase I had never heard coming from a serious director. I tried to explain that the audience wants contact; that they'll never appreciate the unbroken photographic sweep if they're irritated by not knowing what's going on or, worse, asleep. He said, no, he'd only shot the close material for protection, he had no intention of using it, and that was the way our discussions went for the remainder of the film.

Now it's all right to work on a loser, which I knew I was doing, but it's torture to see solutions and not be allowed to attempt them. The whole thing culminated with Benton's announcement that the musical score would be a solo piano, which I knew at once would accentuate every mistake in the film and stand out in a pretentious, self-conscious way. Convinced of imminent disaster, I made a final plea to Jaffe. I felt that I was fighting for the most basic right—to be able to use my knowledge to keep my end of a team enterprise aloft. I was overruled.

When I was younger, attitudes like this didn't bother me. I could look at the horrid editing stalls in Fox's back building and dismiss the implications because I was too involved in climbing the ladder of success to worry about being well used. But by the late sixties and early seventies my dissatisfaction grew to the point where I began to feel there must be something wrong with me. I began to doubt whether there was any justification for my perennial discontent, and wondered if I wasn't just wrong for the part. Was I being neurotic, irrational? Or was the system I worked under irrational? Although in the coolness of reflection, or in the balancing presence of my wife, I could comfortably denounce the whole show-business star mentality, the blunderbuss about *auteur* directors, the way people in charge treat subordinates like machines, another voice said, "It's *you*, Ralph. You will never be satisfied. You're incapable of it."

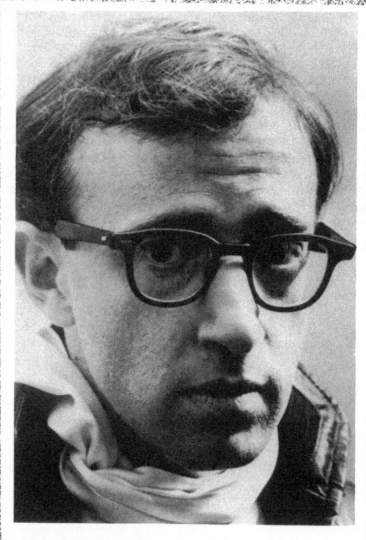

Woody Allen during his early days as a director.
(Courtesy Museum of Modern Art)

17 ■ *Take the Money and Run*

The Film They Wouldn't Release

> It has the texture of a collage—blackout sketches,
> sight gags, fake *cinema verité* interviews,
> old newsreel footage, parodies of all sorts of other
> movies . . . and the kind of pacing—or maybe it's
> just momentum—that carries the viewer
> over the bad gags to the good ones.
> —FROM VINCENT CANBY's first review of
> *Take the Money and Run, The New York*
> *Times,* August 19, 1969

I've watched Woody Allen grow from a novice film director to one of the major forces in the movie business today. From a shy, tentative, unsure comic to a man who has total control over his pictures, including hiring, casting, and advertising. From someone with little sense of film pace or composition to a self-taught master of the medium. He has Prussian discipline. He's the only director I know who finishes a film and then, without any time off, without drinking or drugs or philandering, without celebration, gloating, or self-punishing regrets, goes quietly to work the following day on his next script. He practices his clarinet seven days a week. He finds time to write short stories for *The New Yorker*. He reads voluminously. When we met, I had kept myself handcuffed to a single occupation for over twenty-five years, despite perennial desires to broaden my scope. In the ten years since, I have ventured into photography, teaching,

■ 241

producing, directing, and now co-authoring a book. Woody's daring and unceasing growth was an inescapable influence.

In 1968 Woody Allen was a successful nightclub comedian who had begun to work in film as a writer and actor. He both wrote and acted in *What's New Pussycat?*, had a role in *Casino Royale*, and transmogrified a pulp Japanese spy thriller into a ludicrous farce called *What's Up Tiger Lily?* Toward the end of that year, when Larry Peerce and I were putting the finishing touches on *Goodbye Columbus*, I read that Allen was making his first film from a script he'd written with Mickey Rose called *Take the Money and Run*, but I knew nothing more until I got a call in January of 1969 from the production manager, Jack Grossberg.

Jack and I had worked together on many occasions, starting in the mid-fifties with TV pilots. I knew him as the heartbeat of every project he worked on. During filming, he serves as the arm of the producer on the set; he is in charge of the budget, the time, the rentals, the supplies; he must know the cost of everything and everyone from the cast and the crew to the painters, the electricians, and carpenters who are hired for an emergency weekend set change. He's an encyclopedia of crucial knowledge from union overtime policies to where to get the cheapest and the best of almost anything. Over the years I've seen him play the strong-arm man, the facilitator, the psychologist, the referee, and the matchmaker. On this day in 1969, Jack was speaking as matchmaker. *Take the Money and Run* was in some kind of trouble; there was a general feeling that a new editor was needed; and Jack hoped that I was the right person to work with the introverted director ten years my junior. He invited me to look at the film, which had been in the editing room for some eight months and had progressed to a finished print complete with titles, sound effects, and music.

At nine-thirty on a Monday morning I arrived at a dilapidated screening room on Forty-third Street. At the time I was unaware of the seriousness of the dissatisfaction, of the fact that no audience had yet been found that would laugh at the picture, that Woody was despondent about it, that the production company, Palomar Pictures, a short-lived subsidiary of ABC, was on the verge of deciding not to release it.

I soon found myself treated to a very unusual experience, a film that seemed to be flying all over the place, with highs as high as the Marx Brothers and lows as low as a slapped-together home movie. It was the saga of Virgil Starkwell—a timid and unlikely desperado—and his woeful life of crime. The story was introduced in authentic documentary style by the familiar voice of Jackson Beck, the commentator for the original Paramount newsreels. As the camera zooms in slowly on a brownstone in a New Jersey slum, Beck intones with grim urgency:

> On December first, nineteen-thirty, Mrs. William Starkwell, the wife of a New Jersey handyman, gives birth to her first and only child. It is a boy and they name it Virgil. He is an exceptionally cute baby with a sweet disposition. Before he is twenty-five years old he will be known to police in six states for assault, armed robbery, and illegal possession of a wart.

To help unravel the bizarre psychology of this pathetic and purportedly dangerous outlaw the viewer is offered interviews with people from Virgil's past. Starkwell's cello teacher says that the boy *blew* into his cello—"He had no conception of the instrument." A schoolteacher relates that Virgil felt up the girls in the class—"Can I say *feel*?" His parents appear wearing bizarre Groucho Marx disguises, so ashamed are they of their worthless progeny. "He was an atheist," says the father. "I tried to beat God into him, but it was very tough. . . . How would you like to see my stamp collection?" The wacky documentary atmosphere, complete with nasty neighborhood toughs beating up the young Virgil and smashing his cello, was made even funnier by the constant propensity of the people being interviewed to trip themselves up, remember irrelevant facts, argue with each other, or waste a lot of time in self-conscious mannerisms.

The film was very primitively shot—which really didn't matter as long as the gags worked—and was held together by a plethora of visual one-liners: Starkwell has an automatic in his hand. He is lurking on a sidewalk, casing a pet shop. He enters. We wait. He comes running out chased by a gorilla. Virgil is assigned to the prison laundry room. He comes across a bra in the pile of dirty clothes, gives it an odd look, then throws it in with the rest of the wash. His girl friend, Louise (who until his imprisonment believed he was a cellist with the Philharmonic), visits him in prison and brings him food. With a rapt expression, she presses a hardboiled egg through the screen in the visitor's room, as Virgil reaches up to catch the bits on the other side. Most of these incidents were delightfully surrealistic and very few were developed beyond a minute or two.

Longer gags included an elaborately planned bank robbery in which Woody's gang pretends to be shooting a film; an outlandish argument between Starkwell and his wife on the morning of the big heist over the color of the shirt he is going to wear ("What are the other guys wearing?" she asks with pulverizing nonchalance); and a fiasco prison breakout in which Woody's "gun," a carefully whittled bar of soap colored black with shoe polish, foams up into a ball of suds in his hand, the result of an untimely downpour.

The most sensational scene, one that I think will make its way into the permanent annals of comedy, was Starkwell's first bank job, in which the overly courteous criminal gets into a desperate disagreement with the tellers, who can't make out his holdup note. With Virgil and the first teller each grasping the note, Virgil tries to clear up the misunderstanding.

> VIRGIL (reading): "I am pointing a gun . . . at you . . ."
>
> FIRST TELLER: That looks like "gub," that doesn't look like "gun."
>
> VIRGIL: No, that's "gun."

They argue until the teller calls a second teller who reads the note and finds another spelling error.

> SECOND TELLER (reading aloud): "Please put fifty thousand dollars into this bag and abt natural"—what's "abt"?

Soon the people on line begin complaining about all the time Starkwell is taking. Again Woody reads the note, and finally the teller says, "Oh, I see—this is a holdup." He asks to see Starkwell's gun. Woody obliges. He then informs Starkwell that he will have to have his note initialed by one of the vice-presidents before he can get any money. Woody complains briefly that he is in a rush, but finally resigns himself and goes to a bank officer's desk, where the argument over his penmanship resumes, a crowd gathers, and the scene ends with a cut to Woody making his single phone call from inside a police station.

The film was packed with funny material. It was frenetic and formless and obviously the work of a very fresh mind. But even as I was enjoying it, I began to feel that it was going on forever. The whole thing was put together in a strange, inept way, with little rhythm and a very bad sense of continuity. Whoever made it had no sense of film pace: it would rush along and then stop, then rush along and then stop again. Truly comic incidents were murdered by weak cuts, awkward juxtapositions, excessive length, or lack of completion. Above all, the film was burdened with moments of utterly inappropriate pathos and seriousness and was capped with a grotesque and offensive ending: leading his gang out of a bank after a holdup, Woody is gunned down by the police in a hideous death scene reminiscent of *Bonnie and Clyde*. The last shot in the movie has the camera pulling away from Starkwell's blood-drenched, bullet-ridden body. It was very chilling. I thought, *Holy Cow.*

The screening room was barely relit before I was confronted with the tremendous anxiety that had accumulated around this film. At frequent intervals throughout the screening I had noticed that bodies were slipping in in the dark, and now with the picture over I found myself surrounded by the imploring faces of Allen's managerial and production team. Jack Grossberg and Woody's two managers, Jack Rollins and Charlie Joffe, were among them. Joffe, who was also the producer of *Take the Money*, spoke first: Could I fix the film?

The picture was so choppy and uneven that I could not be certain on such short notice that it had enough solid material to survive an overhaul, and, avoiding a commitment, I asked to see the script. The first thing I discovered when I read the script later that day was that it contained a wealth of jokes, many of them very funny, that I had not seen in the film. When I questioned Grossberg about this, he assured me that all of this material had been photographed, as well as a considerable bunch of jokes that Woody had improvised or invented while shooting. With that assurance, I took the job: Joffe and I met, agreed on a fee and a title—"editorial consultant"—and shortly thereafter he called to say that it was time for me to meet the director.

The attitude of Woody's managers seemed to be that their young ward was a delicate orchid who might wither if approached incautiously. I was instructed to meet them at the corner of Seventy-second Street and Madison Avenue, and from there they ushered me to a nearby seafood restaurant where Woody was sitting alone at a corner table, quietly eating his dinner.

Woody was very serious and very soft-spoken. He didn't put on airs. He wasn't "on." He didn't betray the minutest desire to impress me or to establish himself as The Director, or The Authority, or The Senior Partner, or Anything. I felt comfortable with him and liked him very much.

We talked generally about the picture. Often, when Woody spoke, I had to lean forward to hear him, for in a gesture of involuntary modesty he put his hand in front of his mouth whenever he was chewing. He told me he was about to leave New York for two or three months to go on the road with his play *Play It Again, Sam,* and that in the meantime all the original film for *Take the Money and Run* would be sent to my cutting room. He made no effort to control what I would do with it in his absence.

A few days later a truck delivered two hundred boxes of film to my office, and for the following two weeks I screened a collection of skits that were so original, so charming, so funny in absolutely unexpected ways that it made this period one of the most pleasurable in all my years of editing. A publisher stumbling upon the unpublished notebooks of a young Robert Benchley might have felt similarly.

Many of the discarded jokes were every bit as good as those I'd seen in the film. Invariably, they had flaws, flaws that could easily be cleaned up or worked around or finessed. But as I discovered when working with Woody on this and subsequent films, he has little patience with his own material when it's not working; as a first-time director without any experience patching or revising in the cutting room, he had immediately removed anything that seemed inadequate. His editor, Jim Heckert, a competent West Coast veteran, was accustomed to the Hollywood system in which cutters are expected to follow orders and was therefore not inclined to raise objections or offer unsolicited solutions. The result was a picture that was too short, with too few jokes, and with enough dead spots to convince an untrained viewer that the entire work was rather flat or mediocre, if not a total dud.

As for the dead spots, they survived because of Woody's obsessive desire to keep a strain of seriousness running through the film. His enduring need to communicate emotional anguish finally surfaced in the form of the indisputably sober *Interiors*; but during the making of *Take the Money* the gravity was strictly in the way.

"When I think of that picture," Woody told us recently, "I think of a very, very unpleasant experience. I felt I was stuck with a bad picture, and I was very pleasantly surprised that it did as well as it did. But it was a negative experience. Not the shooting, not the cutting, but once

I started screening it and realized I had serious problems. My instinct from the first when I was making films was to always go for pathos and for a down ending. I shot the ending very brutally. I had been wired for hits by A. D. Flowers, the special-effects man who did all the stuff for *The Godfather* and a million other films. The window panes behind me smashed, blood spurted out—I mean it was a real killing. I remember showing that film with that ending to the people who backed the picture, and they were just stunned. It was a bad screening. There were just the four heads of Palomar, me, and Charlie Joffe. There was no laughter. Occasionally the guys would laugh a little bit, but there was no audience bursting with laughter, and it was all very down. And then I get killed. And they said to me, 'Is that really how you want to end the film?' They were very nice about it, they were being very polite, but they couldn't hide their disappointment. I knew they were talking about not releasing it."

I subsequently learned that Woody had held many screenings of the film and all of them had been demoralizing. "I was really not aware," he says, "of how awful the thing looked, unmixed and with all the sound bouncing around. And I had no idea of the psychology of screenings. I've since been at a rough-cut screening with Sidney Lumet. He welcomes people at the door, he sits them down, he tells them exactly what's happening—where the opticals are going, when, and why. You're watching the film for twenty minutes and then suddenly you'll hear a voice pipe up and it'll be *Sidney*, saying, 'There's an optical going in right here!'

"We'd post a notice at the USO at Forty-third Street and Seventh Avenue and we'd get twelve or fifteen soldiers. And they'd come up to this little tiny screening room at Sixteen hundred Broadway at five-thirty in the afternoon, and they would see this thing with no titles, no explanation, no sound effects, no music or anything, and we would die with it."

While Woody was on the road with *Play It Again, Sam,* I began to reconstruct the movie. I put back some scenes, extended or recut others, juggled the material to create a rhythm, which in some cases meant moving whole scenes from one part of the film to another, and trimming almost everything to quicken the pace. I took a scene—in which Virgil robs a pistol from a jewelry shop, uses it to hold up an armored truck, is cornered by police in an alley, and opens fire only to have a flame shoot out the top of what is actually a cigarette lighter—lifted it from the middle of the movie, and made it the pretitle sequence. Since the bank-robbery ending with Woody getting blown away by rifle fire would have to be replaced, I took the initial portion, which is very funny—about two gangs holding up the same bank at the same time—and moved it toward the middle of the film where some plotted action was needed.

Since the film was haphazardly plotted, it didn't matter too much where one scene or another ended up, and thus I was able to move things around at will to serve the rhythm and the pace. This sometimes created transition problems, and to cope with them, I created a new transitional device by chopping up pieces of the long interview with Starkwell's parents I found in the rushes but which had barely been used in the first version of the film. I now introduced this wonderful material—in which actors Ethel Sokolow and Henry Leff carry on at length about their son, Virgil—wherever I needed a bridge between two segments of the plotted action that failed to connect in a natural way. Because I could not use the parents everywhere, I also kept track of the spots where Woody would have to write some additional transitional material. Here we returned to the three devices he'd originally employed. If you watch the film carefully, you will see how these elements—the parents, the Jackson Beck narration, Woody's own voice-over narration, and Beck's interviews with Starkwell—bind together the otherwise loosely related material.

The first thing I wanted Woody to tackle when he returned were the maudlin patches. Of immediate concern was an early scene in which Woody meets Louise (Janet Margolin) sketching in the park. After circling nearby with an eye on her purse, he is engaged by her in a conversation and takes a liking to her. We then see them walking through the park in misty weather in a romantic sequence that looked like something out of Renoir. The lovers walk up a distant hill with frilly music in the background and something like Vaseline on the lens, and the viewer feels as if he's stumbled into another movie. I said, Woody, it's a lovely scene, but write some jokes, narrate it, tell us what it was like courting her, what you were talking about behind those trees. And I discovered that if he agreed with me, he could go into a corner and emerge a few hours later with everything that was needed on scraps of paper. His narration for the previously unspoken courtship scene came to over three hundred words. As he and Louise drift into dots on the landscape, he tells us that he knew he was in love because he felt nauseous, that "after fifteen minutes I wanted to marry her, and after a half hour I completely gave up the idea of snatching her purse." We see them now from a high angle, standing on a slope facing each other, while on the sound track Woody recalls his anxiety over telling Louise that he was a cellist: "Once she asked me some questions about Mozart. She got suspicious because for a minute, you know, I couldn't place the name." As the camera circles the young lovers, Woody reflects on his attitude toward women: "In prison, I remember the psychiatrist asked me if I had a girl, and I said, 'No.' And he said, well, do I think that sex is dirty. And I said, 'It is if you're doing it right.'" Needless to say, any similarity to Renoir was obliterated.

As Woody and I reconstructed the movie, I found several instances where scenes could be salvaged merely by replacing the music. The film hit a down note again when Virgil was preparing himself for a date with his new girl friend. Woody had aimed for a Chaplinesque atmosphere—"the worst side of Chaplin," he now concludes—by showing the rundown hotel room, the pathetic outcast pulling the toilet plunger in order to get his shower running, opening a defunct refrigerator to reveal his clothes hanging inside, opening the freezer portion to remove his shoes, combing his hair and posturing before the mirror in a hopeless attempt at the debonair. I realized that what made it maudlin instead of funny was the mournful music that accompanied the wordless scene. I laid in a piece of upbeat Eubie Blake ragtime in its place, and the effect was magical: "The sequence was heavy and oppressive and unfunny," says Woody. "And without changing a frame, just changing the music, the thing became funny." Woody's spirits took a definite upturn around this time, and his confidence in the material grew.

Making changes in the score meant re-enlisting the services of the composer, Marvin Hamlisch, whose involvement amplifies all the enchantment the memory of this period arouses in me. Of all the composers I've worked with, and there have been many, for composers often work directly with editors, none compares to Hamlisch in knowledge and ability. His mind is so free and so quick to make connections that if he accepts your intent, he can write a new piece of music in virtually any style in an astonishingly short time. Hamlisch and I had an immediate affinity, and a few years later when he was stuck on a passage in his score for *The Prisoner of Second Avenue*, he sent me a plane ticket to Los Angeles so that we could spend some time on it together.

Until hired to score *Take the Money and Run*, Marvin had been surviving mainly as a rehearsal pianist. Pulled onto the film by Jack Grossberg, who was familiar with his work and knew that he had scored *The Swimmer*, a Frank Perry picture whose release had been delayed, Marvin showed all the talent and none of the confidence of a future multiple-Academy-Award winner. His collaboration with Woody, as important as it was for the picture, was not easy for Marvin, whose expressiveness turned melodramatic alongside Allen's unswerving calm. According to Jack, the worst moment for these two emotionally opposite men had been the recording session for the main title sequence, an original ballad with which Hamlisch was justifiably pleased. Woody's impassive reaction—"What was *that*?" he shrugged when the band finished playing—had so upset the young composer that when Allen left the room, Marvin lay down on the floor and wept.

Once I joined the project and began requesting alterations, Marvin got in the habit of making frequent calls to the cutting room. Incapable of withstanding a moment's wait, he would insist on playing new arrangements right over the telephone, as Woody and I, our minds elsewhere, struggled to be receptive. "Marvin was wonderful," says Woody, "but he really used to drive us crazy. He'd call six, eight times a day, obsessed about everything and nervous about everything. Could I come over and hear a piece of music, could Ralph come over, what kind of cue should he have for this section, would I buy this piece of music, does this sound good, should it just be piano, should it be piano and trombone, should it be funny, could we extend the scene a little bit 'cause it would help—a million questions about everything."

But ultimately the important thing about Marvin was that he could grasp immediately the kind of music we needed in order to transform the tone of a scene, and he unfailingly provided it. A typical example was the escape from the chain gang, Woody's farcical salute to *The Defiant Ones*, a 1958 film in which Tony Curtis and Sidney Poitier spend more time than they care to in each other's company. In Woody's version, Virgil and four other prisoners, one of them black, bust out of the prison camp chained together. After making their way across a field with guards and dogs in hot pursuit, they come upon a roadside diner and after considerable antics steal four bicycles. The idea was good, but the sequence was not nearly as funny as it should have been until I eliminated the diner scene and cut directly from the harrowing escape with the guards shooting at their backs to a shot of the four chained convicts riding down a country road on bicycles with Virgil, also chained, trotting alongside. To amplify the change in context, mood, and level of absurdity that was implicit in the new transition, I replaced the chase music that originally accompanied the bicycle shot with a piece of Quincy Jones bossa nova. Hamlisch immediately liked and understood the alteration and wrote an original piece of bossa nova that took the joke all the way to its completion. For other scenes, we simply told him what tone we were looking for, and he composed impeccably appropriate music. I worked with Marvin again on *Bananas,* a film for which he created one of the great unacknowledged film scores.

When I went through the rushes, I found that Woody had shot about a half dozen endings for the movie, all of them sentimental, weakly amusing, or sad. I told him he had to shoot a new end—a demand that I would repeat on three of our next four films together—and suggested that he return in some way to the interview technique that began the picture. The next morning Woody arrived in the cutting room, having written a new scene in which Jackson Beck narrates the events that led to Virgil's capture and in a parody of TV journalism, interviews those who were close to him near the end or had something to do with his arrest. Louise reflects that Virgil's been depressed lately: "You know, he never made the Ten Most Wanted List. It's very unfair voting. It's who you know." Woody's real-life ex-wife, Louise Lasser, was enlisted to play a neighbor astounded to discover that the schlemiel next door was a criminal: "I actually believed that he was an idiot. I mean I really believed it. And I wasn't the only one. Like, everybody thought so. . . . To think that idiot was a criminal! I just can't believe it. . . . You've never met such a nothing. I can't believe it! That there was a mind working in there that could rob banks! It's phenomenal! Phenomenal!" Virgil's roommate: "Thought I saw his picture on, uh, the post office. I didn't remember whether it was on the wall or a stamp." Then there was Stanley Ackerman, the assistant director on *Take the Money,* a former actor, pressed into service to play the part of a photographer who by sheer accident made a film of Virgil's spectacular arrest. Asked to recall how it all happened, Ackerman gets hilariously sidetracked in details about taking his pants to the cleaners and what he had for breakfast that morning—"I think it was two fried eggs, toast . . . I don't know whether it was orange juice or grapefruit, but I, I remember I had a juice"—that you just want to kick him and say, "Get on with it!"

Finally, in a scene that was shot just before the film was released in August 1969, Woody is back in his cell being interviewed by the narrator and reflecting on his life of crime as he whittles pensively on a bar of soap and asks, "Do you know if it's raining out?"

When the *Times* critic Vincent Canby discussed the picture for a second time on Sunday, August 24, he made another stab at capturing the film's charm, one that comes closer than he could possibly have known to the truth about how the film was edited: "The movie has a sort of loose-leaf form. You have a feeling that scenes, perhaps entire reels could be taken out and rearranged without making much difference in total impact, which is good because it all looks so effortless."

Ralph and Woody on the set of SLEEPER.

18 ■ Scenes from a Marriage

Working with Woody on *Bananas, Sleeper,* and *Love and Death*

W hen Woody Allen approached me with the script for *Bananas* early in 1970, we were, in our respective crafts, in close to opposite positions in the motion-picture pecking order. Woody was just beginning as a director, whereas I had been cutting film for twenty-five years. With only one picture behind him, Woody was still relatively untested, whereas my reputation within the industry was firmly established, particularly by my work on *A Thousand Clowns* and *Minsky's*. The circumstances of our first collaboration reinforced my position as an elder statesman: Woody had exhausted his creative resources on *Take the Money and Run*, and the decision to release the film could clearly be linked to my involvement. Never before had my contribution as an editor been so tangible, nor a director's position with me so vulnerable.

The working style that evolved as Woody and I edged our way

around the ego traps and pitfalls of this subtle terrain might be described as a Dance of Deference. From the first moments we bent over backward in an effort not to force our opinions on each other. "Do you think we can bring that sequence in here?" I might ask. "Well, there's a problem with that," he would respond, "because we want to set up the laugh for the next shot." "Well, why don't we cut away before the sequence ends, go in for the laugh, and then come back?" When decisions had to be made, this invariably was the tone of the exchange.

If I pointed out that something in the script or the filming didn't work, Woody's impulse was never to become possessive and defend what he had done, but simply to get rid of it. Often I had to fight him to save a joke that was faulty but not beyond repair. Out of the extreme politeness and respect grew a partnership, and it was for his grace in partnership that I most valued Woody. It accounted for my willingness to cut five of his next six pictures and to tie my last years as an editor to the beginnings of his remarkable filmmaking career.

As much as I liked Woody, my first impulse when I signed on for *Bananas* was to do something that would solidify my position and prevent the slave-master mentality from reasserting itself in the cutting room. I told Woody I wanted a more significant role in the making of the film and asked for the title associate producer, a request to which he immediately consented.

As associate producer, a position I'd wanted merely as an interpersonal prop, I now felt compelled to do something extra, and so, despite my conviction that an editor is less than useless on the set, I embarked for Puerto Rico to be on hand for the filming of scenes about the banana republic whose regime is threatened by a guerrilla revolt. It is difficult to describe how out of place I felt. I particularly remember one dreary, predawn morning on a cliff outside San Juan. Woody was filming a scene in which government troops disguised as a rumba band were cha-cha-ing through the jungle to launch a surprise attack on the rebels. I crouched on the cliffside, cold and uncomfortable, watching the cameraman, the production designer, the unit manager, the production secretary, the makeup man, the gaffers, the grips, the actors, and all their assistants rushing about in that hectic harmony that would ultimately yield an acceptable take. My lonely alienation in the midst of this commotion seemed a high price to pay to maintain the balance I wanted between me and the director. And when the Xavier Cugat look-alikes dropped their preposterous instruments and pulled revolvers from their puffed-out sleeves, only to have their performances spoiled by a sudden downpour, of all the people who went running for cover, I alone could not even feel the camaraderie of shared disappointment. It was the last time I worked on location. I kept the associate-producer title on *Sleeper,* but by the time we got to *Love and Death* I realized it was superfluous and dropped it.

Like much of Woody's material, the rumba ambush never made the picture, despite his ultimate success in circumventing the elements and getting it properly filmed. It was a hit with the cast and the crew, but wasn't funny on screen. Stationed on location, I saw that many jokes that seemed sensational on the set failed to translate into film humor. Because Woody's comedies are based on a continuous stream of jokes and skits, a larger than usual portion of our editing work entails a search for the moments that work and a careful weeding out of the ones that do not.

In a scraggly guerrilla camp a sleazy South American comic is ushered onto a makeshift bandstand, and the rebel troops are told that the visitor is Bob Hope. As Hope's theme, "Thanks for the Memory," blares out over the camp loudspeaker, the seedy character, who couldn't pass for Bob Hope in a million years, begins delivering a string of one-liners, and the troops won't laugh (which makes him all the more hilarious to us). He tries and tries, until Woody, playing Fielding Mellish, the nebbishy New Yorker who gets caught up in the insurrection, says, "Hey, that's not Bob Hope!" Everyone panics, suddenly aware that the whole thing is an ambush, and, just then, government planes appear overhead dropping bombs. The scruffy troops scatter for cover, but the comic, whose military purpose has already been served, keeps pitching his monologue, growing more and more desperate for laughs as he drones on.

It was technically a complicated scene, shot from several camera angles, with three fighter planes loaded with phony explosives. All the elements—the dive-bombing planes, the ground-level explosions, the scattering soldiers, the tenacious comic—were captured perfectly. But when we screened the material, it looked more like documentary war footage than a comedy scene and was thus rejected.

There was always some material that both Woody and I liked but that had to be removed because it went limp before screening audiences. One of my favorite examples concerned the visit of the San Marco director, Emilio Vargas, to the United States to improve his public relations. His itinerary includes a guest appearance on the Cousin Brucie Show, a teenage rock-'n'-roll program on afternoon TV. Vargas, played by Carlos Montalban ("El Exigente" in the Savarin Coffee commercials), gives the adolescent kids a rousing speech on discipline and other topics of fascist concern, and then Cousin Brucie opens the floor to questions. Will the Beatles break up soon? a boy asks. A girl wants to know Vargas's opinion of double dating. Another what his favorite sandwich is. Why this charming gag failed to raise a chuckle escapes me even now, but in comedy so many elements have to be just right that even the best jokes sometimes perish on the screen.

Occasionally the reactions of screening audiences helped us uncover a joke that hadn't been intended. We had one scene in *Bananas* in which Woody arrives at the San Marco palace for a state dinner with a gift of cake for dessert. Vargas immediately protests, "These are prune, I like cherry," whereupon he and his henchmen get into a terrible row over what type of cake tastes best. Vargas tries to enlist Woody's support for cherry, but Woody, in a daring non sequitur, asserts a preference for toasted corn muffins. At this, Colonel Diaz goes into a rage: "Anything is better than a corn muffin! A lousy, stinking, toasted corn muffin!" and only quiets down when armed guards arrive to quell the disturbance. As far as the cake device was concerned, this scene was supposed to have been the joke. But when our test viewers saw Woody arriving at the state palace and emerging from a limousine timorously bearing the tiny white cake box by its string, they howled. Except for Vargas's initial statement of displeasure at the sight of prune and Diaz's subsequent insistence that Woody should be eliminated at once ("I could kill him now—he brings cake for a group of people; he doesn't even bring an assortment!"), we cut the rest of the skit. The joke had already succeeded.

With so much of his material being removed, trimmed, or modified in the editing, Woody's cool professionalism was an especially refreshing trait. Not since Helen van Dongen had I worked with someone whose fastidious attention to detail and businesslike attitude about weak or faltering material matched my own. When a scene died, Woody never looked back. "You have to subordinate everything to the laugh" is his attitude, because he knows that if you lose the audience for a minute, you pay for it in that sequence and you pay for it again in the next—when you have to rev them up anew.

Having learned from *Take the Money* how many of his sequences fail to make the film, Woody packed *Bananas* so full of jokes that another movie could have been made from its outtakes. If he thought he needed 150 jokes in an hour and a half, he wrote and photographed 300. And he made them tighter, a joke at every turn, so that the pace would never slacken. His approach to screening was becoming equally methodical. Afraid that viewers might not respond freely if they knew he was present, Woody hid under the control console, a desklike structure in back of the Movielab screening room, while I gave the rough-cut speech. He emerged when the lights went out, stayed to hear the reaction, and then disappeared again just before the film ended.

As in *Take the Money*, the original ending of *Bananas* was weak. The idea was funny, but the execution was faulty, and it could not be fixed. An inadvertent rebel hero, Woody is invited to give a revolutionary speech at Columbia University, only to be accosted by a black mob intent on knocking off the honkey lecturer as a "gesture to white America." Woody runs for cover, a bomb goes off, he emerges from the sooty rubble in blackface, and is instantly mistaken for a Brother by three black men with rifles. It was one of those things that never made the transition from paper to the screen.

I said, "Woody, the end doesn't work," a sentence that turned out to be something of a ritual for us. He didn't stir. I said, "Why not do something that relates to the beginning of the picture?" In the opening scene Howard Cosell narrates an on-the-spot Wide-World-of-Sports assassination of a government minister. Woody sat and thought, and the next morning he came in with a new ending for the film. Howard Cosell is witnessing the wedding-night bridal-suite confrontation between Woody and Louise Lasser, playing the girl who slighted him until she discovered that he was the hero of a Caribbean insurrection. The whole thing would be filmed just like a prize fight—ABC-TV's you-are-there coverage of their nuptial union.

Lasser enters the room, carrying her bridal bouquet, sits on the edge of the bed, and pulls off one of her boots. Cosell: "Here comes the bride. She's got a lot of fans." Sounds of cheering. "And I think that it is apparent that she is in very good physical condition. And here comes Mellish!" Woody enters with a towel around his neck, his trainer and his handler behind him. As they begin to massage his arms and shoulders, he makes the sign of the cross. "And it's started!" says Cosell, as the lovers tangle. "The two are working together. It is swift, rhythmic, coordinated." Woody gets a cut over his right eye; a doctor examines him and allows the action to resume. Then, from under the undulating bedspread, Woody's arm pops out, his fingers in a "V." Cosell: "That's it! It's over. It's all over. The marriage has been consummated." Cosell then interviews the newlyweds, who discuss their coition like two prizefighters. Louise: "I just had no idea that it would be so quick, you know. I was expecting a longer bout." Woody: "I was in great shape. I thought I had her in real trouble."

Bananas was a better film than *Take the Money*, but it was still unstructured and frenetic without much refinement of plot. With *Sleeper* Woody took another major step. It was a classic comedy in the tradition of Chaplin and Keaton with a sophisticated plot, intricate sets, and a risky dependence on special effects and complicated machinery. It went beyond anything he had attempted before. "It's always good to give the critics a moving target," Woody once quipped, referring to his self-imposed growth. But this lightheartedness can be deceptive. *Sleeper* proved a monstrous challenge, and tension pervaded every aspect of its production.

The picture was earmarked as United Artists' Christmas release, and its firm deadline could be broken only at serious cost to the company, the director, and the relationship between the two. Woody began shooting on April 30, 1973, on a two-million-dollar budget that allotted fifty days for filming. By the time I arrived in California in August he was several weeks into fifty-one days of additional photography, which had already consumed the $350,000 fee he was due as co-author, actor, and director. The robots, the mechanized props, the stunt shots, and, most exasperating, his own performances were either failing or not meeting his exacting standards. In some cases the failures were so repeated—wires and towropes snapping or flying into the frame—that after innumerable takes he moved on and left perfection to the editing.

Woody does not like the assembly to begin before he has finished filming, but with the release date in severe jeopardy, Jack Grossberg prevailed on him to have me come out to the old Culver City Studios where the picture was being shot and begin cutting at once. I sensed the tremendous stress Woody was under the moment he greeted me on the set, and I could see that despite all his efforts, he was beginning to show signs of impatience with the production team. The stress seemed to exaggerate a conflict between Woody and Jack, thereby ending a long and fruitful relationship. We agreed that I would begin cutting seven days a week while the filming was still in progress.

Sleeper was being made on the remnants of the David O. Selznick lot where *Gone With the Wind* had been produced. In the middle of this lot, amid the huge concrete buildings, was Woody's headquarters, which now doubled as the cutting room—a pretty three-room cottage surrounded by a lawn, a garden full of daisies, and a tall white picket fence. It had been Clark Gable's dressing room. Each morning I arrived by cab at the compound at eight-thirty, passed through the guard post, and rode through the deserted lot to our little house. Everything was very still at those times, except for the sounds of Woody, who had risen before me, playing New Orleans jazz on his clarinet. With the help of a California editor and two assistants, I assembled a substantial portion of the film in rough form by the time Woody and I returned to New York in September. By the end of the month—with each of us, working with an assistant, editing separate segments and then conferring over the results—we completed a rough-cut version of two hours and twenty minutes. During the next two months of refining, some fifty-two minutes would have to be removed.

As often happens with Woody's films, we rejected some of the most impressive material, frequently causing more pain to me than to the author himself. A dream sequence, shot in the Mojave Desert, in which real people were used as chess pieces, is, I think, one of the finest pieces of cinema Woody has ever created. Allen plays a white pawn that is about to be sacrificed. The black knight, a vicious character who has just killed another white pawn, first by smashing him with a mace and chain and then running him through with a sword, says, "You're next," as Woody quakes. In addition to the knight, a black bishop (who is menacingly tapping a large crucifix), the black queen, and a tough little black pawn are all moving in on him. Woody: "Hey fellas, it's only a game. We'll all be together later in the box." The disembodied voice of the man playing black announces his decision to take the white pawn, and, ignoring Woody's pleas, the black knight charges. Woody, hysterical, runs helter-skelter across the board, breaking all the rules of chess. He pauses long enough to feel up the black queen and then dashes off into the desert pursued by the knight. The scene worked magnificently on the screen, and though it failed to fit the needs of *Sleeper*'s plot and comic pace, I saw in it a forecast of major future accomplishment.

By mid-October we had the film down to a hundred minutes and coming close to its final shape when Woody took off for New Orleans to record the score, playing clarinet with the Preservation Hall Jazz Band. His own band later recorded additional material for the film. Toward the middle of November, perilously close to the time when we would have to go into the sound studio to spend a week on the mix—getting each sound in the film (a person's voice, a slamming door) at just the right level—we hit the final snag.

In keeping with the established routine, I again objected to the ending, which was flat and relied entirely on a corny visual gag. To redo it, Woody returned to California for a Sunday shooting about two weeks before the picture was released. Diane Keaton, by then working on *The Godfather,* had to switch back into her role as the light-headed Luna on her day off. It was only through a whirlwind of overlapping labor that we made the Christmas release.

Sleeper was a trying experience for Woody, but it wasn't long before he was applying solutions to many of the problems it raised. By the time we got to *Annie Hall,* he had, with characteristic efficiency, tackled the nuisance of last-minute additions and retakes by including in his original budget two weeks of postproduction photography. And in anticipation of the problem he always has with his scripted ends, the only ending that appeared in the screenplay he presented me was a note that indicated, "Ending to be shot."

Having cut all but one of Woody Allen's first seven pictures (*Everything You Always Wanted to Know about Sex* was produced while I was directing the documentary *Turner*) and having been professionally associated with him longer than with any other director, I am struck by how little I've said about the personal quality of our working relationship and what he is like as an individual. When Woody and I work, our conversation is generally quiet and sober with few displays of emotion, least of all enthusiasm. At times we spent hours earnestly hashing out problems with the plot or the continuity or about what new material Woody needed to write or shoot. The tone of these conversations was easy and professional with surprisingly little kidding around, personal reflection, or anything approaching intimacy. Woody is very private, very reserved, excruciatingly—at times, maddeningly—controlled. He never snacks when he works; he never betrays what he's feeling. His paltry lunches, sometimes no more than a glass of club soda, are symbolic of his stoicism.

I do not count Woody as a close friend, and yet we have so much in common I feel emotionally allied with him. We are both Jewish, both from Brooklyn, both perennially joyless, pessimistic about our chances for happiness, and easily sucked into low spirits. We are both mostly self-educated and have similar passions, such as Russian literature and jazz. We both abhor pretension, whether it be in dress, choice of eating place, or the obnoxious self-importance of many people who work in film.

Having been a stammerer and always somewhat withdrawn and uncertain about myself, I immediately identified with Woody's extreme timidity, an issue that arose again and again as we moved through public places and faced his fans. With colleagues, silence is his primary tool for both protection and control, and it works an unsettling devastation whether on a room full of smooth executives at United Artists or a group of garrulous production people on the set. I knew from my own experience that this was the strategy of a proud but insecure man. As a boy I found that if I got angry, I stammered, I blocked, I made a fool of myself. But shut up, and the effect is potent. Maintain that silence, keep from saying the words that put others at ease, that grease the social flywheels, and more sociable people falter and even go to pieces. In Woody, I'd found a man who had taken my own nonverbal protection to its extreme, and I sympathized with all it represented.

At times I caught myself in a reverie in which I studied his life for clues to my own. How could I fail to be captivated by the courage and willpower it must have taken a man of his makeup to come out from behind the comedians and TV personalities and start performing himself the jokes he once wrote for them? Our choices had been different: despite my gloominess and insularity, I had married and had the emotional security of a family; whereas Woody, more consumed by his alienation, had spent more time living alone and had turned his absorbing introspection into the raw material of his work. Did he look at my life, see in it his own abandoned options, and similarly wonder? I don't know, for we never discussed such things.

Although our similarities remained unspoken, they were the hidden cement of our relationship. Our silent bearing, so threatening to other people, had the familiar quality of home to us. It was certainly rewarding for me to contribute to the films of a man whose struggles I identified with and whose material I liked and respected. And I believe it was comforting for Woody, who feels so out of step with the world, to work with someone who understood his references, values, tastes, and anxieties.

It should be obvious by now that, as a filmmaker, Woody has very little in common with the characters he portrays in his films. The insecurity and fears are truly his own, but the behavior is not. He is not a bumbler. He is not ingratiating. He rarely makes an effort to be affable to strangers. He is not particularly "Jewish" in his mannerisms, speech, or personal habits. Despite his scuffed shoes, ill-fitting chinos, army fatigues, and dilapidated felt hat, he is, when working, much more the style and image of the detached corporation executive. And interwoven with this are the shyness and the ambivalence about stardom. For despite his power, Woody has a fade-into-the-woodwork manner that becomes more and more incongruous the more famous he becomes. He is like an elephant in midtown, who, secretly believing he's a cockroach, pretends not to be there.

None of the popular accounts I've read come near to capturing the man I know—cerebral, cautious, judgmental, shrewd at covering his tracks, with a gentle but very mindful, even calculating, interpersonal style. He is smart, very smart, *frighteningly* smart. Often he knows where the interviewer from *The New Yorker, Newsweek,* or *The New York Times* is heading before the interviewer himself knows; and, thus, he is in almost as much control of his public persona as he is of his film persona. The public reports stress his unhappiness ("My one regret in life is that I am not someone else"), but despite all the words that have been written about his two decades of psychoanalysis, only a few intimates know the particulars of his pain. In the ten years we've worked together, including the occasional times we've socialized, we've never shared a heartfelt concern, an uninhibited laugh, an open display of despair or anger. Neither of us is spontaneous about feelings, and Woody is one of the few people I know who is substantially less spontaneous than I.

From what I have seen, Woody prefers to operate in a stoic professional manner, unencumbered by allegiances and obligations. On the other hand, he is exceedingly generous with the people he values. Ex-wives and girl friends star in his films, and actors with walk-on parts get title credits. My lead credits in *Annie Hall* and *Interiors* are, to my knowledge, the only instances in which an editor has been so honored. Marshall Brickman, the co-author of *Sleeper* and *Annie Hall,* said, when we interviewed him, "I want to repay my debt to Woody." He has helped make or advance the careers of many associates, and they love and respect him for it, and probably in many cases regret that they cannot quite touch him with their gratitude.

As a director, Woody is not free of egotism and all its attendant problems. These are givens in show business. But it is here that all his awareness and self-control have paid off most handsomely. For unlike so many directors I have known, Woody simply has not allowed the ego issues to get in the way. He's kept focused on his main concern, which is the work, and has refused to fall into playing The Director. Repelled by anything resembling authoritarian posturing, he's gone overboard at times to avoid it, appearing on the set in the frowsiest outfits and speaking in the softest, most uncommanding voice.

For several years the opportunity to work with Woody was the only thing that kept me cutting. He never behaved as if I was there merely to service him or to follow orders. He never expected me to cater to him or to second his every thought. He never saw my independent judgment, my disagreements, or my challenges as anything but assets to his films. And thus, though he maintained complete control of every project, it was always a free association when we worked.

Woody seemed to understand that as long as he had the ultimate authority, he didn't have to fear the opinions of others. He was always ready to try it your way, and if your way succeeded, so much the better. Above all, he wanted to learn from the people with whom he worked, people with decades of experience in areas that were foreign to him—and he *has* learned, so that now, if need be, he could easily edit a picture on his own.

The growth in Woody's expertise and his natural desire to use it reactivated all my old self-hatreds about having remained an editor. My unhappiness about having to be a secondary creative force and about being too cowardly to seek the primary spot could no longer be shunted aside, blamed on the nature of the industry, or attributed to unpleasant experiences with directors. If I failed to take the steps that my ambition and desire for fulfillment demanded of me, I had only myself to blame. By the time we finished *Interiors,* during which Woody was also going through great anxieties as a result of the dangerous new terrain he was treading, we both sensed that our decade-long collaboration was nearing an end.

Although Woody works harder than anyone I know, he does not find much pleasure in it. He is in his best spirits when writing his scripts, because then, as he says, "You don't have to meet the test of reality." Otherwise, by Woody's own account, he does not enjoy filmmaking, and he does not think highly of his own work ("I see his films," says Woody of Ingmar Bergman, "and I wonder what I'm doing"). At no matter what stage of production, Woody manages to focus on the negative.

On filming: "I don't enjoy the process. You have locations in freezing weather, or night shooting, and you're constantly worrying about cutting down on expenses. It's no fun to live in a hotel room in a foreign country or a different state and get up at six every morning. It's no fun at all."

On editing: "When you're editing, you have the anxiety of making the film come out. You cut one scene maybe twenty times, you see it over and over—it loses its punch. . . . The cutting-room reality wraps itself around you like a wet blanket."

On finishing: "You can never seem to get the color the way you want it. When it comes time to take out the records you were working with and put in the real music, it's always a disappointment. When you're dead positive that this is the end, that it's finished, the distributors call up and say the first weekend's business is not what it should be. There's never a time when it's just a *fait accompli,* when the thing opens and everybody loves it, and audiences flock to see it—never."

But the most difficult aspect of filmmaking for Woody is *people*—meeting them, dealing with them, managing them. When he arrives at 8:58 A.M. in a room full of sound engineers, sound editors, and assistants at the mix, he does not join in the morning ritual of coffee and conversation, does not pause to receive their greetings, but rather moves double-time in the direction of his chair, keenly hoping to avoid the small talk. Unlike almost everyone else, Woody never eases gradually into work. If he had his way, work would begin the moment he arrived and continue for twelve hours a day, seven days a week with nothing but short, carefully timed meal breaks until the job was done. Socializing, schmoozing, kibitzing are anathema to him. He'd prefer not to have to be introduced to the sound editor's new assistant, and he will do almost anything to avoid a handshake. Those he gives—watery handshakes, no grip in them at all—seem to be moments of torture during which he won't know what to do with his eyes. He will either look away, or he will stare steadily into his opposite's eyes. Either way, the recipient will probably feel ill at ease.

All told, the impact of Woody's entrance will be to dampen

whatever spirit existed in the room. Some, especially those who are working with Woody for the first time and are perhaps hoping to prove that they are capable of acting natural around a celebrity, will try to keep the spirit aloft, keep tossing cheerful morning words, for to fall silent now, they believe, would admit a degree of uptightness that can only make matters worse. But at 9:02 Woody's soft, flat, unreassuring voice—"Jack, can we begin now?"—unexpectedly pierces the awkward banter, sinking any hopes for a relaxed, fraternal atmosphere. Work begins at once, and for the next four hours no one will dare suggest so much as a coffee break.

Although he manages to have things his way, Woody appears none the happier for the experience. By and large, the more people he has to come in contact with, the more taxing he finds the production. Woody seemed particularly miserable during the making of *Love and Death*, much of which was shot in Hungary with the assistance of the Russian army. He found Budapest windy and cold, the Hungarian staff undependable, and the battle spectacles—with hundreds of extras and teams of special-effects men flown in from London—an ordeal. To make matters worse, his long stays in Paris, a city he loves, were compromised by the aggressive attention of the Parisian press.

About halfway into the filming I came to France and spent ten days screening the dailies and conferring with Woody about future photography. One night Diane Keaton, Woody, Davida, and I went out for dinner to a restaurant off the Champs Elysées. The moment we left the hotel the *paparazzi* burst out from behind parked cars, where they'd been awaiting Woody's exit. Walking backward, flashes constantly popping, they led us the full eight blocks to our destination, jamming themselves right through the restaurant's revolving door to get their final shots. An awful price to pay for fame, I thought, especially for someone as shy as Woody, who doesn't know how to handle praise, let alone adulation, and is nervous coming to dinner if any of the other guests are strangers.

"I always had difficulty with people, men and women, on a social level," Woody told Frank Rich for an *Esquire* magazine profile in 1977. "Before, when I was shy and unknown, I thought that if I could only make it in some way, it would really help relieve me socially and I could relax and go to parties and do things. But then, as soon as I did become known, *that* became the problem—I thought, '*My God*, I'm *well known*—I can't go out.' There are times when I feel like—though it isn't true—but I feel like a prisoner in my own home, when I feel like, oh, I don't want to go down and get the papers because some people will say hello to me. So I stay in.

"I was telling my analyst just a while ago that I had a certain admiration for Howard Hughes—I mean, I'm sure he was a *terrible* man—but what I was referring to was that he was living out a certain reclusive quality that I liked. Like Bergman living on that island, until all that mess happened. My idea of a good time is to take a walk from my house to the office and not for the entire walk have to worry about hearing my name being called from a passing car or being spoken to at all. That would be perfect."

Woody refers to his misery in public places in a scene near the beginning of *Annie Hall*. A hoody-looking character recognizes him outside a movie theater where he is waiting to meet Diane Keaton. As Woody squirms intensely, the man calls to his friends, "Hey, dis is Alvy Singer!" and presses him for his autograph. "Jesus!" Woody says when Keaton finally arrives. "What'd you do, come by way of the Panama Canal? . . . I'm standing with the cast from *The Godfather*." Except for the jokes, the discomfort is true to life.

People find it impossible to accept that a public man can be so shy, that the lovable comic character of *Bananas, Play It Again Sam, The Front*, and *Annie Hall* is not open to their most outrageous advances. I have in mind a lunch break during the editing of *Sleeper*. Woody and I were eating at a Horn and Hardart cafeteria on Eighth Avenue near Fifty-seventh Street when two middle-aged women passed our table and stopped about ten feet down the aisle. After exchanging a few words with her companion, one began retracing her steps until she was standing alongside the movie star. "Are you Woody Allen?" she demanded. Quietly, without looking up from his food, he said, "Yes." At that she walked away, rejoining her friend, who was standing with her arms folded a few tables away. As Woody and I resumed our conversation, I noticed that the first woman, having conferred with her friend, was on her way back. "Are you *sure* you're Woody Allen?" she said, looking down at the top of his head. "Yes," he mumbled. Again she left, and I assumed his agony was over. But to my amazement, the second woman now loomed over us, staring boldly at the trapped man. "Can you identify yourself?" she said, whereupon I rose and made shooing motions, and the two of them left.

During the cutting of *Interiors*, Woody and I occasionally ate lunch at an obscure Hunan restaurant on Broadway in the Eighties, a few blocks from the brownstone where I now live and work. As we neared the restaurant, I saw a teenage girl across the avenue who, I knew by the shock of recognition on her face, had spotted him. Wild with adolescent glee, she started running, charged right through the restaurant doors, and arrived at our table, ecstatic and out of breath, just as we were sitting. She wanted his autograph. Woody said no without ever looking up, and she went away crushed. "Why don't you give her the autograph?" I asked, feeling sorry for the girl. Woody just shook his head, as if to indicate the plethora of demands his public makes on him. They run up to him, they shout from buses, they accost him in countless lobbies, and they have no idea what he's like, that he's not the delightful bundle of uncertainty he portrays in his films, that he prefers to be left alone. As I waited on line to buy our tickets for *That's Entertainment* outside the Ziegfeld, Woody hiding in a nearby doorway, as I asked the sound editor's assistant to let us work alone while we made some changes during the mixing of *Interiors*, as I moved reflexively in innumerable ways to shield him from the impact of his fame, I've wondered if his distress wasn't the other side of the looking glass. Was this the kind of anxiety I would feel if I had chosen a less anonymous career? If I had chosen to act on my desire for recognition instead of my fear of it? If, indeed, I were yet to take the path that had opened before me since *A Thousand Clowns* and begin directing films?

Love and Death represented the climax of Woody's love affair with esoteric humor. It was something that was always apparent in his other films. In *Bananas* a baby carriage flies out of control down the steps of the capital as the rebels take the city. The dictator, seeking American aid, misses the CIA offices and walks into the UJA office instead. In *Sleeper* someone tells the awakened Woody two hundred years after he was put into frozen suspension that World War III was started when someone named Albert Shanker got hold of the atom bomb. How many viewers know that the baby carriage is a reference to *Potemkin*? That UJA stands for United Jewish Appeal? That Albert Shanker is the aggressive and much publicized president of the New York teachers' union? These jokes are like a special reward for people who share Woody's background and tastes. *Love and Death* is brimming with these esoteric references, mostly to Russian literature, and because of my love for the originals, it is one of my favorite Allen films.

The picture is special to me also because of the score. Woody proposed the music for *Love and Death* during my expedition to Paris, suggesting that we back the film entirely with Stravinsky, a choice that seemed appropriate considering the Russian setting and themes. When we started cutting, I listened to a lot of Stravinsky and found him too overpowering for the film. He was like a tidal wave, drowning every part of the picture he came in contact with. As an alternative, I introduced Woody to three compositions by Sergei Prokofieff. Prokofieff was a great composer of ballet, opera, and orchestral works, but, unlike Stravinsky, he had written film scores, too. *Love and Death* was scored with two pieces of music I had known and loved since my OWI years—"Lieutenant Kije," from an old Soviet film of that name, "Alexander Nevsky," composed for the Eisenstein film—as well as a third piece, the "Scythian Suite." It was a heartwarming moment for me, the first time I sat through the screen credits and saw "Score by S. Prokofieff"—in part because of my fondness for the composer, but more because of my fondness for the director and the freedom he had given me to contribute to his work.

A pensive moment on ANNIE HALL.
(Photo: Brian Hamill)

19 ■ *Annie Hall*

It Wasn't the Film
He Set Out to Make

The cliché about sculpture, that the sculptor finds
the statue which is waiting in the stone, applies
equally to editing; the editor finds the film
which is waiting hidden in the material.

—TOM PRIESTLY, British film editor

If anyone had predicted in the fall of 1976, when I first started cutting *Annie Hall*, that the picture would win the New York and the National Film Critics Awards, four top Academy Awards, the Directors Guild Award, and four British Academy Awards including Best Picture and Best Editing, I would have dismissed the idea as uneducated speculation. *Annie Hall* was at that time an untitled and chaotic collection of bits and pieces that seemed to defy continuity, bewilder its creators, and, of all Allen's films, hold the least promise for popular success.

Those who have seen the film remember it as a very sophisticated, very affecting story in which Diane Keaton appears in Woody Allen's life like a wonderful, deliriously spastic bird. He is beguiled by her goofy charm, which swirls and swoops alongside his brooding seriousness. But Woody, wanting to mold her, to make her deeper and better educated, sends her into analysis and college courses, drags her to grim documentaries, and buys her books on death. The daffy girl grows; she becomes more independent; she hangs out with her professors. ("Adult education," cries Woody in a stunning reversal, "is such junk! The professors are so phony! How can you do it?") Worst of all, she begins to trust her own judgment, which includes an alarming taste for the "Mellow." And Woody—"If I get too mellow, I ripen and rot"—loses her. Most painful, he loses her to a mantra-ridden West Coast record producer whose life style and values are antithetical to his own.

Despite the intensity of the hurts and sorrows, audiences found *Annie Hall* very funny; and perhaps because for the first time Woody dealt with issues that were very close to their hearts, this movie has made him one of the foremost directors in America today. It was a story told with great wit and humor, which generated more continuous laughter than any previous Allen film, and with a denouement that left many viewers in tears. This love story was not, however, the intended focus of the film.

Throughout 1976 and the first half of 1977 Woody had in mind a film that would be called "Anhedonia," meaning the inability to experience pleasure (a title choice that at United Artists, at least, generated very little pleasure indeed). "Woody wanted to take a risk and do something different," recalls co-author Marshall Brickman. "The first draft was a story of a guy who lived in New York and was forty years old and was examining his life. His life consisted of several strands. One was a relationship with a young woman, another was a concern with the banality of the life that we all live, and a third an obsession with proving himself and testing himself to find out what kind of character he had. Woody is not a frivolous person. He has his commercial side, as one must to survive in the business, but I think he's genuinely concerned with his philosophy, he feels advancing age, and he worries about death. And he's always intuitively tried to use his personal material in his work."

Woody had turned forty in 1975. He found himself to be a man who had taken life very seriously, had struggled to develop and to overcome his limitations, and yet was still extremely dissatisfied with himself, at odds with his environment, and unsure about exactly how much he could blame certain of his own shortcomings on society's. "I'm a complainer," Woody admits, "a big whiner," and in creating Alvy Singer, a character he describes as "mildly misanthropic and socially discontent," his purpose seemed to be to put his own perpetual discontent into a comic context and thereby burst an inner tension and doubt over its legitimacy. His ambivalence, his emotional division over this issue, persists:

Q: "Are the character's constant complaints legitimate or are they neurotic?"

Woody: "I think the character's complaints are all completely legitimate. The degree to which he obsesses over them in the movie gets to be seen as neurotic, but to me that's not neurotic."

Q: "But in the movie you make fun of his obsession, imply that he's carrying it too far."

Woody: "Right. Because I recognize that as the more rational point of view. I just don't happen to hold that."

The first cut of what has come to be known as *Annie Hall* was two hours and twenty minutes long and took us about six weeks to complete. Far from being the story of a love affair—"The best love story of the decade," said Pat Collins of New York's WCBS-TV; "One of the most endearing romantic comedies in the history of movies," said Gene Shalit on WNBC-TV; "A love story told with piercing sweetness and grief," wrote Penelope Gilliat in *The New Yorker*—it was the surrealistic and abstract adventures of a neurotic Jewish comedian who was reliving his highly flawed life and in the process satirizing much of our culture. Diane Keaton makes a brief appearance after Woody's reference to her in the opening monologue and disappears for ten or fifteen minutes thereafter. The movie was like a visual monologue, a more sophisticated and more philosophical version of *Take the Money and Run*. Its stream-of-consciousness continuity, rambling commentary, and bizarre gags completely obscured the skeletal plot. "The thing was supposed to take place in my mind," says Woody. "Something that would happen would remind me of a quick childhood flash, and that would remind me of a surrealistic image. . . . None of that worked."

In the version that Woody and I screened for Marshall Brickman late in 1976, the opening monologue was very long and repeatedly broken by cuts to scenes that amplified Woody's grievances and hang-ups. It was loaded with some of the freest, funniest, most sophisticated material Woody had ever created, and it hurt him to lose it. With a voice-over narration, Alvy Singer takes us to the Brooklyn neighborhood where he was raised and introduces his family.

MOTHER: It's not the same now that the element has moved in.

ALVY (appearing on the scene as an adult and addressing the audience):   The element. Can you believe that? My mother was always worried that 'the element' would move in. It's like a science-fiction movie.

And with that we are presented with the opening scene of a black and white SF film called *The Invasion of the Element*: "Little did the small and serene community in Brooklyn realize," says the stern-voiced narrator, "that they were about to be invaded by the element." A moving van arrives and a black family emerges. White women faint.

We proceed to Woody's grade-school class, a scene that we eventually used in abbreviated form. Woody, a problem pupil who probably would have won his teacher's vote for "least likely to succeed," asks his little classmates to tell the viewers where they are today. Donald, the model student, runs a "profitable dress company." We cut to Donald's present-day home, Woody asking questions like a visitor from another planet: How can Donald possibly enjoy such a drab, predictable, plastic, suburban life? Donald escorts Woody around the house, while undisciplined children (one of whom, we find out from the proud father, can sing all the words to a detergent commercial) make a racket in the background and Donald's over-dressed, overcoiffed wife chirps, "Who is this guy? . . . Is he saying something about our house?" A TV set is running continuously, tuned to a cheap giveaway show.

ALVY: This is the worst kind of show.

TV HOST (responding right from the picture tube):   What do you mean this is the worst kind of show? This show is very popular.

ALVY: This is a popular show?

HOST: That's right. We give away a lot of prizes—that's fun.

ALVY: You're tranquillizing with the trivial—that's what Kierkegaard said.

HOST (genuinely bewildered):   Who? Who? Kierkegaard? What show is he on?

They continue to argue, while Donald's wife gets into a conversation with a female contestant ("Darling, where did you get that suit?").

We return to the classroom. There are other destinies to unravel, including that of Judy Horowitz, a little beauty whom Alvy worshiped. We see her today, fat, surrounded by kids, caked with makeup and cosmetic fakery.

Various gags take Woody from being a peculiar child who never had a "latency period" to a full-blown neurotic adult. We see two kids under the old Coney Island boardwalk. A chum is giving Little Alvy (played by Jonathan Monk) a condom, as Woody explains on the sound track: "When I was ten I knew I should carry around an emergency contraceptive." Another shot under the boardwalk. This time it's Woody with a girl friend and he's removing the latex relic. "By the time I got to use it, it was dust. It's now powder."

As his mother complains about his isolation—"You always saw the worst in people. . . . Even when you became famous, you still distrusted the world"—we see snatches of Woody on the Dick Cavett and Ed Sullivan shows. It's the end of the prologue, about thirteen or fourteen minutes, only a fraction of which will be used.

If we were to look at the first cut now, something we cannot do because it no longer exists, the first dramatic shot that would recall the movie as we've come to know it would hit the screen at this point—the long shot of Woody and Tony Roberts (Rob) approaching the camera as Woody carries on about anti-Semitism. ("I was having lunch with some guys at NBC, and I said, did you eat yet or what? And Tom Christie said, 'No—Jew?' ") Woody then goes to meet Diane at the movies; the thug pursues Woody for his autograph; the Columbia professor pontificates on the ticket line about Fellini and McLuhan, and, in a stunning coup, Woody produces McLuhan from behind a placard. After several minutes·of this familiar material, we'd then be surprised to find that Woody and McLuhan begin a conversation about Woody's college days, particularly an incident for which he was expelled from school after just one year. This triggers a complete flashback scene to a dean's office in which Woody is being reprimanded for burning another dean in effigy.

Returning to the present we'd again find a strand of the movie we know: Alvy and Annie in bed after viewing *The Sorrow and the Pity* for the second time, Annie unwilling to make love to him, and then the flashback to Woody's first wife, Allison Portchnik (Carol Kane), whom he meets at an Adlai Stevenson rally. But we would hardly have time to feel at home with this material before we'd be off on a strange second flashback built on the first. Little Alvy, faking a fever by holding his thermometer over the radiator, is visited by his voluptuous cousin Doris. Doris brings him comic books about Hitler, Nazi spies, German submarines, and similar subjects. As she reads to him, he swoons over her and begins to drool. ("Alvy, you're drooling.") Another cut in time. We are in Nazi headquarters. Two officers are speaking in German. The subtitles: "We caught two from the resistance. We tortured the Frenchman, Sartre, but he refuses to talk. Here's the American." He produces Woody, who steadfastly declines to implicate his associates. The Nazis put a gun to his head and threaten to execute him on the spot. Suddenly Woody pulls a hand puppet from his pocket: "Because of my moral convictions," says the intrepid resistance fighter, "I cannot name names. But *he*"—the puppet—"can," and he proceeds to provide the information they want ventriloquially.

We are now in the home of Alvy and Allison, where Woody is awakening from the former scene. "Why!?" he cries. "Why am I always the coward?" Allison: "Not the same dream?" It is obviously familiar ground. Before we return to Woody and Diane, herding wild lobsters at their beach house, Allison has to put up with his lamentations about cowardice, testing, the Warsaw ghetto, and the earthquake in Chile: "I should be there," he moans, "I'm not helping my fellow man."

Time and again, if we could view this first cut, we would be surprised to find the film dwelling on issues that were just touched in passing in the version we know. From an anxiety about proving himself and being tested to a distaste for intellectuals and an envy of athletes, Woody seemed to be intent on covering every issue of his adult life. Once we got it on the screen, the problem was obvious: "It was like the first draft of a novel," says Brickman, "like the raw material from which a film could be assembled, from which two or three films could possibly be assembled." When Woody and his second wife, Robin, a tough, uptight New York intellectual (played by Janet Margolin, barely recognizable from her tenderhearted role in *Take the Money*), attend the literary cocktail party, they stay much longer, plenty of time for Woody to establish "how creepy the thinkers are." Cutting about the room, we overhear a plethora of one-liners that would burn holes in the pages of *The New York Review of Books*:

> SIDNEY: My book was called *Alternate Modes of Perspectives.* His was *Alternate Styles of Perspectives.*
>
> NORMAN: I'm going to say one word that will refute your entire argument: Beowulf.
>
> NEEDLEMAN: I'm inner-directed, he's outer-directed, but his outer direction is inner-directed.
>
> DWIGHT: I'll review yours and you review mine.

Failing to seduce Robin in the bedroom where she discovers him alone amid the piles of coats, watching the Knicks game, Woody turns back to the TV set. "Knicks ball—out of bounds—Jackson to Bradley—shot! No good! Rebound—Kierkegaard. Passes to Nietzsche—fast break to Kafka! Top of the key—it's Kafka and Alvy—all alone—they're both gripped with anxiety—and guilt—and neither can shoot! Now Earl Monroe steals it! And the Knicks have a four on two—"

As we move into the second half of this original version, Annie finally begins to emerge, because almost all the present-tense material relates to her in some way. But despite the importance of Alvy's problems with Annie—her need to smoke pot before they can make love, his unnerving visit to her Wisconsin home, his jealousy, his anxiety about her moving in with him, her infatuation with Los Angeles and with Tony Lacey, the West Coast record producer played by Paul Simon, and Alvy's great sense of loss when she leaves him—his relationship with her is also a taking-off point for innumerable flights into the past, into fantasy, into current dramatic action that further amplifies his personal themes. Among the scenes that would lead us away from an involvement with the Keaton-Allen love affair as we watch the second half would be:

• Alvy's fantasy trip to California. He and Annie are visiting Rob in Beverly Hills. Rob speaks in a strange zombielike voice: "I prepared these two pods—one for each of you. When you sleep they will take over your bodies, and you will then be happy citizens of Los Angeles."

• A scene on the boardwalk from Alvy's teenage years in which the Surf Avenue Angels, unamused by his banter, can't decide whether to throw him into the water or break his head with a baseball bat.

• A fantasy in which Woody and Shelly Duvall (playing the *Rolling Stone* reporter he dates after breaking up with Annie) are transported from the "transplendent" Maharishi gathering at Yankee Stadium to the garden of Eden, where they discuss sex, anatomy, and the female orgasm with God. The Latter is in the midst of declaring that He is "for all time creating man and woman" when Woody brashly advises, "Well, don't put the sexual organs too close to the excretory ones—it'll only cause problems later."

• A ten-to-fifteen-minute sequence in which Alvy, Rob, and Annie take a tour—in time and space—of the "old neighborhood" in Brooklyn where the two men grew up, including a flashback scene of Little Alvy in the schoolyard taking his temperature with a thermometer he carries with him at all times, as well as other images of Rob and Alvy as boys; a contrast shot of Alvy's coarse, feuding parents and Annie's refined, courteous parents; an incredible sequence in which Woody imagines his parents speaking with the Halls' civility (Father: "Make me a martini." Mother: "Of course, sweetheart. How would you like it, dear?" Father: "On white bread with mayonnaise"); visions of Alvy's boisterous relatives at a post-World War II coming-home party for his cousin; a discussion of the afterlife during which a street elevator rises from the ground bearing the Devil, who takes the trio on a guided tour of Hell—all nine layers ("Layer Five: organized crime, fascist dictators, and people who don't appreciate oral sex"); a fight between two men in a junk-food establishment, Rob and Alvy trying to intercede on behalf of the smaller man and escaping with their teeth only because the bully in the brawl recognizes Alvy as a TV personality.

• A jailhouse scene in which Woody, arrested for his reckless parking-lot driving spree in Los Angeles, is thrown in with a bunch of tough cons and wins them over by entering their joke-telling session with a tour-de-force performance.

All told, this first cut was as different in its way from the movie that became *Annie Hall* as the first cut of *The Night They Raided Minsky's* was from the film that was finished eleven months later. Woody and I were both discouraged by what we saw, but Marshall Brickman, who had had very little experience viewing first assemblies, was despondent.

"I was very disappointed," says Marshall. "I thought that the first twenty-five minutes didn't work at all. I felt that the film was running off in nine different directions. I kept saying to myself—you always feel this when you see the first assembly. And yet there was that persistent and very convincing notion that I was *right*, that it didn't work. The film never got going—actually until Paul Simon appeared, which is pretty late into the film. It was a very commentative film—and Woody of course is brilliant at that—and it was funny, but, I felt, nondramatic and ultimately uninteresting, a kind of cerebral exercise. Stuff that's wonderful fun to write is often less fun for the audience to see, and all that stuff that Woody and I had written was cerebral, surreal, highly intellectual, overliterate, overeducated, self-conscious commentary. And just for a moment I had a sense of panic: we took a chance, and it didn't work; we will be humiliated; is there any way to stop the project?

It was clear to Woody and me that the film started moving whenever present-tense material with him and Keaton dominated the screen, and so we began cutting in the direction of that relationship. We were still, as far as we knew, working on the same film, about a comic who can feel no joy and about his jaded view of the world. But we sensed immediately where the life was, and Woody, with his sure commercial sense, had no hesitation about trimming away much of the first twenty minutes in order to establish Keaton more quickly. After several weeks of working and reworking the material, we hit on the formula that got Woody swiftly through his opening monologue and childhood scenes—first his mother taking him to a doctor (he's upset and refuses to eat because the universe is expanding—a short scene extracted from the middle of the movie); then the classroom scene where the grown Woody defends himself against his third-grade teacher, and his classmates tell where they are today (Donald says he's a "profitable dress manufacturer," and we move on to the next child—no foray into the suburban home, no conversation with the television); a glimpse of Woody on the Dick Cavett show, his mother complaining that he always saw the worst in people, and the opening narration is over. Six minutes. Now Alvy and Rob are on the street in the present time, Alvy complaining about anti-Semitism, and the audience senses the action is about to begin. A minute later Woody is waiting to meet Diane at the theater; she arrives late in a bad mood, she's missed her therapy session, and she refers (in much too loud a voice) to their "sexual problem."

We spend five minutes with Annie at the theater and in bed

afterward. Annie tries to reassure Alvy about her unwillingness to have sex by referring to his sexual problems with his first wife, Allison Portchnick, and in a four-and-a-half-minute flash-back to the Stevenson rally where Woody meets Allison and the bedroom scene where he avoids her by favoring an obsession with the Kennedy assassination we put Allison away for good. We had to get back to Annie, because if she was going to be the dramatic focus that would hold this picture together, we could not stray from her for long. As Woody and I saw the picture heading in her direction, we realized that the other relationships had to be trimmed. Gone are Cousin Doris, the Nazi comics, and the interrogation dream he relates to Allison. After another three minutes with Annie and the lobsters and a glimpse at her former lover, we flash back to Woody's second marriage. It's Robin and Alvy at the cocktail party, but the movie is more and more about relationships now, and the anti-intellectual humor of this scene began to pull the picture off course. Out went the academic one-liners and the philosophers' basketball game. Robin had to be gotten through with, and with severe cutting, Woody's second marriage was off the screen in under three minutes.

In the emerging movie, twenty-four minutes have elapsed when Woody and Rob arrive at the Wall Street Tennis Club for the scene in which Annie and Alvy first meet. The pace until now has been brisk. The two main characters have been introduced, and we've learned something about their personalities, their backgrounds, and the conflicts between them. Light-headed, devil-may-care Midwestern girl who grew up in a Norman Rockwell painting meets urban Jewish comedian who has enough awareness for both of them and hang-ups to match. To the extent that we've focused on Woody's background, it has been to serve the portrayal of this relationship, which, we were now beginning to realize, was completely taking over the film. The tennis-court meeting, coming as it does one-quarter of the way into the picture, has the refreshing effect of a new beginning. We've been alerted to the problems; now we shall see the chronology, how it all happened.

Allen and Keaton stay on the screen together for the next nineteen minutes—at the tennis court, driving uptown in her Volkswagen, and at her apartment afterward; on their first date and then in bed; at the bookstore where he buys her books about death, strolling through the park where they make fun of passersby, and on the dock where he tells her he loves her; in his apartment as she moves in; at the beach house where he refuses to let her smoke pot, her spirit leaving her body during sex as a result. Only then did we cut to a younger Alvy, pretending to enjoy the routine of a horrible comic for whom he is being hired to write material, a scene that proved a useful transition to Woody's onstage appearance in Wisconsin prior to his visit to Annie's home.

When Brickman saw this new version with so much of his original material removed, he felt as if his "flesh had been ripped off," but he realized that his initial panic had been unfounded and that a legitimate film was emerging. Woody, too, had mixed feelings: "There was a lot of material taken out of that picture that I thought was wonderfully funny," says Woody. "I was sorry to lose just about all that surrealistic stuff. It was what I had intended to do. I didn't sit down with Marshall Brickman and say, 'We're going to write a picture about a relationship.' I mean the whole concept of the picture changed as we were cutting it. It was originally a picture about me, exclusively, not about a relationship. It was about me, my life, my thoughts, my ideas, my background, and the relationship was one major part of it. But sometimes it's hard to foresee at the outset what's going to be the most interesting drift. The guesses we started out with, many of them were wrong. But we wound up with the right guesses."

As the movie evolved, we struggled, twisted, stretched, and pulled in order to build a story rationale into the transitions. Marshall Brickman was in favor of abandoning the original time-shifting structure entirely and putting the film together in straight chronological order—opening with the tennis meeting and proceeding to the break-up—but this would not have simplified our task. A typical problem was finding a logical place to have Annie move into Alvy's apartment. The script called for her to move in after two flashbacks to Woody's childhood, the Invasion-of-the-Body-Snatchers fantasy visit to Beverly Hills, and the scene with Woody and the abominable comic. I realized, after many trials and errors, that in terms of emotional buildup the logical place for her to move in came much earlier, after they profess their love for each other on the pier. Shifting the material around into logical and dramatically appropriate positions was as time-consuming as it had been for *Take the Money and Run,* and when we were unable to force a juxtaposition, Woody again had to shoot new scenes.

When you shake a picture down to this extent, some essential ingredients are bound to fall out. Little episodes, verbal asides that were meant to bridge the continuity, cling to the extraneous material and are lost. Among the scenes that we eliminated was one that focused on Alvy's negativeness. It had included an important piece of transitional material in which Woody whines about a West Coast obligation: "Now I've got to go to Los Angeles. . . . I hate L.A.. . . . They want me to be on one of those meaningless awards shows. . . . My agent says the masses like it." Without these lines we had no way of explaining the cut to California, and so among the additional material Woody filmed was a scene at a party in which the carving up of a fresh shipment of cocaine paves the way for the transitional lines:

> COKE FIEND: It's great stuff, Alvy. Friend of mine just brought it in from California.
>
> ANNIE: Oh, do you know something? I didn't tell yuh, we're going to California next week.
>
> GIRL: Oh really?
>
> ANNIE: Yeah.
>
> ALVY: On my agent's advice, sold out. I'm gonna do an appearance on TV.

Although this scene was written and shot just for this information, audiences were always much more focused on the cocaine, and when Woody sneezes into what we've just learned is a two-thousand-dollar cache, blowing white powder all over the living room—an old-fashioned, lowest-common-denominator, slip-on-the-banana-peel joke—the film gets its single largest laugh. ("A complete unplanned accident," says Woody.) The laughter was so great at each of our test screenings that I kept having to add more and more feet of dead film to keep the laughter from pushing the next scene right off the screen. Woody and I both prefer to let laughter intrude a little into the next shot, even to the extent of letting the audience miss a few lines, rather than compromise the pace, but in this case the laughter was so sustained we had no choice but to hold the scene for what seemed to me an interminable and embarrassing length of time (actually about five or six seconds). Even so, the transitional information was lost on many viewers: when they stop laughing and spot Alvy and Annie in a car with Rob, who's discussing how life has changed for him since he emigrated to Beverly Hills, they are momentarily uncertain about how or why the couple got there.

The more we became involved in the plot of the relationship, the more we had to prune. Even scenes involving both Keaton and Allen had to be dropped if they stalled the dramatic flow. One of the funniest examples, which included the major portion of Colleen Dewhurst's performance, took place at the Hall home in Wisconsin. Dewhurst, as Annie's mother, is taking snapshots after dinner as her husband serves drinks and argues with Annie about art. Suddenly Mom remembers a dream she had the night before and asks Alvy to interpret it. She was having a fight with a man—"It was not Dad, Annie, but he was wearing your dad's bathrobe"—over who had control of the TV set. She gets very mad and breaks the aerial off, and when the man demands it back, she runs upstairs and flushes it down the toilet. "So what do you think about that, Alvy?" Woody: "Are you kidding?" Dewhurst: "No. What would your psychiatrist say?" Woody: "You must be joking. It's obviously a phallic dream." Dad: "A what?" Woody: "A phallic dream . . . it represents an unconscious impulse toward castration." The entire family is scandalized.

"My own feeling," says Woody, "was that the whole section ran too long. Ralph felt that the scene just didn't come off, and it was hurt by the material before it, and we should move the story along." With a ruthless editorial momentum, we chopped off the next scene, too, in which Annie's brother (Christopher Walken) confesses to Alvy about a wish to drive head on into oncoming vehicles.

"It was that way till a week before we completed the thing," recalls Woody, "and we stuck the brother back in—we were getting such good responses we started to put back one or two things that we liked."

Like Colleen Dewhurst, Shelly Duvall also lost most of her performance. Half the Maharishi scene was cut, as was the trip to the Garden of Eden. Duvall is reduced to little more than a walk-on part, although one of the lines she speaks in her zonked-out nasal monotone—"Sex with you," she tells Woody as they're lying uncomfortably in his bed, "is really a Kafkaesque experience"—is one of the most hilarious of the film.

As we plowed through the second half of the picture, we had no time for references to Woody's childhood or what had become by now gratuitous raps at the culture. We plundered the long trip to Brooklyn for a few useful moments and discarded the rest, including the conflict in the junk-food establishment, causing the loss of Danny

Aiello's only scene, one in which he gave a very good and very funny performance.

Of all the things we removed from the film the cut that Woody resisted most strongly was the one in which he was thrown into jail after his parking-lot mishap. The movie was speeding toward a conclusion and could not afford to stop for this charming incident. His attachment to it was one of his few lapses in plot sense. "You work so closely on the thing, shoot it every day for months," explains Woody, "and it's very hard to maintain objectivity. I thought the jailhouse sequence would be an interesting end for the movie. The character I was playing had a more human experience. He was thrown into this context with these terrible-looking people and these lowlifes, and it turned out they were not so bad, that his initial fear of them was not really justified, and that by telling some jokes with them—you know, it had a warmer feeling to it."

As usual, Woody was in a terrible quandary about how to end the film. On three separate outings in October, November, and December of 1976 he shot additional material for the last segment, much of it an attempt to show the process by which Alvy comes to miss Annie. He shot scenes in which he's calling Annie on the West Coast over and over again, scenes in which he's doing public-service commercials for educational TV, scenes with a new girl friend with whom he seems to be living while still unable to overcome his longing for Annie. He would audition this material for me in the cutting room and we would try to insert it in the movie. But finally I urged him to forget all of these dramatic transitions and have Alvy say "I miss Annie—I made a terrible mistake," on a flat cut from the scene in which Annie and Alvy are sorting out their things in his apartment—which is finally how the last segment gets underway.

The final moments gave Woody the biggest problems. Several conclusions were shot. One of them, true to Woody's inclinations, was a real downer. He meets Annie, repatriated in New York, dragging her new boy friend to see *The Sorrow and the Pity*. The former lovers achieve "maximum awkwardness," and then, the awkwardness serving as the tear-jerker, they say good-bye. As I had done on *Take the Money and Run* and *Bananas*, I suggested he return to the beginning of the film for a clue about how to end.

In the opening monologue he attempts to summarize his attitudes toward life and toward women. He relates an old Groucho Marx joke—"I would never wanna belong to any club that would have someone like me for a member"—and says, "That's the key joke of my adult life in terms of my relationships with women."

Woody agreed that returning to this material in some way was his best option. He had hardly given it any thought before we were in a cab heading down to the studio, Woody scribbling notes on a piece of scrap paper on the way. The reading (which I do not remember and of which there is no record) came close to providing the finale we wanted, but it wasn't close enough. The following day he said he wanted to try something else, so again we jumped into a cab and Woody jotted down some new ideas as we rode. "It was no big planned thing," he recalls. "I mean we were sitting grousing all day, looking at footage, cutting, recutting, dealing with other problems. I remember sitting with Ralph in the cutting room at five o'clock preparing for a seven o'clock screening that night and saying, let's go down to the sound studio and I'll put a jump at the end of the picture and wing the joke about the eggs. At five-thirty that night we got into the recording booth, ran back uptown and stuck that joke in, and it stayed forever."

The joke about the eggs was a tired old vaudeville gag that Woody adapted to his context. "It was great seeing Annie again . . ." Woody narrates, as Annie and Alvy shake hands and part after a reminiscing lunch near Lincoln Center. "I realized what a terrific person she was, and how much fun it was just knowing her. And I thought of that old joke: You know, this, this, this guy goes to a psychiatrist and says, 'Doc, uh, my brother's crazy. He thinks he's a chicken.' And, uh, the doctor says, 'Well, why don't you turn him in?' And the guy says, 'I would but I need the eggs.' Well, I guess that is pretty much how I feel about relationships. You know, they're totally irrational and crazy and absurd and, but, uh, I guess we keep goin' through it because, uh, most of us need the eggs."

I suggested that Woody read the lines against the picture—that is, read them while simultaneously viewing the image of him and Keaton on the screen saying good-bye, something he rarely cares to do. When he was finished, he said, "What do you think?" I knew his inclination would be to do a dozen more readings, each with slightly different accents and pauses and carefully timed stammers. I said, "Leave it alone. Let's just walk away from it." And later that night when I saw that ending with an audience, I knew my instinct was right. They were grabbed, the picture was wrapped up, and the ending gave every-thing that came before it a new coloring: this was not just an hour and a half of light humor, but something more poignant.

At one point during the editing of those last few minutes, after it was decided to have Alvy and Annie meet for the Lincoln Center lunch, Woody said something to me like, "What about memory—shouldn't we have them discuss old times?" It was an incident I had forgotten about until, during the writing of this book, I asked my assistant, Sandy Morse, what had struck her most about the cutting of that picture. As soon as the subject of memory arose, I knew what we needed to do. Sandy, who was relatively new to the cutting room then (she has since edited Woody's *Manhattan*), was startled by what followed. I rattled off descriptions of pieces of film I wanted her to get for me—a shot of Annie and Alvy driving uptown from the tennis courts, a shot of Woody squeamishly putting a wild lobster in the pot, a shot of them at the beach, a shot of them in bed (Annie reading and Alvy reaching over to kiss her), shots of Annie arriving at Alvy's apartment with her luggage, Annie holding up the porno negligée Alvy bought her for her birthday, and perhaps a dozen others—many more than we finally used. Sandy quickly fetched me the reels, and I held them up to the light, showing her which frames I wanted—twenty feet of this, three feet of that, eight feet of this . . . make this number one, this number two, and so on. She spliced them all together on a single reel, and I edited them down to a reprise of Keaton singing her nightclub number, "Seems Like Old Times" (all the memory moments are silent). One of my favorite cuts in that montage was Woody and Diane on a pier. He points, and we cut to what they "see," which turns out to be another memory cut of them kissing. That little transition helped augment the power of the reprise, although I put it together so intuitively I was hardly aware of its existence until Woody and I screened the film some time later. The creation of that sequence was an insignificant moment for me, because after years in the cutting room, manufacturing similar sequences for *The Pawnbroker*, *A Thousand Clowns*, and *Goodbye Columbus*, it was as natural an option for me as an old vaudeville joke was for Woody.

"I'll never forget," says Marshall Brickman, describing the moment he first saw the film with this new conclusion, "suddenly there was an ending there—not only that, but an ending that was cinematic, that was moving, with that simple recapitulation of some of the previous scenes, with that music. . . . The whole film could have gone into the toilet if there hadn't been that last beat on it. I think every writer of comedy wants to send them out with something like that, to keep them laughing, extremely hysterical, for an hour and twenty-eight minutes, and then for the last two minutes turn it around and let them walk away with something they can chew on."

There remained, however, the problem of the title. Brickman came up to the cutting room, and he and Woody engaged in one of their title sessions, Marshall spewing forth proposals—"Rollercoaster Named Desire," "Me and My Goy," "It Had to Be Jew"—with manic glee. This seemed to have little impact on Woody, though, for he remained committed to "Anhedonia" until the very end. "He first sprung it on me at an early title session," remembers Brickman. "Arthur Krim, who was the head of United Artists then, walked over to the window and threatened to jump." Nevertheless, with the release date approaching, UA hired an advertising firm and asked them to make a presentation for a campaign based on that title. Their proposal, which was ingenious but which would have added several million dollars to the release budget, was to take out advertisements in newspapers across the country, ads that would include a definition of the obscure word and look like the front page of a tabloid newspaper. Banner headlines would scream: "ANHEDONIA STRIKES CLEVELAND!" or "ANHEDONIA STRIKES TUCSON!"

Woody, meanwhile, was adjusting his own thinking, and during the last five screenings, he had me try out a different title each night in my rough-cut speech. The first night it was "Anhedonia," and a hundred faces looked at me blankly. The second night it was "Anxiety," which roused a few chuckles from devoted Allen fans. Then "Anhedonia" again. Then "Annie and Alvy." And finally "Annie Hall," which, thanks to a final burst of good sense, held. It's now hard to suppose it could ever have been called anything else.

The cutting of every film presents different and unexpected challenges. You never know what problems you're going to face or what skills you'll need to summon. *Annie Hall* received intensive editorial attention, but it was not "saved" in the cutting room. Despite Woody's self-deprecating quips ("You know what we had to go through to get it," he said to me when I congratulated him on the Academy Awards), the quality was all there in the first cut. Anyone reading the unabridged shooting script would be overwhelmed by the authors' comic genius. The special job in editing this picture was to find the plot amid all the brilliant skits.

Annie Hall did not entail a lot of cutting from one angle to another, a lot of emergency opticals, or any fancy editorial footwork of the sort that is so often praised or called "dazzling" by people with a limited knowledge of film editing's true scope or purpose. In the entire picture there were only 382 cuts—compared to 1401 in *The Night They Raided Minsky's,* a very different sort of comedy (of equal length), a film that was in such trouble that it had to be not so much edited as remade. The job with *Annie Hall* was, as Eisenstein said, to allow the filmed material to guide you. Somewhere in that two-hour-and-twenty-minute first assembly was a story that worked, and when the commotion and anxiety from viewing the first cut settled, Woody and I set out to find it. Out of the vast amount of material that Woody thought was going to comprise his first personal commentary film, we found a love story about two very different, perhaps incompatible, people; and once he allowed his original intentions to fade and we let the film lead us in this new direction, it proved to be a love story that was a touching fable of our times.

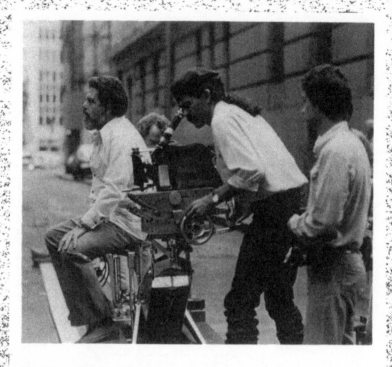

Shooting Thurber's THE GREATEST MAN IN THE WORLD with cinematographer Tony Mitchell.
(Photo: Ken Howard)

20 ▪ Swan Song

In 1971 Glenn Turner, an eccentric self-made millionaire, the head of an evangelic movement called Dare to Be Great, and the founder of a controversial pyramid business scheme that soon tied him up in fraudulent-practices litigation all over the country, decided he wanted a public image, as he was about to launch a political career. Through a chain of people in public relations and film, I was recommended to him as the man who could make his biographical movie.

Turner's opulent corporate headquarters were located in Orlando, Florida, but he spent a lot of his time giving inspirational speeches at Dare to Be Great meetings, in prisons, to fraternal organizations, and anywhere that people wanted to hear him. I first met him in San Francisco, where he'd gone to spur on a group of students who were cleaning up a damaging oil spill, and he promptly gave me the pitch he had delivered to millions of his followers: "I hear you're the greatest film editor in the world. I want you to know that you can do whatever you want to do. You're going to make a great documentary."

The man had been an ugly boy with a harelip and a speech impediment, defects he still had, which was remarkable considering the depth and breadth and intensity of his following. He had climbed to prominence by telling millions to dare to be great, and now he was telling me, a former stammerer who had hidden himself in the cutting room, that I could make a film. He was a secular offshoot of the Southern Baptist preacher tradition, a middle-American phenomenon that was alien to me and that aroused my suspicion. But he was also an outsider, with a great sense of himself and what he could achieve. I admired his defiance of the authorities that impugned him, and I was moved by his determination to uplift the emotionally downtrodden. As I sat and listened to him in his room at the Fairmont Hotel, I was charmed by his earnestness and sincerity, and struck by my reaction: he was manipulating me with his dare-to-be-great formula, and I was inspired.

We agreed that I would make a documentary by following him, observing him, and interviewing him at various times and locations of my choosing over the course of the next three months. He would finance the whole thing and give me complete editorial control.

Making the film was the most gratifying professional experience of my life. The portrait was sympathetic, and yet the undertones of desperation, of mass-movement hysteria, were evident. A sentimental man with much to give, implied the film. A world saver. And, yes, a demogogue of sorts who, through the mobilization of pain, could become dangerous. "You really captured me," said Turner when I screened it for him.

The picture was dramatic and fascinating to watch even for people in New York City, where Turner had received practically no press attention and was almost unknown. The network executives who saw it were moved to superlatives, but were unwilling to purchase it. Turner was prepared to buy an hour of prime time and air the picture at his own expense, allowing the stations to make an additional profit by selling advertising as well. But the networks' editorial policies, which often entail a Pablum objectivity in which almost every subject gets put up and put down in equal measure, precluded the purchase of independent material or, in this case, even the airing of such material as an advertisement. Privately I was told that they believed a prime-time presentation of this picture would make Turner a political powerhouse overnight, and they did not want that responsibility. Just after the networks demurred, a large syndication company, which provides programs to nonnetwork stations all over the country, announced its intention to purchase the picture. Terms were agreed upon and the contract was being drawn up when the company withdrew from the deal for what I was convinced were political reasons. Ultimately the picture was shown locally in the South and Southwest on a number of independent stations.

Without Turner around to incite me, I drifted into a period during which all my old hesitations about leaving the cutting room—not wanting to promote myself, fear of failure, financial insecurity—restrained me. It was during this time that I conceived this book, partly in the hope that it would give me the momentum I needed to move on.

In 1977 another opportunity arose, this time to edit and co-direct an equally unusual film. It was the brainchild of Carl Gurevich, a single-minded, sensual gourmand who wanted to do a documentary on the sexual fantasies of ordinary people. I could tell from Carl's evangelical commitment to the sexual revolution that this project might be as meaningful in its way as the Turner film. In any case, it was not going to be pornography—the objective was an R rating.

Acting Out did not live up to Carl's quixotic intention of showing dream-come-true orgasms on the screen. Many of our volunteers had cross-sexual fantasies, degradation fantasies, perversion wishes of one kind or another. Those with hearty heterosexual appetites often found that put on the spot in the settings they requested and with the porno actor or actress of their choice, they were unable to rise to the auspicious occasion. But at certain moments in this film something poignant about the sharing of private dreams seemed to emerge instead. In any case, I found great pleasure in being able to shape the interviews and enacted fantasies into a documentary statement.

In 1978 Robert Geller, the TV producer for whom I had done some emergency editorial repair work in the past, invited me to direct "The Greatest Man in the World" by James Thurber as a part of the PBS "American Short Story" series. In the meantime I took the aggressive (for me) step of circulating a proposal for a documentary concept of my own. Woody Allen and I shook hands after *Interiors* to end a six-picture cutting-room relationship, and, via a path I only now can trace, I found myself emerging from the shadows and moving into the brightened area at the edge of the director's spotlight.

At this point, a few observations. My first concerns the recurring question of how much editing is too much editing. Take the scene in *Annie Hall* in which Allen and Keaton wait on line at a movie theater arguing about their faltering sex life while a man behind them pontificates on Fellini, Bergman, and McLuhan. This scene remained on the screen for nearly three minutes without a single cut, and yet is properly edited, a fact that is easily overlooked in this era of heavy editing.

Since the sixties there has been a trend toward frenetic, clever, or flashy editing regardless of the tone or style of the film. Richard Lester's reliance on editorial tricks in his famous Beatle pictures, while helping to shake filmmaking out of its stodginess, has been, for this reason, largely a corrupting influence. Picked up and promoted by television and advertising, flamboyant editing has had a faddish appeal, with the result that less care has been given to scripting, filming, and directing the actors.

Regardless of its extent or style, editing should not impress or call attention to itself. As an audience, we no more want to see the wheels and gears and levers responsible for the effect the film is having on us that we want to see the pencil marks on an author's first draft or the invisible wires in a magic show. But as much as I dislike conspicuous or excessive editing, I would never set a limit on the amount of editing that is legitimate. Some pictures require a lot of fast cutting, others extensive editorial revision. Editing is a tool that should be used as needed, and filmmakers who distrust it because it interferes with the photographic purity are handicapping themselves with excessive ideology. On the whole, the editors for whom I have the most respect do not cut according to formulas or habits of mind, but face each new assignment with trepidation, because they know routine solutions do not exist.

Observation Two: Because editors are among the few film collaborators who must struggle with almost all the major issues—plot, continuity, performance, special effects—they are natural candidates for directors. With so many years spent making films work, when I direct a film, my intuition abounds with insights the moment I think of a scene or a transition or a characterization. I hear the music. I imagine the cuts. I see the performances I want, even the character type. And I believe this would be true for many editors. Yet compared to the other breeding grounds, relatively few directors have come from the ranks of career editors. Why the film industry has made such poor use of this obvious talent pool has to do with the nature of the editors, with the nature of the film business, and with the nature of power.

For all their quiet acknowledgment of recent years, editors are part of an oppressed class in filmmaking. Although, in addition to their formal duties, they serve the director as cheerleader, coach, therapist, idea man, and relief pitcher, they are the lowest-paid and least recognized of the top members of the movie team. And because they are also expected to play the role of savior if a picture is not working, they are often the first to be indicted for its failure.

To be a successful film editor one has to carefully weed out all the personal qualities—self-assertion, authority, exuberance over one's own ideas—that are expected in directors. The profession selects in favor of caution, timidity, self-abnegation, tact, "a diplomacy," says British editor James Clark, "which would normally put us straight into parliament." In its extreme, the role of editor is like the old-fashioned role of wives of great men, women whose contributions to history are acknowledged only in the form of folklore. To defy this role is a dangerous thing, for one gets branded with whisper labels like "aggressive woman" or "uppity nigger." Aram Avakian (*The Miracle Worker, Jazz on a Summer's Day*), the editor (and director) whose cutting I most admire and have at times been awed by, resisted playing by these rules, and his editorial career has been damaged as a result. All told, an array of mutually influenced internal and external forces make it as unlikely for an editor to become a director as it does for a woman to head a major corporation.

Observation Three: Having spent so many years in the back rooms, I would naturally like to see filmmaking emerge from its hero myths and be recognized as a collective enterprise. I believe in collaboration, in the excitement of team effort, and in every man's right to credit for his work. As a director, I'm too mindful of the odds and the challenges to want to surround myself with slaves or yesmen who will push me and my blunders into permanent embrace. But as much as I feel directors will benefit from a broadening and diffusing of the spotlight, it is difficult to imagine them voluntarily accepting a cut in their power.

To hold power in filmmaking is to have the option to say, "That's where I dollied in for a close-up," or "I'm in the midst of cutting my new picture" when the work being described actually belongs to someone else. It wasn't long ago that the producer held such prerogatives. He optioned the book, hired the scriptwriters, gave the script to one of his in-house directors, told him which of the contracted stars to use, put a loyal "personal" editor on the project, and saw the result as his own creation. Thus, *Gone With the Wind* is associated with producer David O. Selznick, not with director Victor Fleming, even though Fleming won an Academy Award for his efforts.

During the casting for "The Greatest Man in the World," I was struck by the availability of top character actors—people who for years have had a starlike luster for me—to play minor roles at relatively low rates of pay. Such is the unfortunate state of the acting business. It is also another aspect of a director's power, for everyone around him is hungry for work, and in many cases he makes the choices. It is only a short step, once this power goes to your head, to assuming that because you chose the actor, his brilliant performance accrues to you; because you chose the cinematographer, his inventive camerawork accrues to you; because you chose the set designer, the imaginative sets accrue to you. You may even believe, as many directors do, that because you can demand revisions in the script and even contribute a few lines of dialogue yourself, you are legitimately credited as co-author.

Of course, anyone who's made a career in filmmaking, unless he's been hopelessly brainwashed by the director mystique, knows how things really stand—how petrified a director is of failure, how keenly he hunts down each member of his team, and how grateful he is (whether he acknowledges it or not) for any original ideas or sparks of inspiration his teammates may contribute. Director Stanley Kramer has argued that if editors have ideas, they should be directors, not editors. But when I make a picture, I *want* an editor with ideas, as badly as a baseball manager wants a thinking runner on the bases. Most directors, regardless of their pose, know that filmmaking is more like baseball than tennis and that they cannot work alone. They plead with producers for extra dollars to hire the actor or composer they fear they cannot do without just as strongly as a manager urges a club owner to purchase a star center fielder or pitcher.

Yes, the director is still the key man on the team. But as Casey Stengel said after winning his ninth American League pennant in ten years, "I couldn't have done it without the boys."

Thank You

We want to thank the people who helped us during the writing and researching of this book. For spending time with us at a tape recorder remembering obscure details from the past we are indebted to Dede Allen, Woody Allen, Monroe Arnold, Aram Avakian, Marshall Brickman, Joe Coffey, Herb Gardner, Sidney Glazier, Jack Grossberg, Alexander Hammid, William Hornbeck, Irving Jacoby, Ely Landau, Daniel Mandell, Helen Gwynne Morgan, Larry Peerce, Helen van Dongen, and Willard Van Dyke. Without them the book would have been impoverished. We also owe thanks to Susan E. Morse, Richard Meran Barsam, Randy Wershba, Charles Silver, Alister Sanderson, and especially Win Sharples, Jr., who dug up valuable information we were unable to get ourselves; to David Williams, Davida Rosenblum, Gene Thornton, and Jack Richardson for reading and commenting on the manuscript and for their encouragement; to Nancy Allen for her dynamite typing; to Harvey Klinger for introducing us to each other and to our publisher, and to Henry Kellerman, Lloyd Gilden, Franklin Heller, Hayes Jacobs, Carey McWilliams, Bob Gould, and Phyllis Kertman for reasons they will know.

Index

Academy Awards, 2, 3, 8, 66, 67, 70, 92, 95, 129, 188, 190, 195, 250, 273, 289, 298

Ackerman, Stanley, 251

Acting Out, 295

actors, and editing, 188–89, 211–24, 227, 285–86

After Many Years, 38

Agriculture, U.S. Department of, 111, 114, 115

Aiello, Danny, 285–86

"Alexander Nevsky" (cantata), 270

"All in the Family," 17

Allen, Dede, 70

Allen, Woody, 6–7, 77, 78, 85, 133, 188, 229, 230, 233, 234, 241–52, 255–70, 273–90, 295, 296

Altman, Robert, 193

American Broadcasting Company (ABC), 242, 259

American Cinema Editors (ACE), 70

American Graffiti, 70

"American Short Story," 295

American Society of Cinematographers, 70

Amish, 12, 13, 14–15

Anderson Tapes, The, 164

Andrews, Harry, 13

Angel Street, 97

"Anhedonia," 274, 289

animation, 34, 126

"Annie and Alvy," 289

Annie Hall, 5, 212, 262, 264, 268, 273–90, 296

anonymity, of editor, 2, 4, 8, 18, 30, 61, 65, 67–69, 70–71, 74, 86, 233, 236–37, 238, 239, 265, 269, 294, 297

Antonioni, Michelangelo, 170

"Anxiety," 289

Apartment, The, 66

Apocalypse Now, 8
Aran Islands, 110
Army Signal Corps, U.S., 95, 97, 149
Arnold, Edward, 218
Arnold, Monroe, 212–18, 219–20, 221–24, 227
"Around the World," 26
Arzner, Dorothy, 41, 61, 63–64
Ash Wednesday, 227
Asher, William, 133, 134, 229, 232
Aubrey, James, 133
Aurthur, Robert Alan, 133
auteur, 239
Autobiography of a Jeep, The, 91, 106
Avakian, Aram, 174, 297
Avco Embassy, 226, 235
Avildsen, John, 8
Avventura, L', 170

baby carriage (*Potemkin*), 53–55, 269
Baby Doll, 92, 130
Bacall, Lauren, 143
Bad Company, 224, 238
Bad News Bears, The, 225
Baird, Eugenie, 132
Balaban, Burt, 136, 137
Balsam, Martin, 187–88
Bananas, 251, 255–60, 268, 269, 286
Bancroft, Anne, 171
bank holdup sequence (*Take the Money and Run*), 244
Baptism of Fire, 94
Basie, Count (William), 81, 164
Beatles, 12, 170, 258, 296
Beck, Jackson, 243, 248, 251
Beethoven, Ludwig van, 85
Bell Jar, The, 227
Belmondo, Jean-Paul, 143, 144
Ben-Hur, 73
Benchley, Robert, 246
Benjamin, Richard, 214, 216, 217, 219, 223, 225
Benton, Robert, 238
Benton & Bowles, 128, 134
Bergman, Ingmar, 230, 232, 266, 268, 296
Bergman, Ingrid, 91
Berle, Milton, 125, 126
Berlin Film Festival, 163, 164
Bernice Bobs Her Hair, 234
Best Years of Our Lives, The, 66, 67
Beyer, Eddie, 190
Bible, The, 170
bicycle montage (*A Thousand Clowns*), 177–79, 184, 186
big bands, 81, 82
Biograph, 38

Birth of a Nation, The, 39–40, 47, 175
Birthday Party, A, 13
Bitzer, Billy, 60
Black, Karen, 236
black and white footage, intercutting of, with color, 15–16, 29–30
blacks, 259, 276; and jazz, 81–83
Blake, Eubie (James Hubert), 173, 189, 249
Blockade, 74
Blood and Sand, 41
Blue Angel, The, 98
Bob and Carol and Ted and Alice, 164
Bogart, Humphrey, 143
Bonnie and Clyde, 70, 238, 245
Bono, Sonny and Cher, 18
Booth, Margaret, 4, 61–62, 64, 65, 67
Born to Win, 83, 235–36
Born Yesterday, 224
Bradley, Bill, 279
Brave One, The, 3
Breathless, 142–44, 145
Bretherton, David, 4
Brickman, Marshall, 204, 264, 274, 275, 278, 280–81, 283, 288–89
Bridge on the River Kwai, The, 77
Bridge Too Far, A, 178
British Academy Awards, 273
British Film Unit, 94–95, 101, 111
Brooklyn College, 84–85
Brooks, Mel, 77, 133, 171, 194–209, 229, 231
Brophy, Edward, 76
Brown, Clarence, 61, 62
Brownlow, Kevin, 61, 62, 63
Brubeck, Dave, 189
Brussels World Fair, 131
Budapest, 267
Bullitt, 3

Caan, James, 78
Cabaret, 4
Caesar, Sid, 195, 234
Cagney, James, 175
Caine Mutiny, The, 231
cameramen, 60, 61, 68, 70, 97, 119, 120, 130, 133, 165, 176, 193, 195–96, 197, 200–201, 216, 230, 256, 298
Canby, Vincent, 241, 252
Capital Story, 91
Capra, Frank, 71, 95
Carnegie Hall, 126
Carroll, Wallace, 96
Casino Royale, 242
Cavett, Dick, 277, 281
Chaplin, Sir Charles, 56, 62, 76, 109, 230, 249, 260

Chase, Charlie, 76
Chayevsky, Paddy, 204
chess sequence (for *Sleeper*), 261
"Chuckles the Chipmunk" (*A Thousand Clowns*), 176, 188–89, 191, 212
Churchill, Sir Winston, 207
Cinderella, 34
Citizen Kane, 142
City College (NY), 101, 107
Clark, James, 297
Cleopatra, 170
Clift, Montgomery, 139, 140
Cline, Eddie, 62
Close Encounters of the Third Kind, 151
close-ups, 7, 34, 35, 37, 38, 40, 41, 49, 52, 53, 54, 55, 62, 63, 64, 76, 77, 78, 127, 135, 148, 157, 158, 162, 174, 175, 183, 187, 201, 219, 238, 297
Coe, Fred, 171–72, 189, 190
Coffey, Arlene, 196
Coffey, Joe, 176, 177, 183, 195–96, 197–98, 200–201, 202, 203, 204, 208
Cold War, 107
Collins, Pat, 275
Colpi, Henri, 4
Columbia Broadcasting System (CBS), 81, 129, 130, 133, 134, 275
Columbia Pictures, 110, 231
Columbia University, 259, 277
comedy, editing of, 22–24, 41, 76–78, 188–89, 195, 202, 205–208, 241, 245–52, 255–60, 261–62, 269–70, 275–89
Coming Home, 92
commercials, television, 126–28, 129, 130, 165, 230
Commodore Record Shop, 82
"compilation" films, 46, 93, 95, 103
concentration camps, 95, 139, 140–41, 146, 147–49, 155, 156–58, 161
continuity, 48, 61, 174–75, 178, 182–83, 245, 273, 275, 284, 296
conventions, editing, 37, 141–42, 143–44, 174–76, 178–79
Cooke, Alistair, 129, 131
Cooper, Gary, 67
Copland, Aaron, 99, 105
Cornell University, 129
Cosell, Howard, 259–60
Country Music Holiday, 169
Crawford, Joan, 141
Crisis, 92
Crisp, Donald, 61
Crist, Judith, 30
Cugat, Xavier, 256
Cummington Story, 106
Curtis, Tony, 250
cutting room, routine of, 6–7, 63–64,

86, 92, 104–105, 112–13, 117–18, 119–21, 127, 172–73, 183–84, 188, 203–208, 222, 236–37, 250–51, 256, 258, 259, 261, 262, 265, 266, 287–89

"dailies": *see* rushes
Daily Variety, 223
"Danger," 151
Daniels, Bebe, 63–64
Dare to Be Great movement, 293
Davis, Bette, 4, 141
De Zeven Provinciën, 56
Decugis, Cécile, 4, 144
Dee, Joey, 237
Defense, U.S. Department of, 3
Defiant Ones, The, 250
Deliverance, 8
"Deutschland über Alles," 206
Devil in a Convent, The, 34
Dewhurst, Colleen, 212, 285
dialogue, editing and, 7, 26–28, 76, 119, 177–78, 183, 187–88, 205–207, 278–79, 281, 282, 283, 284, 286–87. *See also* script
"Dick Tracy," 212
Dictionary of Film Makers, 134
Dietrich, Marlene, 98
directional cutting, 48, 175, 183
director mystique, 230–33, 234–39, 265, 297–98
"director's cut": *see* first cut
Directors Guild: *see* Screen Directors Guild
Disney, Walt, 126
dissolves, 28, 34, 36, 37, 141, 143, 153, 162
Divorce American Style, 18
Dix, Richard, 73
Dmytryk, Edward, 231
Dr. Mabuse, 48
Dr. Strangelove, 170
Doctor Zhivago, 77, 170
documentaries: British, 94–95, 96, 101–102, 111; Nazi, 90, 94; Russian, 46, 93, 94–95, 96, 102, 110–11; in U.S., 5, 74, 86, 89–107, 109–123, 129, 130, 174, 190, 262, 294–95
Dog Day Afternoon, 70, 152
Doña Flor and Her Two Husbands, 175
Doniger, Benji, 98
Donnelly, Ruth, 76
Don't Drink the Water, 234
Don't Look at the Camera, 83
double exposure, 34
double feature, 64–65, 75
Douglas, Kirk, 139
Dovshenko, Alexander, 47, 95, 102

"Down with the Story and the Plot," 56
"dream balloon," 38, 166
Dreiser, Theodore, 85
Duncan, Isadora, 23
Dunne, Philip, 91, 96–97, 99, 102
Duvall, Shelly, 280, 285

Earth, 102
"East Side, West Side," 134
"East Toilet, Ohio" pictures, 99
8½, 170
Eisenstein, Sergei, 40, 45, 47–57, 60, 77,
    174, 211, 220, 230, 270, 290
Ekland, Britt, 12–13, 15–16, 21–22, 23,
    25–28
Elephant Boy, 110, 115
Elgar, Peter, 103
Embassy Pictures, 208
End of St. Petersburg, The, 42
Esquire, 267
Evans, Robert, 221, 222, 225
*Everything You Always Wanted to Know
    about Sex,* 262
Ex-Convict, The, 36
Exorcist, The, 11

Face in the Crowd, A, 130
Fail Safe, 3, 152, 169, 173, 181
Fairbanks, Douglas, Sr., 56
Falk, Peter, 222
Falkenberg, Paul, 3
Faulkner, William, 129
Fellini, Federico, 170, 230, 277, 296
Ferro, Pablo, 16
Fields, Bob, 225–26
Fields, Verna, 69–70
Film Quarterly, 114
film libraries, 3–4, 14, 22
Film Society (London), 42
Film Till Now, The, 112, 117, 122
Filmgoer's Companion, The, 69
"final cut," director and, 30, 62, 65,
    230–31, 235
Fine, Morton, 141
Firebird Suite, 105
first cut, 11, 13–14, 21, 29, 30, 66, 121,
    172, 190, 202, 234–35, 247, 259,
    261, 275, 277–81, 289, 290
Fishbein, Dr. Morris, 184
Fitzgerald, F. Scott, 234
Fitzgerald, Geraldine, 146
Fitzstephens, Jack, 161
Fixer, The, 212
Flaherty, Frances, 111
Flaherty, Robert, 93, 107, 109–11,
    113–23, 126, 202
flash cuts, 146–49, 152–53, 154–55,
    156–58, 160–61, 223

flashbacks, 35, 141–42, 145–49, 152–58,
    160–62, 165, 187, 277, 278, 280, 282
flat cut, 143, 286
Fleming, Victor, 298
Flowers, A. D., 247
Fool Killer, The, 169
For Love of Gold, 38
For Whom the Bell Tolls, 66
Ford, John, 95
Foreign Language Section (of Overseas
    Motion Picture Bureau, OWI), 90, 100
Fourth Symphony (Tchaikovsky), 105
Fowler, Gene, Jr., 91
France, 142, 170, 267
Frankenheimer, John, 212
French Connection, The, 11
Friedkin, David, 141
Friedkin, William, 11, 13, 15, 17, 18–19,
    29, 30, 229, 232
Front, The, 268
Frontier Films, 92
*Funny Thing Happened on the Way to the
    Forum, A,* 12

Gable, Clark, 261
Gambler, The, 78
Gance, Abel, 62
gangster pictures, 75–76, 96, 134–37, 140,
    169
Garbo, Greta, 61
Gardner, Herb, 77, 169, 171–74, 176–79,
    181–82, 185–91, 196, 204, 233, 234
Garrison, Greg, 237
Gehrig, Lou, 66–67
Geller, Robert, 295
"Gentlemen," 23
geographical cutting, 143–44, 145, 159
Germany, 41, 69, 94
Getaway, The, 225
Giant, 70
Gibbs, Antony, 4, 178
Gilded Putrefaction, 48
Gilford, Jack, 212
Gillespie, Dizzy (John Birks), 164
Gilliatt, Penelope, 275
Gish, Lillian, 53, 64
Glazier, Sidney, 195, 196, 198, 199–200,
    201, 202–203
Goberman, Max, 105–106
Godard, Jean-Luc, 4, 142–44
Godfather, The, 212, 247, 262, 268
Goldwyn, Samuel, 66–67
Goldwyn Studios, 4
Gone Are the Days, 169, 233
Gone With the Wind, 261, 298
Good Times, 18
Goodbye Columbus, 187, 211–25, 227, 238,
    242, 288

Goodman, Benny, 81
Gordon, Barry, 176
Gorki, Maxim, 49
Gosh-Darned Mortgage, The, 63
Gould, Morton, 105
Grable, Betty, 224
Gradus, Ben, 98
The Grapes of Wrath, The, 74
Grayson, Helen, 106
Great Train Robbery, The, 37, 38
"Greatest Man in the World, The," 295, 298
Greed, 65
Grierson, John, 94, 111
Griffith, D. W., 37–40, 41, 46–47, 49, 60, 62, 166, 174, 175
Griffith, Richard, 112, 117
"Griffith last-minute rescue," 39, 40, 49
Grossberg, Jack, 195, 196, 242, 245, 250, 260
Group, The, 83, 152, 184
Gurevich, Carl, 295
"Guy Lombardo Show," 131–33
Gwynne, Helen, 90–91, 99, 101

Hallelujah Chorus, 27–28, 50
Halliwell, Leslie, 59, 69
Hamilton, Chico, 29
Hamlisch, Marvin, 249–51
Hammid, Alexander (Hackenschmied), 92, 97, 106, 107
Handel, George Frederick, 27, 173
Hard Day's Night, A, 12, 170
Hardy, Oliver, 22, 76, 77–78
Harlem, 82–83, 84, 104, 140, 146, 147, 154, 156, 158, 163
Harris, Barbara, 177, 179, 184, 185, 188
Hathaway, Henry, 66
"Hathaways, The," 213
Heart Is a Lonely Hunter, The, 139, 140
Heckert, Jim, 246
Help!, 12, 28, 170
Heron, Nan, 61
Hertzberg, Mike, 199–200
Hester Street, 234
Hickson, Rosemarie, 90–91
High Noon, 3
Hiller, Arthur, 139, 140
Hines, Earl, 81
Hiroshima Mon Amour, 4, 142, 145
Hitchcock, Alfred, 2, 55, 230
Hitler, Adolf, 94, 206, 207, 278
Hollywood Reporter, 90
Hope, Bob, 257
Hornbeck, William, 59–60, 62, 67, 70–71, 95
Houseman, John, 91

How Green Was My Valley, 96
Hughes, Howard, 268
Hurt, Marybeth, 6
Hurwitz, Leo, 102
Huston, John, 95
Huston, Walter, 102
Hutton, Marion, 133

I Am A Fugitive from a Chain Gang, 74
"I Spy," 130
Iceman Cometh, The, 151
Impossible Voyage, The, 34
In Cold Blood, 164
Ince, Thomas, 41
Industrial Britain, 111
Institute of Film Techniques (City College of New York), 101
Interiors, 5, 6, 246, 264, 265, 268, 269, 295
Intimate Lighting, 236
Intolerance, 39–40, 46–47
It Happened One Night, 95
Ivens, Joris, 91, 93, 112, 115
Ives, Burl, 139

Jacktown, 169
Jacobs, Lewis, 69
Jacoby, Irving, 96, 101, 102, 103, 107
Jaffe, Stanley, 213–14, 216, 218, 222, 223, 224–25, 238–39
James, Henry, 85
Jaws, 70, 151
jazz, 29, 81–83, 84, 91, 146, 154, 164, 261, 262, 263
Jazz on a Summer's Day, 174, 297
Joffe, Charles, 245, 247
Jones, Quincy, 146, 159, 164, 251
jump cutting, 143, 144, 159
juxtaposition, editing as, 2, 3, 154, 174, 178, 221, 245, 283. See also flash cuts

Kael, Pauline, 83, 165, 184, 226
Kafka, Franz, 279, 285
Kane, Carol, 278
Kaplan, Boris, 131
Katz, Sid, 129, 130–31, 170
Kaufman, Boris, 91, 165
Kauffmann, Stanley, 221
Kazan, Elia, 130
Keaton, Buster, 62, 76, 260, 262
Keaton, Diane, 6, 212, 267, 268, 273, 275, 277, 278, 279, 281, 282, 285, 287, 288, 296
Kell, J. Sherman, 62
Keller, Frank, 3
Kelly, Gene, 163
Kennedy, John F., 282
Keystone Cops, 41
Keystone studio, 59–60, 62

Kierkegaard, Sören, 276, 279
Kirk, Andy (Andrew Dewey), 81
Kleptomaniac, The, 36
Klugman, Jack, 215
Knack, The, 12, 170, 178
Knight, Arthur, 76, 107
Kramer, Stanley, 298
Krim, Arthur, 289
Krumgold, Joseph, 106
Kubrick, Stanley, 170, 171
Kuleshov, Lev, 46–47, 48

Lahr, Bert, 16, 29
Land, The, 111, 114–16
Landau, Ely, 139–40, 164–65
Lang, Fritz, 48
Lasser, Louise, 251, 259
Last of the Mohicans, The, 96
Last Year at Marienbad, 4
Laurel, Stan, 22, 76, 77–78
Lawrence, Marc, 76
Lawrence of Arabia, 77
Leacock, Richard, 119, 120
Lean, David, 77
Lear, Norman, 11–14, 16, 17–19, 24–25,
    29–30, 190
Leder, Herb, 134
Leff, Henry, 248
Lefthanded Gun, The, 171
Legion of Decency, 164
Lehman, Ernest, 163
Lenin, V. I., 45, 47
Lerner, Irving, 96, 103, 106
Lester, Richard, 12, 28, 170, 296
Levine, Buddy, 76, 81–82, 84
Levine, Joseph E., 195, 197, 208
Lewis, John, 164
"Lieutenant Kije" (Suite), 270
Life of an American Fireman, The, 35–36,
    37, 39
Little Caesar, 75–76
Liveliest Art, The, 76
Lloyd, Harold, 62
Lloyd, Norman, 102, 105
Lombardo, Carmen, 132
Lombardo, Guy, 3, 131–32
Lombroso, Cesare, 82
London Can Take It, 95
Lonedale Operator, The, 39
*Loneliness of the Long Distance Runner,
    The,* 4
Lonely Villa, The, 39
Long Day's Journey into Night, 139, 140,
    152, 173, 190
long shots, 39, 51, 52, 54, 62, 135, 157,
    174, 175, 183, 201, 238
Lorentz, Pare, 122
Lost Horizon, 95

Louisiana Story, 107, 109–14, 116–23,
    126, 136, 175
Love and Death, 257, 267, 269–70
Love-Life of a South Seas Siren, The,
    93–94
Love Story, 139, 225
Loved One, The, 4
Luciano, Michael, 4
Lumet, Baruch, 151–52
Lumet, Sidney, 65, 83, 92, 139–41, 145,
    151–53, 159, 161–62, 164, 165–66,
    169; 173, 181, 184, 233, 247
Lumière, Louis, 33
Lunacharsky, Anatoli, 45, 48, 56
Lunceford, Jimmie, 81

MacCann, Richard Dyer, 106
Macdonald, Dwight, 165
MacGraw, Ali, 214, 216, 217, 219, 225
MacNaughton, R. Q., 101
Mad Dog Coll, 140
Maddow, Ben, 102
Mademoiselle, 4
Madison, Larry, 98, 106
Major Barbara, 77
Malcolm X (Malcolm Little), 86
Man of Aran, 110, 111
Mandell, Daniel, 4, 66–67, 71
Manhattan, 288
Mankiewicz, Joseph L., 164
Mansfield, Jayne, 145
Marat/Sade, 8
March, Fredric, 67, 91
Margolin, Janet, 248, 278
Martin, Dean, 237
Marx Brothers, 242
Marx, Groucho, 243, 286
Marx, Karl, 46
Masefield, John, 74, 75
Massey, Raymond, 130
May, Elaine, 65
MCA, 3
McCullers, Carson, 139
McGuane, Thomas, 225
McLean, Barbara, 4
McLuhan, Marshall, 277, 296
McQueen, Steve, 225
Méliès, Georges, 33–34, 35
memory cuts: *see* flash cuts
Meredith, Burgess, 106
Metro-Goldwyn-Mayer (MGM), 4, 64,
    65, 66, 110
Messiah, 173
Meyers, Sidney, 92, 100, 102–104, 105,
    106, 107, 112, 134, 229
Mezzrow, Mezz (Milton), 83
Midnight Cowboy, 92

Milford, Gene, 129, 130–31, 170
Miller, Glenn, 81
Milton, David Scott, 236
Miracle Worker, The, 171, 297
Mitchum, Robert, 175
mixing, 65, 100, 226, 262, 266, 269
MKR Films, 130–33, 169–70
Moana, 93, 115
Moby Dick, 57
Modern Jazz Quartet. 164
Monk, Jonathan, 277
montage, 15, 16, 17, 23, 24, 26, 48,
   67, 131, 163, 177, 181, 182, 183,
   184, 186, 288
Montalban, Carlos, 258
Morris, Henry, 80
Morris, Howie, 229, 234–35
Morse, Sandy, 6, 288
Mostel, Zero, 194, 197, 198–99, 200,
   204, 205, 207–208
Mother, 49–50, 93, 101
Motion Picture Association of America
   (MPAA), 164
Moussorgsky, Modest, 105–106
Moviola, 3, 5, 6, 63, 99, 100, 101, 104,
   106, 112, 121, 127, 153, 172, 173,
   188, 204, 222
Mozart, W. A., 249
Mulligan, Gerry, 189
Murder by Death, 64
Murder Incorporated, 135–37, 222
Murder My Sweet, 231
Murder on the Orient Express, 152
Museum of Modern Art, 97, 100
music, and editing, 5, 17, 23, 26, 27–28,
   29, 83, 92, 104, 105–106, 122, 129,
   131, 132–33, 173, 177–78, 181, 186,
   189–90, 223, 236, 239, 249–51, 269–70
Muzhukin, Ivan, 47
My Fair Lady, 170

Nanook of the North, 93, 107, 110, 111,
   115
Nash, N. Richard, 133
Nashville, 193
National Broadcasting Company (NBC),
   81, 277
National Society of Film Critics Awards,
   273
Native Land, 102
NBC Symphony Orchestra, 106
negative cutting, 64, 69, 104–105
Network, 152
New Leaf, A, 65
"New Look," 12, 13, 14, 17, 18, 21, 28
New Republic, The, 221
"New Wave," 142, 170
New York, 30

New York Film Critics Circle Awards,
   273
New York Review of Books, 279
New York Times, The, 99, 194, 198, 241,
   252, 264
New Yorker, The, 83, 183, 241, 264, 275
Newman, David, 238
newsreels, 14, 23, 30, 46, 66, 93, 141
Newsweek, 264
Nichols, Dudley, 109
Nietzsche, Friedrich, 279
Night and Fog, 4
Night Mail, 101
Night They Raided Minsky's, The, 8,
   11–19, 21–30, 34, 49, 78, 92, 190,
   209, 226, 255, 280, 290
Northwest, U.S.A., 102–103, 107
Nykvist, Sven, 230

Obelisk Films, 126
Odessa steps sequence (*Potemkin*),
   51–56, 269
Office of Education, U.S., 107
Office of War Information (OWI), 86,
   89–107, 112, 129, 130, 137, 149, 270
Olivier, Sir Laurence, 139
"Omnibus," 129, 131, 181
On the Waterfront, 92
One Day at War, 96
O'Neill, Eugene, 140, 152
opticals, 28, 121, 141, 202, 247, 290
Orchestra Wives, 96
Ormandy, Eugene, 121, 122
Ornitz, Arthur, 176
Orphans of the Storm, 64
Other Side of the Mountain, The, 227
outtakes, 48, 106, 259
Overseas Motion Picture Bureau (of
   OWI), 89–92, 95, 107. *See* Office
   of War Information

Pacino, Al, 212
Pale Horseman, The, 103
Palomar Pictures, 242, 247
Panagra Airlines, 126
Parade's Gone By, The, 61
"parallel" action, 37
Paramount, 63, 64, 93, 110, 220–21, 224,
   243
Passer, Ivan, 83, 235–37
"Patty Duke Show, The," 133–34, 169,
   170, 232
Pawnbroker, The, 139–41, 143, 145–49,
   151–66, 173, 222, 288
Peerce, Larry, 4, 212–13, 216, 218–19,
   220–23, 225–27, 233, 237–38, 242
Perry, Frank, 250
Peters, Brock, 158, 159

Philadelphia Academy of Music, 122
Philip Morris, 130
Piano Concerto No. 2 (Rachmaninoff), 105
Picker, David, 14, 189, 236
Pictures at an Exhibition, 105
Pinter, Harold, 13
Place in the Sun, A, 70
Plath, Sylvia, 227
Play It Again, Sam, 246, 247, 268
Plow that Broke the Plains, The, 122
Poitier, Sidney, 250
Polonsky, Sonya, 6
Porter, Edwin S., 34–37, 38, 39
Portrait of the Artist as a Young Man, 86
Potemkin, 50–57, 93, 269
Preservation Hall Jazz Band, 262
Pretty Baby, 175
Pretty Boy Floyd, 134–35, 136
Pride of the Yankees, The, 66–67
Priestly, Tom, 8, 273
Prince, Harold, 226, 235
Prisoner of Second Avenue, The, 250
producers, and editing, 8, 11, 13–14, 17–19, 24–25, 29–30, 65, 66–67, 222, 230, 234–35, 238, 239, 298
Producers, The, 18, 194–209, 226, 231
projection, 60
Prokofieff, Sergei, 85, 270
Proletkult Theatre (Moscow), 48
propaganda films, 42, 46–48, 49, 50–57, 71, 86, 90, 91, 92, 93, 94–96, 102–103, 105, 106–107, 111, 211. *See also* documentaries
Psycho, 55
Public Broadcasting System (PBS), 295
Public Enemy, The, 75
Public Health Service, U.S., 91
Pudovkin, V., 42, 47, 49–50, 95, 101, 174
Puerto Rico, 256
Purlie Victorious, 233
Pygmalion, 77

Quiet One, The, 104

Rachmaninoff, Sergei, 105, 106
Ramona, 39
raw footage, 5, 7, 11, 92, 172, 181, 183, 190, 219. *See also* rushes
Real Glory, The, 66
Realart, 64
Reisz, Karel, 174, 175–76
Renoir, Jean, 109, 230
Resnais, Alain, 4, 142
retakes, 66, 119, 127–28, 193, 198–99, 219, 260, 262
reverse shooting, 34, 170

Revillon Frères, 111
Rich, Frank, 267
Rich, Lee, 225, 226
Richards, Paul, 188–89, 212
Richardson, Tony, 4, 170, 178
Riefenstahl, Leni, 94
Ringling Brothers, 84
Rise of the American Film, The, 69
Riskin, Robert, 91, 95–99, 102
Ritz Brothers, 76
River, The, 122
RKO Radio Pictures, Inc., 3
Robards, Jason, Jr., 12, 13, 16–17, 21, 22, 23–24, 25–28, 173, 176, 177, 178, 179, 185
Roberts, Tony, 277
Robinson, Edward G., 218
Rockwell, Norman, 282
Rodakievicz, Henwar, 91
Rohmer, Eric, 4
Rolling Stone, 280
Rollins, Jack, 245
Roosevelt, Franklin Delano, 90, 106
Rose, David, 29
Rose, Mickey, 242
Rosen, Chuck, 196
Rosenblum, Davida, 84, 208, 209, 223, 267
Rosenblum, Jack, 74, 80, 82, 84, 85
Rosenblum, Paul, 226
Roth, Philip, 212, 214, 216, 221
Rotha, Paul, 42, 93, 112, 117
Rothstein, Max, 112, 126
rough cut: *see* first cut
rushes, 60, 64, 91, 98, 99, 114–17, 126, 127, 134, 172–73, 199, 202, 203, 218–19, 221, 225, 226, 236, 237, 238, 248, 251, 267
Ruth, Babe (George Herman), 66

Sabatini, Rafael, 184
Sadoul, Georges, 134
Sailor from Gibraltar, The, 4
Saks, Gene, 188, 189
Salt, Waldo, 92
San Francisco, 1945, 103, 105
Sartre, Jean-Paul, 278
Savitt, Jan, 81
Scarface, 75
Scheuer, Philip K., 169
Schulman, Arnold, 214
"scratch" score, 189, 190, 236. *See also* music, and editing
Screen Directors Guild, 231, 273
"Scythian Suite," 270
"Sea Fever," 74
"Search, The," 129–30
Seberg, Jean, 143, 144

"Seems Like Old Times," 288
Segal, George, 236
Selznick, David O., 261, 298
Sennett, Mack, 41, 59–60, 62
Separate Peace, A, 227
Serpico, 70, 152
Seurat, Georges Pierre, 145
Shalit, Gene, 275
Shane, 70
Shanghai Express, 98
Shaw, Artie, 81
Sherwood, Robert, 96, 106
Shub, Esther, 46, 47, 48, 93
Silone, Ignazio, 85
Silver, Joan, 234
Simon, Neil, 133
Simon, Paul, 279, 281
Sixth (*Pathétique*) Symphony
  (Tchaikovsky), 105
Sleeper, 257, 260–62, 264, 268, 269
Slow Dancing in the Big City, 8
slow motion, 34, 145, 162, 165
smooth cut, 39, 40–41, 77, 174–75
Snow White and the Seven Dwarfs, 74
Sokolow, Ethel, 248
Something for Everyone, 226, 235
Song of Ceylon, 101–102
Sorrow and the Pity, The, 277, 286
sound editor, 91, 161, 202, 226, 266
sound film, 75–76
Sound of Music, The, 170
Soviet Union, 42, 45–57, 69, 93, 95,
  96, 110–11, 211
Special Day, A, 175
special effects, 28, 34, 247, 260, 296.
  See also opticals
Spielberg, Steven, 151
Splendor in the Grass, 130
splicing, 6, 7, 17, 60, 61, 62, 64, 92,
  104, 120, 121, 128, 136, 288
Sporting Club, The, 225–27, 237–38
*Springtime for Hitler: A Gay Romp with
  Adolf and Eva at Berchtesgaden*, 194–95,
  205–206
Stalin, Joseph, 45, 79, 101, 211
Standard Oil of New Jersey, 111, 116,
  121–22, 123, 126
"Stars and Stripes Forever," 178
Steeltown, 91
Steenbeck editing machine, 6
Steiger, Rod, 139, 145–49, 153, 154, 156,
  158–59, 162, 165, 218
Steinberg, Saul, 5
Steinkamp, Frederic, 65
Stern, Bert, 174
Sternberg, Josef von, 98–99, 211
Stevenson, Adlai E., 278, 282
stock footage, 3, 14–17, 22–23, 27, 28,

29–30, 35, 41, 49, 93, 179, 186
stock music, 105–106, 178
stop-motion, 34, 170
Strand, Paul, 102
Stravinsky, Igor, 105, 270
Strike, 49
Stroheim, Erich von, 65
Sugarland Express, The, 70, 151
Sullivan, Ed, 277
Sussan, Herb, 132, 133
Susskind, David, 134
Swedes in America, 91
Swimmer, The, 250
synchronizers, synchronization, 5,
  76, 104, 106, 113, 126, 134, 183,
  219

Take the Money and Run, 234, 241–52,
  255, 258, 260, 275, 278, 283, 286
Tarantula, 24
Target for Tonight, 95
Taste of Honey, A, 4
Tchaikovsky, P. I., 85, 105
Teaching Film Custodians, 126
Technique of Film Editing, The, 174
television, 3, 8, 17, 93, 97, 107, 123,
  125–34, 144, 151, 152, 165, 169,
  175, 176, 196, 197, 212, 227, 230,
  234, 237, 242, 251, 258, 263, 276,
  294–95, 296
Ten Days That Shook the World, 211
Tennessee Valley Authority, 96, 97
Thalberg, Irving, 65
That's Entertainment, 269
Thing, The, 24
This Property Is Condemned, 151
This Sporting Life, 8
Thomson, Virgil, 105, 121–22
"Thoughts," 29
Thousand Clowns, A, 18, 169–74, 176–79,
  181–91, 196, 212, 222, 226, 255,
  269, 288
Three Stooges, the, 76
Thurber, James, 295
Tissé, Edouard, 60, 230
Tolstoy, Count Leo, 85, 231
Tom Jones, 4, 170, 178
"Tomorrow Belongs to Me," 4
Too Much Johnson, 61
Toscanini, Arturo, 106–107
Toscanini: The Hymn of the Nations,
  106–107
Tourneur, Maurice, 61
Town, The, 98–99
Transfilm, 129
TransAtlantic Tunnel, 73
Traube, Shepard, 97

travelogues, 93, 126
Trip to the Moon, A, 34
Triumph of the Will, 94
Tropic of Cancer, 134
Trotsky, Leon, 211
Truffaut, François, 4
Trumbo, Dalton, 3
Tucker, Forrest, 22
Tuesday in November, A, 91
Turin, Victor, 93
Turksib, 93
Turner, 262, 294–95
Turner, Glenn, 293–95
Twelve Angry Men, 151
20th Century–Fox, 4, 135, 137, 239
"2000-Year-Old Man," 195, 201
Two Tickets to Paris, 169, 237

United Artists, 12, 14, 174, 177, 189, 190, 191, 236, 260, 263, 274, 289
United Artists Television, 133
United Nations, 103, 126
United Service Organizations (USO), 247
Up the Down Staircase, 195

Valentino, Rudolph, 41, 61
Vallee, Rudy, 15
Valley of the Tennessee, The, 91
van Dongen, Helen, 91, 93, 112–21, 123, 173, 202, 258
Van Dyke, Dick, 130
Van Dyke, Willard, 89, 91, 92, 96–99, 102–103, 107
vaudeville numbers (*The Night They Raided Minsky's*), 13, 16, 17, 23, 24, 26, 28, 34–35
Verdi, Giuseppe, 106
Vertov, Dziga, 46, 49, 91, 93
Victory in the West, 94

Wagner, Richard, 207
Walken, Christopher, 285
Walker, Don, 189–90
Wallant, Edward Lewis, 140, 151, 153, 154, 165

"Wanted," 130
War and Peace, 57
Waterston, Sam, 6, 7
Watt, Harry, 83, 101
WCBS-TV, 275
Webb, Chick (William), 81
Webster, Nick, 233
wedding scene (*Goodbye Columbus*), 212, 214–18, 219–24
Welles, Orson, 142
Wenning, Kathy, 234
Westerns, 41
Weston, Jack, 213
Whatever Happened to Baby Jane?, 4
What's New Pussycat?, 242
What's Up Tiger Lily?, 242
White, Merrill, 3
Why We Fight, 71, 95
Wilder, Billy, 66
Wilder, Gene, 194, 197, 203, 207–208
Williams, Elmo, 3
Wilson, Woodrow, 40
Window Cleaner, The, 106
Wisdom, Norman, 12, 16–17, 21–22, 23–24
Wise, Robert, 69
Wiseman, Joseph, 13
Witness for the Prosecution, 71
Wizard of Oz, The, 74
WNBC-TV, 275
women, and editing, 4, 6, 46, 47, 48, 61–62, 63–64, 65, 69–70, 91, 93, 112–21, 173, 234, 258, 288
Wood, Sam, 66–67
Wray, Fay, 95
Wright, Basil, 101
Wyler, William, 66, 95

"Yankee Doodle Dandy," 206
"Yes, Sir, That's My Baby," 173, 178
Yorkin, Bud, 16
"You Are There," 151
You Can't Take It with You, 95
Young Lions, The, 231
"Your Show of Shows," 195, 234

Zinnemann, Fred, 163